Utilitarianism

... ever gentle on my mind.

Utilitarianism
A Contemporary Statement

Robin Barrow
Professor
Simon Fraser University
Canada

Edward Elgar

Published by
Edward Elgar Publishing Limited
Gower House
Croft Road
Aldershot
Hants GU11 3HR
England

Edward Elgar Publishing Company
Old Post Road
Brookfield
Vermont 05036
USA

British Library Cataloguing in Publication Data
Barrow, Robin 1944–
    Utilitarianism: a contemporary statement
    1. Ethics
    I. Title
    171.5

Library of Congress Cataloguing in Publication Data
Barrow, Robin.
        Utilitarianism: a contemporary statement/Robin Barrow.
            p.   cm.
        Includes bibliographical references.
        1. Utilitarianism.   I. Title.
    B843.B36   1991
    171' .5–dc20   90–28072
                                                                                            CIP

ISBN 1 85278 097 5

Printed in Great Britain by
Billing & Sons Ltd, Worcester

Contents

1. What Lies Ahead?

In his celebrated book, *After Virtue*, Alasdair MacIntyre introduces 'the disquieting suggestion' that 'we have ... lost our comprehension, both theoretical and practical, of morality.'[1] He concedes that we still use moral language and hold what we are pleased to call moral beliefs. But could it be, he asks, that we do this without any adequate grasp of the underlying conceptual scheme that makes coherent sense of the moral domain? Are we perhaps in the same situation as we would be if we had only fragments of scientific knowledge and information, but lacked understanding of the body of scientific theory that would enable us to make sense of the fragments?

MacIntyre's hypothesis, even as starkly presented here, seems to me plausible, although his explanation of the state of affairs, his working out of the implications and his conclusions may be another matter. It may very well be the case that our moral understanding is confused and fragmentary, and that it does not extend far enough to enable us to make sense of our beliefs. If that is so, MacIntyre is also correct in his further suggestion that 'analytic philosophy', if it is interpreted to mean an activity that is exclusively 'descriptive and descriptive of the language of the present at that',[2] would not be able to help us. For, if we do not go beyond the way that we do talk, and hence the way in which we do think, we cannot escape the disjointed, incomplete and very possibly contradictory understanding that we have. (MacIntyre does not in fact say that analytic philosophy is 'exclusively' descriptive of the language of the present. He uses the equivocal word 'essentially', but I take him to mean by that, 'to all intents and purposes', or 'as near as makes no matter'.)

However, 'analytic philosophy' does not have to be interpreted so narrowly. One may think of the attempt to analyse morality, or any other concept, not merely as an attempt to describe our use of moral terms, but as an attempt to show a certain amount of respect, though by no means an unqualified respect, for the thinking that is suggested by our language, while at the same time endeavouring to tease out unrecognized implications, to imagine or conceive of possibilities, and to structure the whole by reference both to the canons of logical reasoning to which we

1

subscribe and to such non-moral knowledge as we have that seems pertinent. In other words, while we cannot ignore the fact of our confused moral understanding, we can to some extent go beyond it and knock some sense into it. (As in fact, of course, MacIntyre himself attempts to do, though he would not call his method 'analytic philosophy'.) It is reasonable to suppose that 'the language of morality is in (a) ... state of grave disorder',[3] and that one cannot rectify this by means of a narrow form of linguistic philosophy. It is not reasonable to suppose that a broader conception of philosophical analysis will not be crucial to any attempt to impose order.

But before embarking on the task of, in part, making use of philosophical analysis to arrive at a coherent account of morality, I want briefly to consider a broader, more populist, thesis. This thesis affirms that morality is dead, both in the sense that, in general terms, moral considerations no longer govern our lives, and in the sense that there is no reason why they should, since what have sometimes been thought of as *sui generis* obligations are no more than conventions, even if they are conventions that arise out of certain particular needs and preferences.

The state of the world today may certainly seem to some to provide evidence for such a view. The prevalence of such acts as mugging, theft, hostage taking, rape, sabotage, fraud, vandalism, terrorism, and murder; the brutality and cynicism of governments, the political oppression, the individual materialism and selfishness, and other such-like evidence, with which we are all too familiar, could certainly be taken as an indication that we neither are, nor aspire to be, particularly moral. And the fact that some of these acts arise out of conflicting values and ideologies may be taken as a sign that there are many competing moralities in existence, as may the fact that, in the opinion of some, the above list of horrors could be augmented by reference to abortion, pornography, euthanasia, cruelty to animals, the provision of contraceptives to the young and drunken driving. It is hardly contentious to observe that there is little uniformity of opinion on what acts are morally acceptable, what makes an action morally acceptable, and even whether the notion of morality has any distinctive meaning separate from notions such as prudence, self-interest, cultural preference or traditional value. Morality, on anybody's view, is certainly confused and very possibly losing its appeal.

However, the question of whether morality is truly dead depends for an answer partly on what we mean by 'dead', and partly on what we mean by 'morality'. Perhaps, for example, an issue such as whether the young should be encouraged to use birth control is not a moral issue at all. Perhaps the revolutionary violence that has become widespread of late is, as some claim, morally justified. And perhaps some of the thinking that passes for moral can be shown to be incoherent in itself and discounted, and therefore no longer constitutes evidence that our understanding, taken collectively, is inconsistent. One thing, at any rate, is very clear: whether morality is dead or not, the moral sense is very far from dead. We may not like the fervour and fanaticism of various particular groups, but we can hardly deny that some of them act with a distinctively *moral* fervour. They believe passionately that what they are doing is morally justified, or even (which may be different, as we shall see)[4] morally right. They do not act purely, if at all, for selfish reasons, prudential reasons, or the thrill of it, but for what they regard as morally compelling reasons. Furthermore, much of the furious reaction to such acts of terrorism as I have in mind is a *moral* indignation. No doubt other elements, such as wounded pride, patriotism, self-interest and fear come into it, but it seems plain enough that many of us, however inarticulately, can still feel a distinctive sense of outrage that we label *'moral* outrage'. Even if certain acts, such as mugging or burning abortion clinics, can arguably be seen as being beyond an objective form of moral reasoning, the nature of the more spectacular events grabbing world headlines, and people's reactions to them, seem to indicate that a *sui generis* sense of rightness and wrongness, which, in anybody's language, is what we mean by a specifically 'moral' sense, is very far from dead.

It may, however, be the case that there is a crisis of moral faith, particularly amongst those who lack religious or ideological conviction, or who recognize logical objections to grounding their moral beliefs in their religion, and who concede the fact that an ideology that does their moral thinking for them avoids the question of whether what they do is truly moral. Such people do not necessarily lack opinions on moral matters, or lack a moral sense, but, being aware of the difficulty of grounding moral judgements in reason and of establishing them as objective truths, as well as being sensitive to the complexities of actual situations, they feel uneasy at putting forward their own convictions as if they were self-evident truths, or condemning those of others, as if they had some expertise and authority that entitled them to judge. Some may go so far as to embrace some explicitly relativistic view of morality; but even those who still believe that some actions are right and others wrong, regardless of time and place, may see this belief as an article of secular faith, rather than a matter of demonstrable fact.

A substantial part of moral philosophy during this century has, whether by chance or design, contributed to a weakening of the idea of moral knowledge, and hence moral certitude. The basic arguments to establish the logical independence of religion and morality are to be found as far back as Plato's dialogues. But in this century their logical separateness has become a philosophical orthodoxy. There is no obvious way, if there is a way at all, in which we can make sense of and validate moral judgements by relying on religion. Coherent secular bodies of thought that give rise to particular moral prescriptions have likewise been dismissed, very often, as ideologies, with the implication that, however well worked out, they rest on unproven and unprovable evaluative premises. More generally, the presumption that moral beliefs could be objectively substantiated by some form of reasoning was given a severe jolt by the logical positivist doctrine that all truths were either analytic or empirical, and that moral (aesthetic and religious) claims, being neither, were literally 'non-sense'. Moral claims were acknowledged to have significance, essentially because they evinced the attitude of the speaker; but they did not amount to propositions that were capable of being true or false.

This so-called emotivist theory of ethics is, of course, far from being regarded as the final word on the subject. Nonetheless, A.J. Ayer's *Language, Truth and Logic*,[5] which presents a bold version of such a thesis, is still widely read, and subsequent developments in moral philosophy have, to some extent, reinforced the tenor of his approach by concentrating heavily on formal features of morality. For example, the influential early work of R.M. Hare[6] concentrated exclusively on making formal points about the nature of moral discourse, such as that it is prescriptive and universalizable, and left many with the impression that it didn't much matter what you did, so long as you did it sincerely and consistently. A great deal of other work on the analysis of various moral concepts is certainly open to the charge of being circular and locked within the assumptions of our time and place in history. At the same time, though few philosophers would be so naive as to conclude directly from evidence of cultural variation that moral beliefs are simply cultural preferences, the increase in our awareness and understanding of cultural variation, thanks to the work of sociologists and anthropologists and the changing world situation, has probably given further impetus to the idea that morality is more or less adequately summed up in Thrasymachus'[7] claim that 'right' is simply 'might' – in other words, that 'morality' is just the name that we give to conventions foisted upon us by the powerful, in their own interest.

In so far as there is a substantive view of morality dominant in the Western world, one might, in any case, say that it is incoherent. That view, which I refer to as the 'liberal-democratic view', assumes a plurality of fundamental moral principles of equal weight. For example, the principles of freedom, equality, and happiness are held in equal regard and, where these principles clash, it is assumed that there is no rational way of determining the superiority of the claims of one principle over another. Furthermore, the fact that these basic principles cannot themselves be shown to be true is generally emphasized. A premium is therefore set on such values as autonomy and on the importance of each individual at any rate having rational grounds, derived from one or more of the principles, for performing particular actions. As against this view, it may be said that, if it is agreed that the basic principles are articles of faith, there seem to be no obvious grounds for insisting that people should reason from these first principles. Why should we not act on faith or by intuition in respect of specific situations as well? Besides, if the various fundamental principles are indeed of equal weight, then it surely follows that, in cases of a clash between them, there is no correct answer to the question of which one we should give priority to. A decision to subordinate everything to the claims of, say, equality could not legitimately be dismissed as 'unreasonable', since, by the premises of the theory, reason does not come into the matter. To act in the interests of happiness would be no better and no worse than to act in the interests of freedom.[8]

Given this emphasis on, variously, linguistic analysis of moral concepts, the formal characteristics of moral discourse, and an intuitively appealing but more or less inoperable set of principles, it is small wonder that some philosophers have expressed dissatisfaction. Philippa Foot, for example, has tried to argue for the idea of substantive virtues and vices.[9] Iris Murdoch turned back to Plato for inspiration in the idea of the Good.[10] G.J. Warnock argued that morality could not be defined simply in terms of formal and procedural values, and that it is also necessarily about what he termed people's 'well-being'.[11] But despite these bold attempts, and other far more comprehensive and detailed theories of ethics of a substantive nature, MacIntyre's view that our understanding of morality, as evidenced by our language, is in a 'state of grave disorder'[12] is hardly surprising.

In this book I attempt to present a coherent and plausible case for a particular moral theory. I hope to avoid the problem of the grave disorder of our moral language by refusing to be entirely bound by the implications of our language, on the grounds that our language may embody incoherent thoughts and that it is possible to stand, at least to some extent, on the outside of a particular form of discourse.[13]

Since the linchpin of the view that I shall argue for is the concept of happiness, it must be categorized as a version of utilitarianism.[14] However, I am anxious that this should not lead readers to approach it as an exegesis on either classical or contemporary utilitarianism. There are a number of reasons why I do not want to adopt that approach. First, there is the very practical consideration that, if it were to be presented as such, some readers familiar with and unresponsive to familiar versions of the theory might be inclined to treat it as a purely academic exercise, whereas I wish to argue that the view of morality here presented ought to be accepted and acted on. Second, I do not wish to concentrate on interpreting familiar arguments, so much as to explicate a view, to present a positive ethical theory, without particular concern for the sources of the various ideas. There are already many excellent disquisitions on utilitarianism and some impressive attempts to reintegrate or modify some of the problematic claims of the founding fathers. I do not see any particular need to add to those, whereas I do see a need to present a fresh account of ethics that purports to be more plausible than any other. Third, while I believe strongly in the educational value of the close study of standard philosophical texts, I have increasingly felt, as a teacher of philosophy, that emphasis falls too often on the quality of argument at the expense of the substance. A minor illustration of that tendency is provided by book reviews that triumphantly expose a mistake here and a slip there, without giving any account of the overall thesis being argued, let alone considering its plausibility. Worse still are those reviews that, when they can conveniently categorize the book as belonging to a familiar school of thought, proceed to produce the reviewer's objections to the school of thought as such, without particular reference to the presentation before them. In much the same way students may display great ingenuity and dexterity in challenging an argument concerning the substance and practical implications of which they have no convictions at all. In the context of this book, I would rather elicit a response that sincerely takes issue with the view of morality that I present, than one that ignores that view in favour of concentrating on particular errors in reasoning, treated in isolation from one another. Finally, to claim to be championing an established doctrine, such as utilitarianism (Marxism, existentialism, etc.), even with modifications, opens one to the unwarranted charge of accepting all those features of the doctrine that one does not have space to reject expressly.[15]

I shall not therefore be at pains to synthesize or extract from classic or contemporary texts, except where I can use specific arguments to establish particular points, or where a *locus classicus* provides a useful way into an issue. This is neither a work of criticism nor of textual exegesis. It is an account of what seems to me to be a convincing ethical theory, which, if readers are disposed to categorize, I incidentally acknowledge to belong in the utilitarian tradition.

However, for the most part, I shall present my statement of the theory by means of focusing on various questions, difficulties and criticisms that have become familiar in moral philosophy, many of them specifically in arguments about utilitarianism. Some of the traditional objections to utilitarianism I shall seek to refute; others I shall accept, and accordingly modify my version of the theory. In dealing with some of these objections I do, where appropriate, make use of established texts and commentaries. For example, in considering whether utilitarianism can coherently admit different qualities of pleasure, I refer to Mill's remarks on the matter.[16] Similarly, in outlining what I regard as the fundamental premisses of utilitarianism, I consider G.E. Moore's objection that good cannot be equated with happiness.[17] But in neither case am I as interested in the question of what their respective positions may be, as I am in the question of what a clear and coherent position on the issue would be. They are introduced because they are, so to speak, dramatically useful to the argument.

Overall, I believe that my account is close to what Bentham and Mill, when they were not transparently at odds with one another, which, in my view, is less often than their very different styles have led people to suppose,[18] actually meant. But that matters a great deal less to me than whether what I say makes sense and avoids obscurity and incoherence. The result, I hope, is a book that provides in the most straightforward language possible: an ethical position, categorized as utilitarian, to be considered on its own merits; an argument for that position; treatment of most of the problems traditionally associated with utilitarian positions; reference to some of the famous problems of interpretation in the classic texts; and treatment of some of the basic problems in moral philosophy such as, most particularly, the nature of an ethical theory. I have relegated most of the references to on-going scholarly debate to the notes, in order to make the argument expounded more readable.

The plan of the book is as follows. In Chapter 2, I discuss the nature of an ethical theory and the kind of 'proof' to which it is amenable. In Chapter 3, I outline an account of the species of utilitarianism that I am going to elaborate and defend. I attempt to redress at the outset what has long been regarded as a weakness in utilitarianism, namely its lack of reference to a principle of justice. The fourth chapter offers an analysis of happiness, since in the absence of that we do not have an adequate understanding of the theory. Readers should pay attention to the concept delineated rather than the word chosen, perhaps, since it is not part of my claim that others necessarily mean what I mean by the word 'happiness'. My concern is to explain what is being valued, rather than to worry about whether it is correctly labelled. Chapter 5 takes up an interesting challenge made by MacIntyre some years ago, to the effect that utilitarianism is necessarily conservative.[19] This has some importance for the more general question of ethical relativism, a matter on which any serious claim to providing a plausible ethical theory must take a stand. Chapter 6 argues for rule-utilitarianism as against act-utilitarianism.

Chapter 7 discusses the traditional problem of whether different qualities of happiness can consistently be acknowledged in utilitarianism. It is argued that they cannot, and incidental attention is paid to the questions of whether Mill intended to suggest that they could, and what Bentham expected us to do with his 'felicific calculus'. Chapter 8 considers a curious but prevalent misunderstanding to the effect that utilitarians do not recognize other values, but assess everything including, for example, works of art, in terms of happiness potential. The conundrum that suggests that nobody can sincerely be a utilitarian, since in championing the theory one shows commitment to the value of truth, which may be at odds with the value of happiness, is also considered. Chapter 9 deals with the suggestion that utilitarianism may lead to the sacrifice of innocent scapegoats, and is therefore morally suspect, and also raises the question of acts of supererogation. Chapter 10 considers the question of whether the theory that has been elaborated is sufficiently in touch with our actual moral sentiments. Are the implications that it has in respect of, say, friendship and promise keeping acceptable to us?

In concluding this chapter, let me note two quite pronounced and rather curious trends relating to utilitarianism. One is a remarkable tendency to seriously misrepresent it; the other is a tendency to adapt it and adopt it, without explicitly noting that one is doing so, and without others seeming to notice that, in one guise or another, utilitarianism has a great deal of serious support as an ethical theory.

Some criticisms of utilitarianism have been surprisingly wide of the mark: for instance, the false assumptions that utilitarians would judge the merits of, say, a school simply by reference to the happiness of its members,[20] or the value of a painting by the pleasure it gives; that they don't care about things such as truth, justice, and friendship;[21] that they believe that the end justifies any means and, specifically, that they believe that everything should be subordinated to economic necessity. (This last misapprehension is not to be confused with MacIntyre's suggestion that utilitarianism is necessarily always interpreted to support the *status quo,* and therefore in certain societies might be identified with economic interest. That, I shall argue, is mistaken, but it certainly isn't absurd.)

But even setting such extreme misunderstandings aside, some curious comments have been made about utilitarianism. Moore, as has already been mentioned, somehow got it into his head that utilitarians such as Mill thought that happiness was to be identified with good, which has no warrant in anything Mill ever wrote and is, as Moore easily shows, a most ridiculous thing for anyone to think. Many commentators write as if Bentham believed that one could accurately measure the amount of pleasure potential in an act by means of his calculus, which nobody in his right mind could suppose and, though Bentham was in many ways odd, he was not out of his mind.

On the other hand, while utilitarianism is thus given a highly misleading and poor press, many recent works in ethical theory could arguably be classified as falling within the utilitarian tradition (once misconceptions about the nature of that tradition have been removed).[22] I mention this merely to indicate that, while a common view amongst moral philosophers is that utilitarianism is a period piece, it is in fact very much alive and a source of considerable inspiration. In 1973 Bernard Williams wrote 'the day cannot be too far off when we hear no more of it'.[23] The judgement was perhaps a trifle strange at the time. In retrospect it was very off-target for, as Quinton observed as recently as 1989, the intervening years have in fact seen 'for utilitarianism ... a remarkable restoration of status'.[24]

Notes

1. Alasdair MacIntyre, *After Virtue* (1981), chapter 1, p. 2.
2. Ibid.
3. Ibid.
4. See Chapter 2.
5. A.J. Ayer, *Language, Truth and Logic* (1936). According to Alan Ryan (*Oxford Today,* Vol. 2, No. 2, 1990) this book much to Ayer's 'chagrin continued to outsell everything else he wrote'.
6. E.g. R.M. Hare, *The Language of Morals* (1952), and *Freedom and Reason* (1963).

7. See Plato's *Republic*, Book 1. There are, of course, other possible interpretations of Thrasymachus' position.
8. This argument is further pursued in Robin Barrow, *Plato, Utilitarianism and Education* (1975). Isaiah Berlin has neatly captured the essence of this view in his essay 'Two concepts of freedom': 'The world that we encounter in ordinary experience is one in which we are faced with choices between ends equally ultimate, and claims equally absolute, the realisation of some of which must inevitably involve the sacrifice of others.'
9. Philippa Foot, *Virtues and Vices* (1978).
10. See, e.g., Iris Murdoch, *The Sovereignty of the Good* (1970).
11. G.J. Warnock, *The Object of Morality* (1971). See also his *Contemporary Moral Philosophy* (1967).
12. MacIntyre, op. cit. p. 2.
13. Cf. T.M. Scanlon, 'Contractualism and Utilitarianism' in Sen and Williams (eds) *Utilitarianism and Beyond* (1982), p. 107. 'The current meaning of moral terms is the product of many different moral beliefs held by past and present speakers of the language ... moral terms are used to express many different views ... and people who express these views are not using moral terms incorrectly, even though what some of them say must be mistaken.'
14. As R.G. Frey, in his introduction to *Utility and Rights* (1985), p. 4, justly observes: 'there is nothing which is "utilitarianism" *per se:* the term refers not to a single theory but to a cluster of theories that are variations on a theme, the components of which can be distinguished.'
15. Cf. R.M. Hare, 'Ethical Theory and Utilitarianism' in Sen and Williams (eds) op. cit., p. 24, faced with a similar problem: 'The ... theory that I shall advocate has close analogies with utilitarianism, and I should not hesitate to call it utilitarian, were it not that this name covers a wide variety of views, all of which have been the victims of prejudices rightly excited by the cruder among them. In calling my own ... theory utilitarian, I beg the reader to look at the theory itself, and ask whether it cannot avoid the objections that have been made against other kinds of utilitarianism.' Amen.
16. See J.S. Mill, *Utilitarianism* (ed. M. Warnock, 1962). Chapter 2, esp. pp. 257–262. (All subsequent references to Mill's *Utilitarianism* are to this edition.)
17. G.E. Moore, *Principia Ethica* (1903). Chapter 1.
18. See, for example, H.L.A. Hart, *Essays on Bentham* (1980), esp. chapter 4, 'Natural Rights: Bentham and John Stuart Mill', which convincingly and appreciably narrows the gap between the two men on this issue at least.
19. A. MacIntyre, 'Against Utilitarianism', in T.H.B. Hollins (ed.), *Aims in Education: the philosophical approach* (1964).
20. Amy Gutmann, in 'What's the Use of Going to School?' in Sen and Williams (eds) op. cit., p. 261, suggests that 'freedom provides a better standard than happiness by which to determine what and how to teach people'. Perhaps it does. Education would provide a better one yet! Utilitarians do, no doubt, hope that their children will be happy at school and that their schooling may make some indirect contribution to their own and others' happiness, but in no sense do they use happiness as a criterion for estimating educational success. They evaluate educational practice by educational criteria. They may then argue for the importance of education by reference to the claim that educational success (as determined by educational criteria) will be of long-term benefit to the individual and/or the community as a whole. As John Gray has well brought out, in *Mill on Liberty: a Defence* (1983), John Stuart Mill in particular shared Helvetius' view that 'L' éducation peut tout'.
21. And this despite, e.g., Mill's explicit reference to 'desirable things (which are as numerous in the utilitarian as in any other scheme)'. (*Utilitarianism*, op. cit., p. 257.)

22. R.M. Hare's work is instructive in this respect. In *Freedom and Reason* (1963) he was at pains to distinguish his own theory from utilitarianism, without necessarily dismissing the latter. His view was that 'utilitarianism cannot ... cover the whole of morality' (p. 121) but that 'a point of contact between utilitarianism and the account of the nature of moral argument' (p. 122) that he was developing could be established. In passing, he cited as awkward problems for utilitarians the question of whether one ought to maximize happiness or distribute it equally, the question of whether higher and lower pleasures should be recognized, and the nature of happiness. He also argued that act- and rule-utilitarianism were not as clearly distinguishable as proponents of either one assumed. As I shall argue, Hare is incorrect on the last point, and the problems cited are by no means insuperable. But what is of immediate interest is the extent to which his later book, *Moral Thinking* (1981) and other more recent writings, move towards a species of utilitarianism.
23. Bernard Williams, 'A Critique of Utilitarianism' (1973). p. 150.
24. Anthony Quinton, *Utilitarian Ethics* (2nd ed. 1989). p. ix.

2. What is an Ethical Theory and of What Kind of Proof is it Susceptible?

The main contention of this chapter is that an ethical theory should be seen as an attempt to explicate what in ideal circumstances would constitute right conduct, rather than as an attempt to provide unambiguous prescription for conduct in the imperfect world we inhabit.[1] By extension, the plausibility of a particular theory is to be assessed by reference to such things as its clarity and coherence, and not in any direct way by reference to how useful it may prove to be as a practical guide to conduct or to how it squares with our sentiments.[2]

This double premiss is extremely important to my overall line of reasoning. But, though it may seem an unusual, even a questionable, assumption, it involves no more than insisting that ethical theory should be treated like any other branch of theory. Scientific theory seeks to tell us how the natural world actually is: it goes beyond appearances, and is none the worse for occasionally shattering our everyday opinions and prejudices. In addition, its quality is not properly assessed by reference to the extent to which it is useful to us in our daily dealings with material objects. Literary theory is not to be governed by the limits implicit in books that have actually been written, although no doubt it should take some account of them. Aesthetic theory is not to be governed by our current capacity for aesthetic response, nor is it to be confined by the limits of what we can readily achieve. In like manner, ethical theory is not to be constructed, nor therefore assessed, by exclusive reference to our current values and our capacity to put it into practice. 'Ought' implies 'can', but the 'can' in question is logical rather than contingent.

In the body of this book I shall attempt to provide a coherent and plausible account of a utilitarian ethical theory, rather than an account of any particular epoch's or philosopher's view of utilitarianism. However, since many criticisms of previous attempts to explain utilitarianism arise out of misapprehensions concerning the theory itself,[3] as traditionally expounded, and concerning the kind of theory that it purports to be, I shall devote this chapter to clarifying my use of basic terms such as 'good', 'right', and 'ethical theory'. In the following chapter I shall outline what I take to be the essential nature of the utilitarian position in question. Subsequent chapters will then examine in detail various questions and problems to which the theory seems to give rise.

As illustrations of criticisms that involve the kind of misapprehension referred to, we may begin by noting the objections (i) that utilitarianism does not make it easy for people to know what they ought to do; (ii) that it flies in the face of the manifest fact of cultural variation in moral values; and (iii) that it presupposes that the right is derivative from the good.

The first of these objections was explicitly noted by John Stuart Mill. In response to those who complained that a utilitarian would have neither the time nor the wherewithal to work out how much happiness, for whom, for what duration, of what intensity and so forth, would follow from various alternative courses of action, he scathingly replied that no more would a Christian have the time or the wherewithal to make decisions in accordance with a thorough review of the Bible.[4] Mill's response is entirely adequate so far as it goes. The fact that an ethical theory spells out in a thorough, painstaking, and schematic way all that is involved in morally right action and all the dimensions that have a bearing on the matter, does not necessarily mean that the individual, before acting, has to go through a checklist of aspects of the situation in a literal, self-conscious way. He does not have to articulate the theoretical justification for action consciously in order to act in the correct way as demanded by the theory. However unreliable they may sometimes be, human beings are capable of a high degree of internalization and intuitive recognition. On any ethical view, they are capable of acting, and acting rightly, without having a philosopher's analysis of the theory at their fingertips. Indeed, not only are they capable of it, but it seems a matter of common experience that they are inclined to proceed in this way. Furthermore, the complexity of the analysis of a theory should not be confused with the question of the difficulty of acting in accordance with it.[5]

But Mill might well have gone further: ethical theories are not *directly* concerned with enabling people to act morally with greater ease or success. They are concerned to elaborate on what is involved in acting morally. They are designed to explain in what morality consists. While such explanation obviously has *indirect* bearing on our capacity to act morally, it is not in itself any objection to a theory that it does not make it easy for us to exercise that capacity, or that it does not tell us clearly what to do in all conceivable situations. It is, perhaps, historically understandable that utilitarianism should have been criticized for being impractical, unwieldy, and lacking in detailed prescription, since men such as Bentham and Mill were intensely practically concerned.[6] Nonetheless, it is quite irrelevant to challenge the utilitarian theory on the grounds that it is difficult to act in accordance with it and that it does not readily yield specific guidance for action, even if such charges were well founded, since those are not the direct concerns of an ethical theory. An ethical theory seeks to explain the nature of morality, and since the truth may well be that it is not always easy to know what we ought to do in particular circumstances, it can hardly be held against a theory that it does not make leading the moral life easy. To do so would be comparable to objecting to atomic theory on the grounds that tables and chairs are more easily dealt with in life on the assumption that they are what they appear to be – namely solid, three dimensional, self-contained objects, rather than a concantenation of hypothetical indivisible particles.[7]

To repeat and emphasize this basic but very important and often ignored point: an ethical theory is not primarily or directly intended to make moral decision making theoretically straightforward and simple, or practically easy. It is supposed to clarify what is the case in the moral domain, and it may be that the moral domain is such that sound theorizing shows that moral behaviour will necessarily be difficult, contentious, and perhaps sometimes even impossible. If, say, Aristotle's view of ethics is ultimately to be reckoned as inadequate, it will not be simply on the grounds that it is not always possible to discern what behaviour constitutes the Aristotelian mean.

The second example of a familiar but misplaced criticism of utilitarianism illustrates a common misunderstanding of a different kind. For, as a matter of fact, as I shall argue in Chapter 5, utilitarianism does not fly in the face of evidence for cultural variation in respect of moral values. It is true that it is a theory that would be classified by many people as 'absolute' and 'objective' (ignoring for the moment the problematic nature of these ambiguous terms), since it clearly states that happiness is good and that we ought to act so as to promulgate happiness, whatever particular peoples or cultures may believe to the contrary. Nonetheless, it is one of the few ethical theories, perhaps the only one, that can both explain and accept a great deal of cultural variation. This comes about because of the nature of its pivotal concept, happiness. As we shall see in Chapter 4, happiness and human nature being what they are, quite different systems of social organization and behaviour may be morally acceptable on utilitarian terms.

It may in any case be argued that, if utilitarianism or any other theory leads to the conclusion that certain cultures' views of morality are mistaken, that raises a question mark against those other views rather than against the theory in question. Whether a clash between some widely held, deeply rooted belief and a new theory should be accounted an objection to the latter is of course difficult to decide in particular instances. In practice, the initial suggestion that the world is round will be vanquished by the commonplace assumption that it is flat. And, of course, sometimes the commonplace assumption is sound, and the theory thereby invalidated. It remains clear, however, that a conflict between some received opinion and the implications of a theory does not in itself discredit the theory. We have to consider the coherence of, and argument for, the theory on its own terms and, similarly, the independent grounds for retaining the conflicting opinion. Thus, we do not say the theory must be wrong because we know the world is flat. We reconsider and come to the conclusion that the argument for supposing the world is round is strong, while that for supposing it flat is not. In the same way, if it were the case (as it may or may not be) that utilitarianism led to the conclusion that certain cultures are morally superior to others, the contemporary sentiment to the effect that this cannot be so could hardly be accounted as an argument against utilitarianism. Rather, one would have to show what is wrong with the argument provided for the theory and/or provide an independent argument in favour of the prevailing sentiment.

The third example of a misconceived objection to utilitarianism similarly trades on a belief that may conceivably be sound, but which has not been shown to be so, and which in any case is strictly speaking outside the purview of the utilitarian's argument. For the utilitarian theory is avowedly a theory about the rightness of actions, and takes it as a premiss that the rightness of an act is determined by whether it maximizes intrinsic good. It is therefore true that the theory presupposes that right is derivative on good in a way that Kantian ethics, where the central concept is that of duty, does not. That is merely another way of saying that the former is an example of what we classify as a teleological theory, the latter formalistic or deontological. But this cannot be regarded as an objection to the theory. Objections to the theory have to take the form of criticism of, say, the utilitarian conception of happiness or its notion of justice. An objection to the idea of a teleological theory as such is quite distinct from an objection to this species of such a theory, and would have to be conducted not by means of making the observation that it is teleological, but by providing independent reasons for eschewing that kind of theory.[8]

One valuable consequence of recognizing this point may incidentally be that we come to see that there is in any case no necessary conflict between a particular teleological theory and a particular deontological theory. The former offers a theory of what makes acts right, the latter a theory of what entitles the agent to moral praise or blame. It could conceivably be the case (to oversimplify grossly) that the utilitarian is correct in asserting that acts are right in proportion to their tendency to promote happiness, and that the Kantian is correct in claiming that to be a moral person what matters is not the consequence of your actions but the spirit in which they are undertaken. However that may be, one cannot reasonably seek to discredit utilitarianism simply by observing that it presupposes that the right is derivative on the good. It expressly outlines a specific thesis about the manner in which an act has to relate to a particular conception of the good to be a right act. Legitimate criticism has to focus on the argument provided in support of that specific thesis. It is, after all, a theory about what makes acts right rather than a theory about what entitles an individual to be judged morally good. Closely related as the two undoubtedly are, they are not necessarily interchangeable. It may be possible to be morally good while doing the wrong thing, and vice versa.[9]

Despite the impropriety of responding to an argument for utilitarianism, or any other theory, by concentrating on assumptions and implications that have not been explicitly dealt with, rather than by focusing on the coherence of what has been said, one would ideally like to give consideration to all such potential objections, however tangential, misconceived, or extraneous. However, since that would constitute too ambitious and unrealistic a programme, I intend instead, in the remainder of this chapter, at least to outline the broad assumptions about the nature of an ethical theory that I am taking for granted and, consequently, the kind of proof to which it is amenable.

So far as 'good' goes, I concur with G.E. Moore in regarding it as a simple (i.e. non-complex) unanalysable term, comparable in that respect to 'yellow'.[10] We can talk about the conditions under which things appear yellow, the contexts in which they appear yellow, and we can discuss what things are yellow; but we cannot define yellow by breaking it down into familiar constituent parts as we can define a 'horse' as a 'solid-hoofed, perisodactyl quadruped, having a flowing mane and tail'. We can try to pinpoint yellow by locating it in relation to other colours on the spectrum, and we can talk about how to modify yellow in real life by mixing various colours. Similarly, we can discuss the questions of whether good is found in conjunction with certain other properties, what we are doing when we describe something as good, and what things are good, but we cannot define it in the sense of break it down into its constituent parts.[11] We can define it only by way of explaining its function, in some such terms as the *Shorter Oxford Dictionary's* 'a term of general or indefinite commendation'. We can say a little more about specifically 'moral good', but that is because we can say something about what is meant by 'moral'. To say that something is morally good is to commend in moral terms as opposed to, say, aesthetic terms. Consequently, assuming that we have something to say about the respects in which the moral domain is distinguishable from the aesthetic (the prudential, the religious, etc.) domain, we should be able to add some detail to our conception of the morally good.

In principle, I have no difficulty with going further with Moore and regarding the good as something that has to be intuited or recognized, just as yellow has to be seen. Indeed, I regard the claim that happiness is a good as a self-evident truth, and the more specific utilitarian claim that it is the only thing good in and of itself as, in the last resort, amenable only to intuition. However, it would be confusing to categorize utilitarianism as an intuitionist theory on those grounds, since the latter term is generally used to refer to theories that claim that a number of goods may be intuited (and, in some cases, a number of rights as well). Furthermore, while I subscribe to the basic intuitionist tenet that the good is something that can only be intuited, I regard that as a somewhat unhelpful observation, unless we can say something more about the conditions under which a person's intuition is to be taken more or less seriously (rather as we may say that a person's judgement that he is looking at something yellow is only to be trusted, given that he is not colour blind, that conditions are in some sense normal, etc.).[12] If we cannot do that, we cannot get beyond the obvious problem that intuitions notoriously differ. I see it as part of the purpose of studying ethical theories to try to arrive at some kind of intellectual preparedness for trusting one's intuition. For, some people might reasonably be accused of failing to intuit that happiness is good, primarily because they do not fully understand what it is that they are being asked to recognize.

I need hardly add that agreement with Moore that 'good' is a unique, unanalysable, quality, and that it can ultimately only be intuited, does not lead to sharing his preoccupation with the naturalistic fallacy and, specifically, does not involve acceptance of his view that utilitarianism involves committing that fallacy, which I shall show to be mistaken in the next chapter.[13]

I also find W.D. Ross's suggestion that goodness is what he, following Aristotle, terms a 'consequential attribute' or a supervenient quality most useful.[14] While goodness is simply what it is, so that people have to be brought to recognize it, rather than come to an understanding of it by way of a definition involving already familiar terms, it surely is the case that it is to be found only as a result of the presence of other qualities. It seems quite inconceivable to me that goodness might in principle be a quality of anything, and that it is merely a contingent matter that some things are never good, as it may be said that anything could in principle be bigger or smaller than it is. Even yellowness might be argued to be a supervenient quality in this way. It is not simply an accident of nature that grass and leaves are generally green. Their greenness is the inevitable consequence of such things as photosynthesis. If they were yellow, they would not be what they are. But certainly if we were to believe, and to be correct in our belief, that, say, happiness, friendship and promise-keeping were good, it would seem more reasonable to suppose that they are so in virtue of certain features they have in common, and that are not to be found together in things that are not good, than that goodness just happened to alight on them, rather as a bee may settle on this flower rather than that. The essence of the claim that goodness is a supervenient quality is that it is something that is invariably to be found with, and that represents something beyond the sum of, certain other qualities. A comparison might reasonably be drawn with an electric current: we can list the things that are necessary to produce an electric current, but the current itself is something more than the mere sum of those things.

Ross devoted considerable attention to trying to determine what qualities led to the emergence of the supervenient quality of goodness. Here I do not follow him. I do not find his specific arguments and claims altogether persuasive and, in any case, it is not of major importance for my purposes to determine what those qualities may be, since I adhere to the utilitarian claim that happiness is the only thing that in itself has the supervenient quality of goodness. In virtue of what characteristics it does so is of less importance to me than the question would be to a theorist such as Ross, who, believing that various things might be good, gains some practical advantage from determining what other qualities when found in conjunction give rise to goodness. I wish only to make it clear that I understand goodness to be an unanalysable quality that is supervenient on other non-moral qualities.

I am assuming that strictly speaking goodness is a property of people and states of affairs, while rightness is a property of actions or conduct.[15] Furthermore, as already indicated, I shall take it for granted that rightness is parasitic on goodness. If there were no such thing as a morally good state of affairs, then there could be no such thing as right and wrong actions. This assumption should not be confused with any claim about the inherent superiority of consequentiality or teleological theories over deontological theories. In fact I do not find those labels at all helpful, since although it will commonly be said, and *prima facie* with good reason, that utilitarianism is to be contrasted with deontological theories, which regard certain acts such as truth telling or keeping promises as right regardless of consequences, the view of utilitarianism that I shall expound, being a species of rule-utilitarianism, would accept that certain actions ought to be performed regardless of the consequences of performing them on particular occasions. Of course, it may be said that nonetheless the utilitarian views them as justified because of consequences; it is merely that in such a case he focuses on the consequence of having a rule of conduct that is rigorously obeyed. But then it is hard to imagine a deontological theorist who would maintain that an action was right, regardless of what the consequences of so maintaining might conceivably be. If promise keeping, for example, is believed to be always morally incumbent upon us, this must either be because some good is believed to come of such conduct or because the conduct is itself being regarded as a good state of affairs (i.e. promise keeping is not being seen as a series of right actions, but the state of affairs of persons keeping promises is being seen as good).[16] At any rate, my concern here is simply one of clarifying usage of terminology. What is viewed as a morally commendable state of affairs I term 'good'; what is viewed as a morally commendable action I term 'right'.

People may be said to be good in so far as they behave morally, in the full sense which includes not merely doing right acts but doing them for moral reasons as opposed to, say, prudential, selfish or unavoidable reasons. Formally, acting for moral reasons would generally be agreed to involve, at least, acting autonomously and with a sense of the rightness of one's conduct. I am not, for example, acting morally, even if I do something acknowledged to be right, if I do it because I was compelled to do it, or if I do it unreflectively simply because I get the urge to do it. If my donation to charity is to be classified as a moral act, I must myself determine to do it, and I must do it at least partly because I believe it to be right to do it. These characteristics of moral behaviour are usually associated with the tradition of moral philosophy deriving from Kant, but they are in no way incompatible with utilitarianism, and indeed are a necessary underpinning for any truly moral theory.[17]

Some, such as G.J. Warnock,[18] have argued in addition that, for his behaviour to be moral, the agent must act with a view to people's well-being. I am not sure that this is correct, although it is very persuasive. At any rate, to avoid the charge of begging certain questions, I shall prefer to say that a person who acts autonomously, in the belief that he is doing right, is formally to be classified as acting morally, even if he does not have a view to people's well-being. This allows, for example, that the individual who determines to tell the truth, because he sincerely believes it right to do so, even when he knows that the consequences will be unpleasant for everybody concerned, is nonetheless acting morally in the sense of playing the moral game rather than any other kind of game. It is of course another question whether what he does is in fact morally right, and I shall argue that it is when we try to answer that question that Warnock's 'view to people's well-being' comes into play. In other words, I am maintaining that being concerned about people's well-being is a substantive moral value, and not part of the definition of morality.

A state of affairs may be described as good in so far as it embodies things that are good. Thus, for an ideal utilitarian such as Moore, a world that is beautiful and friendly is to that extent a good world. Others might regard societies as good in so far as they involve freedom. The hedonistic utilitarian will, of course, be concerned ultimately only with the amount of happiness in a state of affairs.

Particular actions or conduct generally are to be described as morally right in so far as they contribute to increasing the sum of goodness in the world. But having said that, which is again a purely formal point about how the word 'right' is being used (and without any specific reference to utilitarianism), it is evident that we need to distinguish between what is right and what is thought to be right. In common parlance, we may reasonably say of someone that she did the right thing in the circum-stances, or that she did right to act in such a way, even when we recognize that as a matter of fact what was done was morally wrong. Whereas a person may be morally good, even when what they do is wrong, provided they act morally (i.e. autonomously and sincerely believing they do right), and whereas, by contrast, a state of affairs either is good or it is not, an act may either be right in fact, or right in the sense of 'the act of a morally good person' despite being wrong. What is right in fact is what does contribute most to the sum of good, but an act may in the other sense be described as right, if it is sincerely thought by the agent to contribute most to the sum of good.

In this regard, I find Ross's distinction between actual and *prima facie* duties offers instructive and useful guidance, although I do not endorse precisely his distinction.[19] What is surely clear is that we can differentiate between what is actually right in the sense of morally desirable behaviour in an ideal world, what it is actually right to do in particular real-life and often imperfect situations, and what a person may be morally commended for doing even though it is judged to be in some sense wrong (or, at any rate, not known to be right). The distinction between the first two has not, I think, been sufficiently emphasized, with the result that many misapplied criticisms are made of ethical theories (particularly, as it happens, utilitarianism) to the effect that they enjoin us to do acts that intuitively it is hard to accept as morally right in all circumstances, most obviously when there is a clash between two principles both of which are central to a theory.

An ethical theory such as Kant's, for example, may claim that both promise keeping and telling the truth are always right, and critics have been known to object that this is incoherent, since sometimes it is literally impossible to abide by one principle without offending against the other. Utilitarianism has frequently been criticized by means of imagining ingenious unfortunate situations in which acting with a view to promoting as much happiness as possible would seem to lead to such practices as sacrificing innocent scapegoats, which seems intuitively morally unacceptable. As I shall argue at various points in remaining chapters, this criticism of utilitarianism is confused on various counts: it takes advantage of inadequate formulations of utilitarianism, such as that it is concerned to maximize happiness or promote the greatest happiness of the greatest number; it fails to take account of the distinction between rule- and act-utilitarianism; and it may be argued that in some real-life situations there have to be scapegoats on any conceivable ethical theory. (See Chapter 6). However, the point to be made here is that this line of criticism against any ethical theory fails to take account of the distinction between what is ideally (i.e. in Ross's terms, *prima facie*) right conduct according to the theory and what, still according to the theory, it is right to do in real-life situations (i.e., one's actual duty).

The proper response of a Kantian to this line of criticism should be: the claim of the theory is simply that promise keeping and telling the truth are right acts. An ideal world would be one in which people never told lies or broke promises or offended against any of the other principles embodied in the theory, and the question of whether the theory is coherent in this respect has to be considered by reference to whether strict adherence to all the principles is logically conceivable or conceivable in ideal circumstances. The fact that, in the world as it is, there is already a great deal of wrong-doing and imperfection certainly means that in practice we face clashes of principle, or embarrassing consequences for acting rightly, but it does not show the theory to be unacceptable. Ethical theories are designed to tell us what kind of a way of conducting ourselves, if we all consistently did so, would constitute a morally ordered world.[20] Putting the matter succinctly, a Kantian ethical theory tells us that telling lies is always a wrong act; it does not seek to answer the question of whether an individual is ever justified in doing this wrong act.

Ross's notion that we have various *prima facie* duties, which is to say duties that we should carry out other things being equal, but that these are to be distinguished from our actual duty (i.e. what we ought to do in particular situations, which might involve clashes of *prima facie* duties or in some other way make it impossible to carry out our *prima facie* duty), has the merit of recognizing that what is unequivocally morally right is not necessarily identical with what we had best do in actual situations. He, however, was tempted to try to systematize some account of, in his terminology, our actual duty. That seems to me to be going beyond expounding an ethical theory, which I take to be solely concerned with determining what is ideally good and right. I cannot imagine that anybody could successfully elaborate a theory that went beyond that and gave us the means of determining what we had best do in all conceivable circumstances in an imperfect world.[21]

In view of these considerations, I shall adopt the following terminology. First, I shall refer to acts that we ought to perform in an ideal world as right acts. And these right acts, I shall maintain, we have a duty to perform, even in the world as it is, where we can. Second, I shall refer to acts that it seems we should perform in particular circumstances in the real world as justified acts. To perform such specific acts will not be termed our duty, but will be regarded as morally commendable. Third, I shall refer to a certain class of acts as morally intentioned. For, as we have just noted, colloquially it may be said that a person who sincerely, if mistakenly, acts with a view to the good or to his duty has acted rightly. To avoid confusion, while conceding that such a person may reasonably be seen as a morally good person, I shall refer to such conduct as morally intentioned, since clearly such conduct might be neither justified nor right. Thus a person who believes that one should keep promises and tell the truth and who, when faced with a clash between these principles, seeks to do that which he thinks will promote most good (as opposed, say, to that which is most convenient or most to his advantage), but in fact fails to do so, performs a morally intentioned act, and as such is to be commended as a moral agent. Should his action indeed promote most good, he has performed a justified act and one that is morally commendable. But whether or not it is a right act is an inappropriate question: right acts are those that are always incumbent on us, and in this case, *ex hypothesi*, we are beyond the opportunity for performing a right act.

At this juncture my concern is to make the terms I shall use clear and precise rather than to unfold the details of the substantive ethical theory in question. However, it may be sensible to indicate briefly how my terminology might get used in substantive terms. Let us suppose that it were agreed that in an ideal world we ought to tell the truth, to keep promises, and to avoid causing gratuitous suffering. In an ideal world, not only could we consistently abide by these and other principles, but the very fact of doing so in one case might make it easier to do so in other cases. At any rate, it would obviously be possible in principle for a community to live in such a way that promises were always kept, the telling of lies and the causing of gratuitous suffering always avoided. When we observe that these principles may conflict, then, we are correct, but they do so only because of human imperfection. An individual faces a conflict either because he put himself into a conflict situation by, for example, making a promise which, if kept, could only cause suffering to others, or because other people or the world in general create problematic situations. On Ross's view these three duties are *prima facie* and one makes an intuitive judgement as to which of them one ought to adhere to in cases of conflict; what one then ought to do is one's actual duty. On the view I am putting forward, one ought always to keep promises, avoid telling lies and causing gratuitous suffering. Those are three firm duties; to behave in accordance with the principles is to act rightly.[22] In so far as a conflict arises, if it is one caused by me (for example, by making an unwise promise), then, though it will not help in determining practice, we can at least say, unequivocally, that my mistake lay in making a foolish promise; the duty to keep promises is still absolute, but the question of what it is right for me to do, having got myself into this mess, does not arise. There is no right act possible now. We can only consider what I am justified in doing, which is to say what it seems likely will contribute most to the sum of goodness. In so doing I act, not rightly, not according to duty, but in a morally commendable way. If in retrospect it seems that what I did was most productive of good, I was indeed justified. If it was not, then my action was not justified, but it was morally intentioned. But the awkward consequences that may arise from my doing my duty, because of the imperfections of the world in general, should be ignored. That is to say, for example, if I have made a reasonable promise then I should keep it, even if circumstances are such that through no direct fault of mine somebody somewhere will be made to suffer.

The agent's motivation will be widely agreed to be an important consideration in determining whether he is acting morally. If my motivation is entirely selfish then, whatever I do, I will not deserve commendation as a morally good person; but my actions can still be regarded as morally commendable (in my terms 'justified'), if they happen to promote the good. Motive, then, is irrelevant to the question of what is right. For right acts are being defined as those acts that ought always to be performed, where they can be.[23]

I have said that ethical theories are concerned with determining how we ought to behave in an ideal world. This important claim requires elaboration. An ethical theory should not be construed as an attempt to explain, or to provide a theoretical underpinning for, what this or any other society is pleased to regard as its moral code. That endeavour would be better classified as an anthropological theoretical task, and to confuse it with ethical theory would be similar to confusing a theory of witchcraft with scientific theory. Scientific theory seeks to explain the physical world as it is, and that explanation can only be hindered by concentrating on some established but erroneous theory of how the world is. In the same way, trying to articulate a theory that makes sense of a specific moral code of behaviour, though it may give us hints and clues that we can make something of, is quite different from trying to articulate a theory that explains what is morally good and right. Similarly, an ethical theory should not be confused with an attempt to provide a coherent theory for our beliefs about morality, in so far as these differ from our practice. An ethical theory is not necessarily shown to be the more unreasonable or unconvincing in proportion to the extent that it is at variance with current moral practice and belief.

Nor are ethical theories, properly speaking, prescriptive. It is true that morality is a prescriptive domain: moral principles enjoin us to do certain things. But an ethical theory is only incidentally prescriptive, because of its subject matter. The theory itself is essentially descriptive: it explains what makes things right; it gives an account of what is the moral case. It is comparable in this respect, if no other, to medical theory, which is likewise dealing with normative concepts such as health and fitness, but which nonetheless does not in itself prescribe specific practice. Medical theory seeks to determine what health and fitness are, and to establish what leads to health and fitness and what the relationships between various other concepts may be and what actions lead to what results. Such understanding clearly has profound implications for how the medical profession should conduct itself but, nonetheless, to maintain that, for example, doctors must prescribe certain drugs in particular situations or carry out heart transplants is to go beyond medical theory, and the soundness of medical theory is not judged by reference to its tendency to provide specific prescription.

In the same way, something such as the Christian system of ethics is not a true ethical theory, but a prescriptive theory, inasmuch as it consists largely of specific rules of conduct. To become an ethical theory, it would need to provide a more coherent explanation of central concepts, such as goodness and rightness, and a fuller explanation of why and in what sense it is right to honour one's father and mother, etc. It would need to concentrate on what is right, in the sense of incumbent upon us in an ideal world, rather than on rules of conduct for an imperfect world. If it be felt that I am here arbitrarily defining ethical theory, and doing it in a somewhat severe way, it may be replied that I am arguing that, at any rate, a theory such as utilitarianism is misunderstood if it is seen as an attempt to provide clear and useful prescription for conduct in the world as it is. Obviously, the hope is that a proper understanding of the nature of morality, a grasp of the criteria whereby right conduct may be determined, will contribute to a better understanding of what conduct may be justified and to reasonable specific prescriptions for action (and it is certainly necessary to those aims). Nonetheless, that is not the direct concern of ethical theory; it is not the concern of the theory of utilitarianism that I shall expound.[24]

An ethical theory, as I understand it, should not be identified with an account of the nature of moral discourse, although a full understanding of the moral domain will involve such an account and some ethical theories are heavily reliant on a theory of the nature of moral utterances. For example, the question of whether concern for well-being should be seen as a necessary part of the meaning of a moral utterance or as part of a substantive ethical theory involving the claim that a moral judgement that ignores such a consideration, while being a *bona fide* moral as opposed to a non-moral utterance, is morally inadequate or wrong, has already been referred to.[25] But, whatever one's view on that particular question, it is certain that a theory that does no more than elucidate the logically necessary implications of moral language is incomplete as an ethical theory.

By way of further illustration of this point, emotivism and prescriptivism may be contrasted. The prescriptivism associated with R.M. Hare, particularly in his early *Language of Morals,*[26] is not an ethical theory (or, if one prefers, it is a different kind of ethical theory to utilitarianism). The reason for this is that prescriptivism as originally formulated concentrates exclusively on the logical properties that make an utterance fall into the moral, as opposed to any other, non-moral, category. But that kind of analysis in itself is notoriously unable to lead to any clear conclusion about whether, for example, the sincere Nazi who recognizes that his views logically involve prescription and is willing to universalize them so as to acknowledge that, if he were a Jew, he too should be treated as he treats Jews, is morally reprehensible or not. Emotivism, by contrast, even in the bare form presented by A.J. Ayer,[27] though it too is clearly grounded in the claim that moral utterances are of a certain logical type, explicitly proclaims that there is no more to morality than the generation of utterances that exhibit a positive or negative attitude and that are couched in such a way as to evince a similar attitude in others. It therefore does constitute an ethical theory even if, in this case, a bold but somewhat unconvincing one. (If a prescriptivist were to argue that there is no more to morality than his analysis of the features of moral discourse revealed, and that the sincere, universalizing Nazi is therefore behaving morally, and not simply making distinctively moral claims, he could claim to have an ethical theory, of course.) It should perhaps be added that there is no necessary incompatibility between the claims made about the nature of moral discourse by either prescriptivists or emotivists and utilitarianism, and indeed I shall take it for granted that a *bona fide* moral utterance is emotive, prescriptive and universalizable.

Because of what an ethical theory such as utilitarianism is, it cannot legitimately be criticized or found wanting either because it fails to give us clear guidance as to what we ought to do in various real-life situations, or because acceptance of the theory is shown to lead in practice to certain dilemmas, in the proper sense of situations where there actually is no one clearly justified way to proceed. Even if we had full understanding of morality, we would still be faced with uncertainty and dilemma, because the world is imperfect. An ethical theory may make it clear beyond all doubt that, say, torturing innocent people is wrong, but it cannot directly determine whether or not such a practice may be justified in a world where, if we do not torture certain innocent people, some other innocent people may be blown to smithereens. An ethical theory may convince us that friendship is good, but it cannot tell us whether or not we are justified in maintaining friendships in every conceivable circumstance, given that some at least of the world's population are already acting wrongly and, specifically, may be abusing friendship. Placing a moral value on friendship, truth telling, or anything else only makes sense, initially, if we envisage ideal conditions.

Nor, as we have said, can an ethical theory such as utilitarianism reasonably be dismissed or condemned simply for failing to square entirely with our current practice or sentiment. This claim may perhaps require a little further explanation, since in some sense a recognition that an ethical theory is incompatible with our moral sentiment is psychologically bound to constitute an objection to that theory. The elucidation of an ethical theory is in essence like the elucidation of any other concept, and in conceptual analysis usage of the word or phrase that betokens the concept must guide but must not dominate us. An adequate review of usage guides us all to the same broad area as a starting point; it ensures that we are at least all trying to talk about the same thing. If, for example, I want to analyse the concept of democracy, it would be absurd to ignore the fact that people just don't call societies governed by absolute, autocratic, hereditary, monarchs 'democratic'. If, for some reason, I nonetheless insist on arguing that such societies are democratic, I must at least acknowledge that I am using the word in an idiosyncratic way that does not appear even to refer to the same kind of concept as others have in mind. My analysis, if it pertains to the concept that others have in mind, however confusedly or hazily, when they talk of democracy, must take account of facts such as that most people talk of Britain as being, however imperfectly, democratic; that the Soviet Union also professes to be democratic, and that people can have serious arguments about whether and in what respects trade unions are democratic.

Attention to such usages ensures that we are all playing the same game or talking about broadly the same thing, and it also furnishes us with a variety of useful hints and clues. It would be useful, for example, to consider on what grounds two such distinct systems of government as that of the United States and Soviet Russia could conceivably regard themselves as democratic. However, it is self-evident that usage cannot dictate our analysis, for two reasons. First, it may transpire that there are incompatible uses and, if that is so, different things are being talked about. They may both be called 'democracy', but they cannot both embody the concept of democracy. They are at best distinct conceptions of democracy and will need to be analysed separately. (If it be said that we have to distinguish between acceptable and unacceptable usage, it is difficult to see how that could be done except in the light of some independently arrived at analysis.) Second, many particular usages, though consistent, will be obscure, incoherent, or self-contradictory. The task of analysis is, therefore, having focused on a particular conception that appears to be what is referred to by an identifiable usage, to tease that conception out by clarifying the further concepts embodied in it, noting logical implications, removing contradictions and inconsistencies, and ensuring that the detailed conception finally arrived at is compatible with whatever claims about it we insist are well-founded.[28] (For instance, it would be important, if we are in favour of democracy, to offer an analysis that represents something we are indeed in favour of.)

If, therefore, I expound an ethical theory that seems to have no point of contact with what people generally presume morality to be about, it is legitimate to object that whatever I am talking about I am not producing a *bona fide ethical* theory. On these grounds, for example, on some interpretations of the first book of Plato's *Republic,* one might say that Thrasymachus' opinion that right is might is not an ethical theory, but a denial of ethics, by contrast with Callicles' view in the *Gorgias* that might is right. Callicles' view, whatever we think of it, is at least concerned to make a distinctively ethical pronouncement: it is morally right to dominate. Thrasymachus appears to say 'all this talk of rightness is just an emotive way of trying to invest naked power and success with an aura of sanctity'. More crudely, if I classify the cultural norms of Swift's Hottentots as a moral code, I would seem to be playing a different game from that engaged in by other ethical theorists. It would, then, be entirely fair to object to utilitarianism, if it were the case that, in a similar way, it had no point of contact with what people normally regard as morality.

However, if a theory does have some clear point of contact with at least some of our normal moral sentiments, if, that is to say, it clearly is an ethical theory of some sort, then its subsequent departure from other of our sentiments cannot in itself be held against it. The issue becomes one of whether the theory can convince us that, starting from the point of contact, its ramifications are more reasonable than those sentiments that it conflicts with. In just the same way, whether democracy requires that children shall have the vote is not to be decided by the widespread assumption that it does not, but by considering in greater depth the implications and meaning of facets of democracy that are agreed upon, such as that it involves equal representation for all citizens.

When, therefore, it is said that utilitarianism conflicts with our moral sentiment, it should be remembered that in principle that may indicate an error on our part rather than on the part of the theory.[29]

Because of the relationship between the good and the right, an ethical theory must contain some reference to what state of affairs is good (as opposed to an account of what goodness means, which, as I have said, cannot be provided in terms of a conventional definition). But because of what an ethical theory is, it must also contain some reference to the distribution of good. For some unaccountable reason, it has often been maintained that utilitarianism does not recognize the principle of justice. But it does, as we shall see. What it does not do, since it is not a deontological theory, is recognize the inherent rightness of certain acts (though, on the face of it paradoxically, it does maintain that there may be certain acts that we ought always to perform, even in the real world). However the principle of justice may also be equated with the principle of fairness, and utilitarianism does have such a principle, as it must do, since a fully fledged ethical theory tells us what is right, and no account of what is right can be complete if it makes no reference to the distribution of the good.[30]

Finally, to come full circle, because of what an ethical theory is, it should be presented and appraised as an explanation of what makes for right conduct and a good society in ideal terms. I believe, and I have tried to suggest here, that a great deal of misguided argument about all manner of ethical theories has been generated by mistakenly assuming that a theory is at fault, if it either has nothing to say about resolving some dilemmas in real life or, more generally, fails to solve some of our perceived moral problems. But it must be the case that, in a far from perfect world, there could be situations, and in all likelihood will be many, where the attempt to perform right acts will involve disastrous consequences or involve confusion between conflicting principles. It is, however, surely clear that commitment to, say, both the principle of promise keeping and the principle of truth telling is, in itself, entirely coherent, and clashes between them only come about in the mess of real-life situations, where, for example, people make unwise promises or there are awkward truths to be taken account of.[31]

If an ethical theory is to be judged by its ability to tell us clearly what we ought to do in any particular real-life situation, it is not to be wondered at that the world thinks moral philosophers have failed, and we will wait forever for an adequate ethical theory. But that is rather like judging the theory behind bridge building by its capacity to tell us directly how to build a good bridge in all situations. Such a demand is entirely misplaced. The theoretical engineer is not necessarily enabled by his knowledge to recognize what he had best do with the unfamiliar materials at his disposal to span a particular crossing in some undiscovered jungle. If, on the other hand, ethical theories are understood as attempts to articulate what would constitute an ideal human society, then many contributions over the centuries are seen to be very revealing and helpful even though, in my view, utilitarianism is seen to be the most compelling. (However, it may incidentally be noted that deonotological theories also have far more plausibility, if interpreted as attempts to analyse the ideal, than if interpreted as attempts to prescribe conduct in real life. It is far more plausible to suggest that in a morally ordered world one should always keep a promise, than it is to claim that one should always do so in fact, come what may.) Put simply, what we may be morally justified in doing is not always in itself a straightforwardly right act and, conversely, an acknowledged right act, on any theory, may in fact promote more harm than good. Ethical theories do have crucial relevance to justified conduct in real life, which is of course why they are of pressing practical importance, but it is an indirect relationship – the theory provides the explanation of the ideal to which we inadequately strive.

To conclude on a positive note, understanding the true nature of an ethical theory provides us with the necessary guidance towards understanding the kind of proof to which it is amenable. 'Proof' is perhaps an unfortunate word to use here, and I only do so by way of passing acknowledgement to Mill's attempt to answer the question 'of what sort of proof is the principle of utility susceptible?'[32] I do not myself think that Mill was guilty of some of the grosser charges on which he has been accused, such as committing the naturalistic fallacy. I do not, in other words, think he maintained anything so crude as: we do value our happiness, therefore we ought to do so, and therefore the general happiness is a good. In the first place, as Kleinig[33] has argued, he was surely concerned with the kind of argument that might cause one to assent to the truth of the principle of utility, rather than with producing a specific argument of that type. But more than that, I believe that his main points were that happiness is a self-evident good, that there is no other putative good that is self-evidently good, and that the acknowledged self-evidence of one good in contrast to all others is a good reason for giving it pride of place.

Whether that is a reasonable interpretation of Mill or not, our concern at this point is not to argue for the principle of utility, but to indicate the kind of proof to which any ethical theory is amenable. It is clearly not the kind of theory the truth or falsehood of which can be empirically demonstrated. Bridges built according to a particular theory that subsequently fall down are *prima facie* evidence against that theory. But we cannot treat, for example, people's misery or lack of freedom as evidence against an ethical theory, since the question of whether such things as people's misery or freedom morally matter is part of what an ethical theory is designed to answer. Nor can an ethical theory be treated exactly like a mathematical theory, because there is not the same universal acceptance of moral axioms as there is of certain mathematical axioms from which theories may be derived.

What we therefore have to do is apply the tests that we apply to any conceptual question: that is, we have to judge the worth of an ethical theory by reference to the clarity and fullness with which it is explicated, its internal coherence and consistency, and its consistency with other of our rationally held beliefs with which it may come into contact. (If, for example, we do not believe in God, or believe that religion and morality are logically autonomous, we cannot consistently produce an ethical theory that is necessarily tied up with religious theory.) If an ethical theory meets these requirements, then it may be said to be amenable to our rational understanding. Obviously it may then come into conflict with our sentiments or psychological antipathy. The task of the author of an ethical theory is to force the reader to recognize, by reason, that an entirely coherent package or system that has some undeniable grounding in what he (the reader) does believe about morality is being offered. If that is the case, it may reasonably be pointed out that any remaining psychological objections are just that: psychological. They do not cohere with what has been agreed to be a coherent explication of the implications of one or more agreed starting point; it is they, the psychological objections, that should in reason be abandoned, and not the theory.[34]

One does not ask of the analysis of a concept whether it is true. One asks whether it is an analysis of the same concept that we, the discussants, had in mind at the outset, and one then asks whether it is coherent. For example, I propose to analyse the concept of indoctrination. We agree, broadly, that indoctrination is essentially about closing the mind, so we are talking about the same thing, very loosely conceived. I then proceed to reason, let us say, that there are certain ways of imparting knowledge that by their nature could not conceivably close the mind. You agree, with the result that we have to accept that indoctrination necessarily involves only a certain way (or ways) of imparting knowledge. Perhaps we go on to agree on certain other criteria, such as that if a person is to be said to be indoctrinating they must proceed with some kind of intention to close the mind.

When we have finished, you might conceivably say: 'Well, that's all very well, but it doesn't square with the belief that I and some other people hold that teachers, merely by dint of being who they are and having influence over children, are indoctrinators.' At this point there is nothing I can do, except point out that the analysis we produced together was shown to be rational and coherent and that, if we are to stand by it, you must put aside your sentiment and recognize that it is incorrect to label teachers as indoctrinators just because they influence children. I cannot say that you have to stand by the conception we arrived at together, and I cannot say that, if you reject it in favour of the broader conception that allows you to maintain your sentiment, you are incorrect. But I can say that you are being inconsistent, and I can say that you are talking about something different. You can do what you like, but you have to choose. Do you want to operate with a broad category (that most of us would probably label 'influence', though that is only a point about verbal usage), or do you want to operate with the more specific conception of indoctrination we have arrived at? What is logically impossible is for you both to accept the latter and call all teachers indoctrinators.

A great deal of criticism of utilitarianism (and other ethical theories), it seems to me, has come about because critics cannot face up to making the choice. They accept what has been argued, and then arbitrarily alight on some moral belief that is not compatible with it and claim that there is therefore something wrong with the theory. But so long as they fail to pinpoint any crucial inadequacies in the conception of the theory, there is no reason to assume the theory inadequate. In those circumstances it would be more reasonable to reject the sentiment.[35]

In the remaining chapters, therefore, I seek to do no more than give a thorough explication of a certain theory of utilitarianism, articulating its central concepts clearly and fully, stressing logical implications and pointing out its internal consistency, clarifying and explaining away popular misapprehensions, and grounding the whole in certain widely accepted assumptions about the nature of morality. If that can be done successfully, we have done all that can be done to establish an ethical theory: we have presented it at the bar of rational appraisal.[36]

Notes

1. The reference to the need for an ethical theory to focus on 'what in ideal circumstances would constitute right conduct', which is introduced in this chapter and elaborated on subsequently, bears a superficial resemblance to Rawls's (1971) 'veil of ignorance', Hare's (1982) 'perfectly prudent preferences', and Harsanyi's (1982) 'true preferences' (i.e., those preferences which a person 'would have if he had all the relevant information, always reasoned with the greatest possible care, and were in a state of mind most conducive to rational choice'. p. 55). However, these authors are concerned, broadly, to distinguish what individuals would believe, if they had full knowledge, from what they might believe in reality. I am concerned to distinguish between what we may all recognize as being the case if we ignore contingent restraints of time and place, and what is the case in particular situations. Thus it is possible to conceive of a society in which promise keeping always contributes to happiness, although it is unlikely that that will ever be the case in societies as they are.

2. F.H. Bradley, for example, in his *Ethical Studies* (1927), invokes 'the common moral consciousness' in his attempt to urge that utilitarianism is immoral. But as Bernard Williams, *A Critique of Utilitarianism* (1973), p. 78, rightly says, 'what is important ... is not whether [Smart], or I, or the reader regard this or that as horrible, but what the implications, carefully considered, are of these principles for one's view of human nature and action, other people and society'. In other words, particular sentiments, though at odds with a theory, do not constitute a refutation of the latter; but, if we cannot live with the overall implications of a theory, when it has been fully articulated, that is to say that we are not persuaded of its truth.

3. 'I believe that the very imperfect notion ordinarily formed of [utilitarianism's] meaning is the chief obstacle which impedes its reception.' J.S. Mill, *Utilitarianism* (1962). p. 255.

4. J.S. Mill, *Utilitarianism* op. cit., chapter 2, p. 275: 'Again, defenders of utility often find themselves called upon to reply to such objections as this – that there is not time, previous to action, for calculating and weighing the effects of any line of conduct on the general happiness. This is exactly as if any one were to say that it is impossible to guide our conduct by Christianity because there is not time, on every occasion on which anything has to be done, to read through the Old and New Testaments. The answer to the objection is, that there has been ample time, namely, the whole past duration of the human species.' Perplexed by the extraordinariness of the objection, Mill goes on to make the celebrated remark: 'There is no difficulty in proving any ethical standard whatever to work ill, if we suppose universal idiocy to be conjoined with it.' (p. 275).

5. In fact, Mill (op. cit.) touches on this issue both when, in response to the charge that utilitarianism sets too high a standard for humanity, he remarks 'this is to mistake the very meaning of a standard of morals, and confound the rule of action with the motive of it. It is the business of ethics to tell us what are our duties, or by what test we may know them' (p. 269) and, more directly, when he points out that difficulties in living by the utilitarian theory have nothing to do with the matter: 'it is not the fault of any creed, but of the complicated nature of human affairs, that rules of conduct cannot be framed so as to require no exceptions, and that hardly any kind of action can safely be laid down as either always obligatory or always condemnable' (p. 277). But though Mill is therefore aware of the point that a number of the intuitively damaging implications of the theory are not the fault of the theory but

the fault of human beings, he did not draw out the conclusion that one should formulate the rules, duties, etc. required by a theory, by assuming an ideal context.

6. As James Steintrager writes, in his lucid study *Bentham* (1977), p. 11, 'In 1768 Jeremy Bentham discovered the principle of utility, that the greatest happiness of the greatest number is the only proper measure of right and wrong and the only proper end of government. From then until his death in 1832, he worked with steadiness and determination to discover means of promoting that end and thus 'to rear the fabric of felicity by the hands of reason and law' [*The Principles of Morals and Legislation*, 1948. p. 2.] 'From the beginning until the end of his life Bentham was above all other things a reformer' (p. 117), one whose ideas, furthermore, 'profoundly attend the course of English politics during the nineteenth century' (p. 11).

   On the other hand, as Mill points out, 'difference of opinion on moral questions was not first introduced into the world by utilitarianism, while that doctrine does supply, if not always an easy, at all events a tangible and intelligible mode of deciding such differences'. *Utilitarianism*, p. 272.

7. Thus we do not accept Elster's (1982) contention that utilitarianism is to be rejected because it fails to do what 'a theory of justice or social choice' should do, namely 'satisfy two criteria'. 'Firstly, it should be a guide to action, in the sense that it should enable us to make effective choices in most important situations. Secondly, we must require of a theory of justice that it does not strongly violate our ethical intuitions in particular cases. If a theory suggests that people should take tranquilisers when the Coase theorem requires them to, then we *know* (his emphasis) that it is a bad theory'. (p. 234) In fact, despite his emphasis, Elster immediately qualifies the second criterion by acknowledging the possible cultural or biological base of some intuitions, and concludes, much more weakly, 'Such problems notwithstanding, I do not see how a theory of justice can dispense with intuitions altogether.' Nor do I, of course, as the remarks in the text about the need to take note of, but to avoid domination by, our current sentiments indicate. (See also note 29, below.) So the second criterion is, while not very helpful, unproblematic and not necessarily damaging to utilitarianism. The first, as I suggest in the text, is to be rejected. Far from being a reasonable criterion of an adequate ethical theory, it suggests a peculiar idea of what such a theory is. As Mill says 'there exists no moral system under which there do not arise unequivocal cases of conflicting obligations ... [But] though the application of the standard may be difficult, it is better than none at all'. (*Utilitarianism*, p. 277).

8. Mill (op. cit. p. 257), after his preamble, introduces the theory as one that 'holds that actions are right in proportion as they tend to promote happiness, wrong as they tend to produce the reverse of happiness', period. It is, in other words, not so much a theory that emphasizes the rightness of actions rather than, say, the moral goodness of people, but a theory concerning the former rather than the latter. Cf. his explicit remarks, in dealing with the allegation that 'utilitarianism renders men cold and unsympathising': 'These considerations are relevant, not to the estimation of actions, but of persons; and there is nothing in the utilitarian theory inconsistent with the fact that there are other things which interest us in persons besides the rightness and wrongness of their actions' (p. 271).

9. J.J.C. Smart, 'An Outline of a System of Utilitarian Ethics' (1973, p. 53) rightly and usefully reminds us of 'the importance of Sidgwick's distinction between the utility of an action and the utility of praise or blame for it', pointing out that 'many fallacious "refutations" of utilitarianism depend for their plausibility on confusing the two things'. (p. 53). 'I beg the reader, therefore, if ever he is impressed by any alleged refutations of act-utilitarianism, to bear in mind the distinction between the rightness or wrongness of an action and the goodness or badness of the agent, and

Sidgwick's correlative and most important distinction between the utility of an action and the utility of praise or blame of it. The neglect of this distinction is one of the commonest causes of fallacious refutations of act-utilitarianism'. (pp. 55, 56) Smart's point is equally relevant to rule-utilitarianism.

10. See G.E. Moore, *Principia Ethica* (1903), chapter 1.

11. MacIntyre (1981, p. 15) remarks that 'Moore's arguments at times are, it must seem now, obviously defective – he tries to show that good is indefinable, for example, by relying on a bad dictionary definition of "definition"'. This is true, so far as it goes. But it does not alter the fact that 'good' is indefinable in this particular way, and it does not show that the contention that it is indefinable in some broader way as well is false. Of course there are things that one can say about 'good' that may be classified as a type of definition. The dictionary, after all, has an entry on the word. But I see no reason to dissent from Moore's fundamental point that goodness is something one has to sense rather than describe. I do, however, concur with MacIntyre in his overall estimate of Moore's arguments. See Chapter 3, below.

12. It is interesting that intuitionism is generally respectfully dismissed, while two philosophers generally so classified, W.D. Ross and H.A. Prichard, are held in the highest esteem. I would add that I am sorry that more of A.C. Ewing's work, particularly his *Reason and Intuition,* is not in print. The subject is admirably dealt with in W.D. Hudson, *Ethical Intuitionism* (1967) and in the same author's *Modern Moral Philosophy* (1970).

13. See G.E. Moore, *Principia Ethica.* op. cit., and *Ethics* (1912).

14. W.D. Ross, *The Right and the Good* (1930), chapters 2 and 3.

15. Ross (op. cit. p. 156), as so often, speaks wisely and to the point here: 'Moral goodness is quite distinct from and independent of rightness, which ... belongs to acts not in virtue of the motives they proceed from, but in virtue of the nature of what is done. Thus a morally good action need not be the doing of a right act, and the doing of a right act need not be a morally good action. The ethical theories that stress the thing done and those that stress the motive from which it is done both have some justification, for both 'the right act' and 'the morally good action' are notions of the first importance in ethics; but the two types of theory have been at cross purposes, because they have failed to notice that they are talking about different things.'

16. Cf. Mill (op. cit. p. 254) in reference to Kant: 'But when he begins to deduce from this precept [the Categorical Imperative] any of the actual duties of morality, he fails, almost grotesquely, to show that there would be any contradiction ... in the adoption ... of the most outrageously immoral rules of conduct. All he shows is that the *consequences* of their universal adoption would be such as no one would choose to incur'.

17. 'Utilitarian moralists have gone beyond almost all others in affirming that the motive has nothing to do with the morality of the action, though much with the worth of the agent'. (J.S. Mill, *Utilitarianism*, p. 270).

18. G.J. Warnock, *The Object of Morality* (1971).

19. W.D. Ross, *The Right and the Good* (op. cit. chapter 2). Ross means by a *'prima facie* duty', 'a conditional duty' or one that I should do unless the obligation conflicts with and is over-borne by another. I am in effect arguing that by reference to the yardstick of happiness, or more particularly by focusing on the ideal of a fully happy community, we can formulate a finite number of duties that are essential to the ideal and, if faithfully adhered to, cannot come into conflict. Thus one can actually do one's *prima facie* duty. (At one stage I considered simply reversing Ross's terminology, on the grounds that what one ought to do ideally is, in my scheme of things, one's actual duty, while what one determines is best in problematic

circumstances is, in a straightforward sense, only one's *prima facie* duty. But such a change would cause more confusion than illumination.)

20. Neither Bentham nor Mill believed that, taking the world as it is, one would attain the desired happiness of all (or even the greatest happiness of the greatest number possible, in so far as that is different) by a simple application of the principle of utility. Bentham emphasized reason and law as the means whereby egoism might be converted to utilitarianism, while Mill emphasized more the notion of education. But both see a need to take active steps to bring about a harmony between, not only individuals, but the inclinations, beliefs, etc., of people in general, and a plausible and possible form of social life, taking account of realities. To some extent, in the course of this book, I am merely spelling out the full implications of this recognition.

21. Certainly few, if any, think that Ross succeeded in this regard. As G.J. Warnock, *Contemporary Moral Philosophy* (1967) p. 5, puts it: the theory of intuitionism 'appraised as a contribution to philosophy, seems deliberately, almost perversely, to answer no questions, to throw no light on any problem. One might almost say that the doctrine actually consists in a protracted denial that there is anything of the slightest interest to be said'.

22. It should be noted that I am not claiming here that these or any other principles necessarily are substantiated by utilitarianism.

23. My use of the distinction between right acts and justified acts has some affinity to Smart's (1973) distinction between right and rational actions, (pp. 45 ff.), and to Hare's (1982) distinction between two levels of moral thinking, (pp. 30 ff.). Cf. also the conventional distinction between objective and subjective duty, and the notion of putative duty. Smart uses 'the word "rational" as a term of commendation for that action which is, on the evidence available to the agent, likely to produce the best results', and reserves 'the word "right" as a term of commendation for the action which does in fact produce the best results'.

24. 'Direct utilitarianism is ... of all utilitarian doctrines the most faithful to the spirit of utilitarianism, and to its demand for a rational, decidable, empirically based, and unmysterious set of values.' ('A Critique of Utilitarianism', 1973, pp. 128,129.) Why and on what grounds does Bernard Williams claim that the spirit of utilitarianism makes this set of demands?

25. See above, p. 20.

26. R.M. Hare, *The Language of Morals* (1952).

27. A.J. Ayer, *Language, Truth and Logic* (1936).

28. For more on this view of the nature of philosophical analysis, see in particular, R. Barrow and G. Milburn *A Critical Dictionary of Educational Concepts* (1986), under the entry 'analysis', and K. Graham, *J. L. Austin, A Critique of Ordinary Language Philosophy* (1977).

29. Consider here this comment: 'The fact that [an ethical theory] has consequences which conflict with some of our particular moral judgements need not be decisive against it. In science general principles must be tested by reference to particular facts of observation. In ethics we may well take the opposite attitude, and test our particular moral attitudes by reference to more general ones ... In this monograph I am not concerned with what our moral customs and institutions in fact are [a 'descriptive' theory, in Smart's terms], and still less am I concerned with the question of why they are as they in fact are ['explanatory']. I am concerned with a certain view about what they ought to be ['normative'] ... In fact it is precisely because a doctrine is false as description and as explanation that it becomes important as a possible recommendation.' (J.J.C. Smart, 'An Outline of a System of Utilitarian Ethics', (1973, pp. 56, 57.) I share Smart's position, though I do not use the phrase 'normative theory', and tend to refer to ethical theory as explanatory, not of course of why moral customs 'are as they are', but of why they are to be

construed as they ought to be. Mill (*Utilitarianism*, p. 252) addresses this issue obliquely when he writes 'But though in science the particular truths precede the general theory, the contrary might be expected to be the case with a practical art, such as morals or legislation. All action is for the sake of some end, and rules of action, it seems natural to suppose, must take their whole character and colour from the end to which they are subservient. When we engage in a pursuit, a clear and precise conception of what we are pursuing would seem to be the first thing we need, instead of the last we are to look forward to. A test of right and wrong must be the means, one would think, of ascertaining what is right or wrong, and not a consequence of having already ascertained it.'

30. See for example Mill (op. cit. p. 268): 'As between his own happiness and that of others, utilitarianism requires him to be as strictly impartial as a disinterested and benevolent spectator.'

31. One advantage of focusing on the ideal is that it avoids the misleading problems that arise when one tries to interpret utilitarianism in terms of Winners and Losers. The question is not which course of action is best, given that one makes this group losers and another that group losers. Any course of action that necessarily leads to losers is wrong in ideal terms. We should be looking for ways of behaving, rules of conduct, that involve no losers if, taken together, they are consistently adopted by all people.

32. See Mill (op. cit.) chapter 4. See also chapter 1, pp. 254, 5: 'It is evident that this cannot be proof in the ordinary and popular meaning of the term ... We are not, however, to infer that its acceptance or rejection must depend on blind impulse, or arbitrary choice ... The subject is within the cognisance of the rational faculty ... Considerations may be presented capable of determining the intellect either to give or withhold its assent to the doctrine; and this is equivalent to proof.' 'Is it susceptible of any direct proof?' asks Bentham, *An Introduction to the Principles of Morals and Legislation* (1948). 'It should seem not: for that which is used to prove everything else, cannot itself be proved: a chain of proofs must have their commencement somewhere. To give such proof is as impossible as it is needless.' (p. 4)

33. J. Kleinig 'The Fourth Chapter of Mill's *Utilitarianism*' (1970).

34. Cf. T.M. Scanlon (1982), p. 109, 'A judgement as to which account of the nature of morality ... is most plausible ... is just that: a judgement of overall plausibility. It is not usefully described as an insight into concepts or as a special intuitive insight of some other kind.'

It may be worth remarking that Scanlon's contractualism (the view that 'an act is wrong if its performance under the circumstances would be disallowed by any system of rules for the general regulation of behaviour which no one could reasonably reject as a basis for informed, unforced general agreement') (p. 110), is not strikingly different from the utilitarian position I shall espouse. He, in common with a number of other philosophers, such as Rawls, focuses on the question of what a disinterested person would say about a rule, whereas I think it more appropriate to focus on the question of what rules would necessarily suit everyone if conscientiously observed by all. He maintains that individual well-being is a good simply because 'an individual could reasonably reject a form of argument that gave his well-being no weight'. (p. 119) That is true, but one may pointedly ask whether that is true of anything else. In trying to explain the source of motivation to moral action, Scanlon contrasts the utilitarian view with his own that 'the source of motivation that is directly triggered by the belief that an action is wrong is the desire to be able to justify one's actions to others on grounds that they could not reasonably reject'. (p. 116) But it is not clear to me why utilitarianism could not embrace this account.

35. Cf. T.M. Scanlon (1982), p. 106: 'A philosophical theory of morality must offer an account of these reasons [that morality provides for action] that is, on the one hand, compatible with its account of moral truth and moral reasoning, and on the other, supported by a plausible analysis of moral experience.'

36. 'I ... renounce the attempt to prove the ... system. I shall be concerned with stating it in a form in which it may appear persuasive to some people, and to show how it may be defended against many of the objections which are frequently brought up against utilitarianism. Nevertheless I should like to indicate my opinion that the choice of conceptually clear and emotionally attractive systems of normative ethics which might be alternatives to it is not as wide as is sometimes thought.' J.J.C. Smart, 'An Outline of a System of Utilitarian Ethics' (1973), p. 5.

3. What is Utilitarianism?

In some shape or form utilitarianism is as old as the written record of moral philosophy. It has been argued, albeit not very successfully, that Plato was a utilitarian in the *Republic*.[1] Certainly when Francis Hutcheson used the phrase 'the greatest happiness for the greatest numbers' in *Concerning Moral Good and Evil*[2] the idea to which he referred was not a new one. Then, in *The Principles of Morals and Legislation*,[3] Jeremy Bentham claimed that 'nature has placed mankind under the governance of two sovereign masters, pain and pleasure', and referred to this as 'the principle of utility'. In 1863 John Stuart Mill, son of James Mill, who had himself adopted a Benthamite philosophy, published his essay *Utilitarianism*.[4] From that moment, ethical theories centring on the moral value of happiness and/or pleasure crystallized around the label 'utilitarian', and found their classical expression in that essay. At this point, ignoring the problems that lie in Mill's statement, we may conveniently summarize the theory in his words as: 'The creed which accepts as the foundation of morals, Utility, or the Greatest Happiness Principle.' It 'holds that actions are right in proportion as they tend to promote happiness, wrong as they tend to produce the reverse of happiness. By happiness is intended pleasure, and the absence of pain; by unhappiness, pain, and the privation of pleasure'.[5]

Nonetheless, confusion is still possible between three kinds of utilitarianism. First, there is what may reasonably be classified as 'economic utilitarianism', so called because of the everyday connotations of the word utility. 'Utility' to the man in the street simply means usefulness. A product has utility, if one can put it to good use. A means has utility, if it will achieve its end. A policy has utility if it will serve its purpose. Hence there arises a sense of utilitarianism that means no more than a means–ends policy or justification. It is this sense of utilitarianism that journalists generally have in mind when they refer to the government acting out of 'utilitarian considerations'. Since it is common for governments (and no doubt individuals) to concentrate on economic ends, it is not unreasonable to regard economic utilitarianism as representative of this type.[6] It could, of course, have other ends (e.g., one might act out of utilitarian considerations with respect to public safety), but what is characteristic of utilitarianism in this sense is that it lacks any specific moral connotations.[7] It is concerned with effective means to an end, and not with the morality of means or ends.

Second, there is what is generally referred to as ideal utilitarianism. This is a type of ethical theory that posits various moral ends and claims that actions are right in so far as they serve as means to one or more of those ends. G.E. Moore,[8] who believed in friendship and beauty, amongst other things, as moral ends, is usually classified as an ideal utilitarian, but one who substituted other values for Moore's would also be so classified, provided he retained the belief that the rightness of actions lay in their tendency to contribute to the ends in question. Ideal utilitarianism, as other forms of utilitarianism, is therefore regarded as a consequentialist ethical theory, meaning one that judges the morality of actions by their consequences, or a teleological theory (one that is directed to the *telos* or end of action), as opposed to a deontological theory, which sees certain acts as being right and others wrong, regardless of their consequences .

Third, there is hedonistic utilitarianism, so called from the Greek *hedone* meaning, roughly, pleasure. Hedonistic utilitarianism involves the claim that happiness or pleasure is the only ultimate end and that the rightness of actions is to be determined by their propensity to produce or contribute to that end. It is hedonistic utilitarianism with which Bentham and Mill are associated and with which I shall be concerned in the following pages.[9]

Simple as these opening paragraphs may seem, problems of meaning and interpretation are already lurking there. The most obvious is the question of what constitutes happiness and what its relationship to pleasure may be. But there is also a certain obscurity about phrases such as 'the only ultimate end' and 'tendency to contribute' or 'propensity to produce'. In this chapter, I hope to explain how any such phrase is to be interpreted, in such a way as to nullify certain standard objections to the theory to the effect that it either endorses any action that produces some happiness, which is implausible, or that it fails to offer any clear guidance as to whose happiness is to count and to what extent. From this point on it is important to remember that I do not purport to be interpreting Mill or Bentham, except when I expressly say so. I shall seek only to clarify my conception of utilitarianism.

The fundamental tenet of hedonistic utilitarianism is that happiness is the sole thing that is morally good in and of itself. To make full sense of this claim it will at some stage be necessary to consider precisely what is meant by 'happiness'.[10] For the moment it will be sufficient to characterize it roughly as a sense of well-being. Happy people (and other sentient beings, if there be some that are capable of happiness) are those who do not suffer from things such as despair, dismay, alienation, loneliness, frustration or disappointment; they are content with the world as they perceive it and their lot in it. This is clearly only a vague characterization, and it ignores further questions such as whether anybody can be completely happy or whether contentment needs to be distinguished from, say, ecstasy or divine discontent. Such matters will be considered in Chapter 4. The more immediately important question is what is meant by the claim that happiness is 'the sole thing that is morally good in and of itself'.

The first point to note is that it is a claim about moral good and not about any other kind of good. Other things such as, for example, beauty and rationality, may very well be good in and of themselves, in some non-moral sense. Indeed, many utilitarians will acknowledge various other goods, including aesthetic values, but they will argue that these are to be distinguished from moral good.[11]

The second thing to note is that the claim is not that 'happiness' means 'good', or that 'good' means 'productive of happiness'. The claim does not involve an attempt at definition. G.E. Moore misleadingly and mistakenly criticized utilitarianism on these grounds.[12] He argued that the theory was obviously incoherent because, of any state of affairs that was agreed to involve happiness or of any action that was agreed to be productive of happiness, it is intelligible to ask 'But is it good?' And, if that is so, happiness cannot be identified with goodness. The reasoning, as far as it goes, is sound. It does seem intelligible to say, 'I know that this state of affairs is a happy one, but is it morally good?' And that does indicate that we do not regard goodness and happiness as one and the same thing. However there are at least three crippling objections to Moore's procedure here.

First, to be precise, this test (sometimes referred to as Moore's open question argument) shows only that we, in regarding the question as intelligible, do not think that happiness and goodness are to be identified. It does not show that they are not to be identified. We might be mistaken, and what seems to us to be intelligible might not in fact be so.

Second, Moore runs together the notions of good and right (see below). The claim, so far, is simply that happiness is the sole thing that is morally good in and of itself. It has not been suggested, and it would not be by a utilitarian, that provided an act is productive of happiness it is morally right. At the very least one would need to consider whether alternative actions might have been productive of more happiness, and in fact the situation is considerably more complex than that and a number of other things have to be considered too. Furthermore, a utilitarian is not committed to the view that any state of affairs involving happiness is a good one. Whether it is or not depends, at the very least, on how much happiness is involved and how it is distributed, and therefore a utilitarian can readily acknowledge that the question whether a happy state of affairs is necessarily a good one makes sense, without being inconsistent.

But the main point to be stressed here is that Moore is incorrect to suppose that the utilitarians he was criticizing (such as John Stuart Mill) did identify goodness and happiness. If I say that triangles are the only figures bounded by three sides, I do indeed make a definitional point. It is true, because having three sides is part of the meaning of triangle, and not because I have observed that triangles, defined in some other way, happen always to have three sides. But if I claim, however contentiously or mistakenly, that Rembrandts are the only beautiful paintings in the world, I equally clearly do not make a definitional point. I am claiming that beauty, defined in some way or other, is a quality only to be found in Rembrandts, which are not defined in the same terms. Beauty and a Rembrandt painting are quite distinct concepts, and I claim that they are always found together and beauty is never to be found in other paintings. One therefore concedes to Moore that it would be peculiar to maintain that happiness and goodness are to be identified by definition (though not necessarily logically absurd, as was pointed out above), since such an identification plainly doesn't fit with the way we generally talk. But there is nothing odd or incoherent at all about maintaining that happiness is the only thing that in and of itself has the quality of goodness. And that is what I understand the utilitarian's fundamental claim to be.

In short, Moore is correct to observe that, rightly or wrongly, we will not accept the view that 'morally good' means the same thing as 'being productive of happiness'. But he is wrong to suggest that utilitarians make this claim. The claim that they do make, which is that happiness alone has the intrinsic quality of moral goodness, is not in any way challenged by the correct observation that it seems intelligible to question it. Utilitarians themselves may question whether a particular action is right, even if it produces happiness. For their thesis is not that anything that produces happiness is *ipso facto* right.[13] They may also question whether a state of affairs that involves happiness is good, for whether it is or not depends on further considerations such as how the happiness is distributed. But the crucial point for the moment is that the utilitarian will concede even that it makes sense to question the fundamental contention that happiness is the only thing that in and of itself has the quality of goodness. If the claim were meant to be a matter of conceptual truth, Moore would be right to worry that it seems intelligible to deny it. But as it is not presented as a conceptual truth, but rather as a claim to be argued for, it is not only irrelevant, but to be expected, that some will quite intelligibly question it.

Third, it should be noted that the utilitarian claim is that happiness is the sole or only thing good in and of itself and not, for instance, that it is the supreme good. Most ethical theories recognize a plurality of values. It is common for these values to be seen as being of equal weight, with the result that the interests of, say, freedom and equality, or truth and happiness, may on occasion conflict. This is generally accepted as an awkward fact of moral life. Since it is certainly the case that utilitarians have been known to value other things, as, for example, Mill clearly valued freedom greatly, it has often been supposed that the distinctive feature of utilitarianism is that it places the value of happiness above other values, while still recognizing that there are other intrinsic values. In particular, it has been argued that Mill regarded freedom as intrinsically valuable and that, as a result, he ran into a certain amount of difficulty in his essay *On Liberty*, notwithstanding the fact that even there he had recourse to the claim that happiness was the supreme value.[14]

I believe this to be an incorrect reading of Mill. He, and any other utilitarian, may certainly be said to have other moral values besides happiness, inasmuch as a fully developed utilitarian system may lead one to value other things extrinsically, even in some cases without qualification.[15] Nonetheless, it remains a case of valuing these other things as means to the end of happiness. Thus, Mill clearly did not value freedom in and of itself, but as a means to happiness.[16] And even when he argues for absolute freedom of speech, it is not on the grounds that this specific value is, like happiness, good in and of itself, but on the grounds that the unconditional guarantee of this freedom is necessary for the survival of truth and the increase of understanding, and that they in turn are necessary for the long-term cultivation and maintenance of happiness.[17] (It may be added, in passing, that the notion of a plurality of principles of equal weight is, in any case, arguably untenable. For in cases where principles clash, either we give more weight to one than another, which is to say that they are not in fact equal, or we decide between them by reference to another principle, which also indicates that all are not in fact equal, or we must conclude that it literally does not matter which principle is given priority. The last option preserves the coherence of the position, but I have yet to encounter a theorist who truly thinks that it does not matter if we give priority to equality today, freedom tomorrow, and happiness the day after.)

Whether the above is a fair interpretation of Mill or not, the species of utilitarianism I am here expounding must be clearly understood to involve the assumption that freedom in and of itself is not necessarily good. It, and various other values, may turn out to be very important, and we may arrive at a principle that enjoins us always to preserve it (or some aspect of it such as freedom of speech). But were we to have reason to believe that maintenance of freedom was ultimately detrimental to human happiness, utilitarians would cease to value it. To say that happiness is the sole thing that is morally good in and of itself is, therefore, to say that in so far as there is happiness there is something good, regardless of the terms on which it is gained or the consequences of its being gained, and there is nothing else of which this is true. This is not, of course, to say that utilitarians do not care how happiness is achieved, or would be unconcerned if, as a consequence of their happiness, people were willing to let civilization collapse, for example, and the human race to extinguish itself. For the fully developed theory involves all sorts of considerations about whose happiness should be considered, the length of time we should be concerned with, quantities of happiness, and fair distribution of happiness. A utilitarian would regard a situation in which a few individuals bought their happiness at the cost of the suffering of the majority and the extinction of the human race as deplorable, since on any reckoning such a situation would involve minimal happiness. He would indeed have to concede that in such a case the happiness of the few constituted a microscopic amount of goodness within an otherwise deplorable state of affairs; but that admission is quite distinct from maintaining that, since a few people are very happy, all is well with the world and that the acts that produced it were therefore right.

Happiness, then, is not simply more important than anything else to the utilitarian; more than that, it is the only thing that he regards as having the quality of moral goodness in and of itself. Yet, conversely, it is not the only thing that he values in and of itself, for he may value aesthetic beauty or friendship in and of themselves from a non-moral perspective; and he may grant moral value to other things such as friendship or truth telling, either because they have extrinsic value in that they contribute to happiness or because they constitute sources of or means whereby people may acquire happiness. Thus a utilitarian may consistently value beauty for its own sake, friendship both for its own sake and as a source of happiness, and freedom of speech as a means to promoting happiness, provided that he continues to maintain that happiness is the only thing that is morally good in and of itself.

Using the distinctions introduced in the previous chapter, it is clear that acts may be justified in that they are the product of the agent's sincere and accurate estimate of their propensity to produce happiness, and that acts may be said to be morally intentioned even if the agent's sincere estimate proves misguided. But in neither case are they necessarily right acts or acts that are necessarily demanded by utilitarian theory. For not only is the utilitarian committed to something more plausible than the thesis that provided an act produces some happiness it is right or that provided some people are happy the state of affairs is good; rather more importantly, he is committed to the view that what we ought to do, what acts are morally right, is determined by consideration of what overall set of acts would combine to produce complete happiness in ideal circumstances.[18]

As we saw in the previous chapter an ethical theory is not an attempt to explain what we ought to do in all conceivable circumstances. It is an account of what makes acts right. Its connection with day-to-day behaviour is to be found in the fact that it furnishes the criteria whereby we determine whether particular acts are right. If happiness is the sole thing that is good in and of itself, then the criterion we need to focus on is the propensity of an act to promote happiness. But, as we also saw, it is no objection to the theory that we often cannot apply the criterion satisfactorily, so that we sometimes do not know whether an act will promote happiness and sometimes indubitably face a dilemma. The theory has to be worked out in terms of an ideal. If utilitarianism is correct, then an ideal world would be one in which everyone was completely happy. It follows that the behaviour in which we ought to engage (right acts), the institutional arrangements we ought to foster, the attitudes that we ought to cultivate and so forth, are those that in combination would produce such an ideal. As we shall see in Chapter 5, it is conceivable that a number of different sets of behaviours, attitudes, etc. would all contribute equally well to the ideal. But it is certain that not any set would do so.[19]

A proper understanding of this point should enable us to clarify somewhat the confusion that surrounds the question of distribution of happiness. The formulaic expressions, referred to above, have traditionally been used in an attempt to provide a succinct and accurate summary of the utilitarian assumption that right conduct is not simply a matter of acting in such a way as to produce happiness, but rather of producing as much happiness as possible. Thus (perhaps paradoxically, in view of the confusion they have engendered), their prime purpose has been to emphasize that, while the utilitarian premiss is that happiness alone has the quality of moral goodness, the utilitarian theory is about how we ought to organize ourselves and behave, given that premiss. It is a theory about which actions are right, and as such has to take account of such things as the distribution of happiness and its reliability. The simplest of these formulae is the injunction that one should 'maximize happiness', the most famous is probably that one should 'promote the greatest happiness of the greatest number'. But neither of these phrases is entirely satisfactory, as witness the objections that have been raised against them.

Both they, and all others with which I am familiar, suffer in the first place from being unclear on a straightforward verbal level. If 'maximize' means 'make as great as possible' it remains unclear how we are to weight intensity or degree of happiness against extent or distribution, or what priority we should give to duration of happiness as against intensity. Talk of 'a tendency' is manifestly imprecise. 'The greatest happiness of the greatest number' is likewise equivocal, and has the additional demerit of being certainly false if it is interpreted to mean, as critics have often done, that the utilitarian would cheerfully countenance a situation in which some gained intense and lasting happiness at the expense of others.[20]

But the main problem with all such formulae is that they are interpreted without taking note of the distinction that I have introduced between the ideal and the actual.[21] The utilitarian should not allow himself to be driven to accepting any of these formulae as summary statements of how the individual should proceed in everyday life. One may be justified in doing that which one thinks will contribute to the greatest happiness of the greatest number in a particular situation (however the phrase is interpreted); but what one does on those terms will not necessarily be right. What the theory demands is that we assess what is right by reference to what kinds of conduct would promote happiness in ideal circumstances.

To repeat the main contention once more: in order to understand any ethical theory, it is necessary to envisage it first in the context of an ideal world, in a situation in which, so to speak, it works; for difficulties that arise in putting it into practice, if they arise from people's wrong conduct or from contingent difficulties in everyday life, rather than incoherence in the theory, cannot reasonably be held against the theory. That artists do not in fact create works according to the principles of a given aesthetic theory does not in itself show the theory to be wrong. Even the fact that they cannot do so for contingent reasons does not necessarily invalidate the theory. Similarly, the fact that telling the truth and keeping a promise may be incompatible on occasion does not show that both are not proper moral injunctions. The fact that turning the other cheek may prove disastrous in the real world, even in respect of moral consequences, doesn't show it is wrong.

What, according to utilitarianism, would be a morally perfect world? One in which everyone would be fully and therefore equally happy. Right actions in those circumstances would be any that maintain the situation, wrong actions any that militate against it. If it could be argued that such a world were inconceivable, then the theory could be said to be incoherent, as a theory that wants everyone always to defer to others is incoherent. But there is nothing incoherent in this ideal, whatever the practical difficulties involved. That is to say, there is nothing inconceivable or logically impossible about the idea of elaborating an ideal community in which all persons are happy and in which social arrangements and modes of behaviour are such as to maintain that happiness. It is important that any such ideal should take account of what we understand about human nature and practical possibility and likelihood. We are not talking, for instance, about a kind of science fiction that posits logically possible, but so far quite unrealizable, material conditions, or human beings of a different order from any we are familiar with. What is required is the imaginative depiction of a community that, while it takes people as they are in the sense of what they appear capable of, and while it presumes that physical and material circumstances will likewise be such as it appears possible they can be in the world as we know it, is nonetheless ideal in that it presumes that, of all the things that people are capable of doing, they will do those most conducive to happiness. No doubt any such ideal will in practice have its flaws, but it is not inconceivable.

The contention here, then, is that utilitarianism is bound to seem at best an unworkable doctrine, at worst an incoherent one, and phrases such as 'maximizing happiness' are bound to strike us as effectively vacuous, if we persist in trying to work the theory out in the context of the imperfect world we are familiar with. Of course, if we start with a community of people some of whom are, variously, selfish, untrustworthy, ill-educated, lacking in self-esteem, embittered, and so forth, and a social situation in which there are various kinds of institutionalized injustice, anomaly and disadvantage, it is going to be practically impossible to arrive at a clear account of what is morally right on utilitarian terms. Even something fairly uncontentious on most ethical views, such as the claim that one should keep one's promises, loses much of its force in an essentially non-moral world. The value of keeping promises seems, on any view, less self-evident in the context of Nazi Germany than in the context of a small, peaceable, farming community in Iowa. But the utilitarian does not need, and should not be trying, to establish that promise keeping does promote human happiness in the world as we know it. He should be seeking to establish that it is one necessary feature of a world that would promote happiness, provided that it was in other respects also organized to that end. In short he needs to work out what set of rules and social arrangements would, taken together, ensure human happiness, rather than whether particular rules will or will not advance happiness in themselves in current conditions. [22]

What is morally right is for us to do those things that are necessary for maintaining a happy world. To perform such acts is our duty. What we ought to do in the particular situations we face that are not covered by rules embodying our duty, is what we have reason to believe would most contribute to the sum of human happiness. But, whereas we may understandably feel that the question of what we are justified in doing is of more pressing concern than the question of our moral duty (which perhaps partly explains Ross's[23] preoccupation with the former), an ethical theory is properly concerned with the latter. Nor need we fear the charge that this makes ethical theory confessedly academic, unrealistic and of little practical importance. For, although we may have to live with the fact that no ethical theory solves all our practical moral problems, the fact remains that only in the light of a clear understanding of what is morally right in ideal terms, can we begin to make sense of moral issues in everyday life. The question for the utilitarian is not whether keeping promises does or does not promote happiness in the world as we know it; for we know very well that, like virtually everything else, it depends on the nature of the society we have evolved. The question is whether there is reason to suppose that in a society in other respects geared to the interests of happiness, the keeping of promises would militate for or against the ideal.

The above should not be interpreted as a cavalier dismissal of questions about practical justification or moral responsibility. As has already been said, to deserve moral commendation an individual must act autonomously with a view to the good, and on utilitarian terms it is therefore praiseworthy that an individual should consider the question of whether his acts are likely to promote happiness. Furthermore, he may reasonably claim justification for his acts, if he sincerely reasons that they are likely to be productive of happiness. But when it comes to the question of what is actually right and what people ought invariably to do, the utilitarian must have recourse to an argument designed to show what kinds of behaviour would in ideal circumstances evidently enhance human happiness.

In the light of the above, it would seem best to dispense with all attempts at a short-hand formula, and to say instead that utilitarianism enjoins us to do those things that would in combination, in ideal but possible circumstances, inevitably tend to contribute to the maintenance of happiness for all. The juxtaposition of 'inevitably' and 'tend to' may seem superficially odd, but it is necessary. The word 'inevitably' reminds us that the theory is not concerned to make a moral duty out of anything that might make people happy, as giving them circuses might, but to assert that we ought to do certain things without which people in general are assuredly never likely to be happy, such as giving them food. But we add the phrase 'tend to' in recognition of the possibility that, human beings being as individual as they are, it is not necessarily a matter of certainty that everyone will always derive happiness from a given rule of conduct. Thus, the fact that certain individuals might be so constituted as to derive no satisfaction from a world in which promises are kept, need not in itself deter us from arguing that on balance, in ideal circumstances, the world will be the happier for observance of the principle that promises should be kept.[24]

Another implication of the above paragraphs is that the quite common criticism of utilitarianism on the grounds that its preoccupation with happiness leads it to ignore or deny any principle of justice is entirely misplaced.[25] The misapprehension is the more extraordinary in view of the fact that Mill has a fairly straightforward chapter 'on the connection between justice and utility'.[26] The problem to some extent seems to arise out of the ambiguity of the term 'justice', which may be taken to refer either to a distinct substantive principle or to a formal distributive principle. What Mill does in the chapter referred to is tackle the question of fairness or impartiality, which is a formal distributive principle. Of course any ethical theory has to include some account of who counts, and to what extent, in respect of the moral good.[27] The utilitarian takes it for granted, quite uncontentiously, that all sentient beings who can experience happiness count equally in respect of the moral good. That is why Bentham is so ready to extend the sphere of morality to include animals, since he believes it obviously the case that they can experience happiness. ('The question is not, can they reason? Nor, can they talk?, but, can they suffer?'[28]) A just world is a fairly ordered moral world – one in which goodness is equally distributed.[29] Thus, with his eye on the ideal, the utilitarian looks for a mode of social arrangement that will provide happiness equally for all. As has already been noted, and will be examined in more detail below, it may well be that a variety of types of social arrangement might equally well provide happiness equally for all, which has important consequences for the utilitarian's capacity to recognize moral worth in many, but not all, different societies. But for the present, we need only emphasize that utilitarians are concerned about justice in the sense of fairness, and that indeed, for all their inadequacy, that is evidently what the various formulae that we have referred to have been trying to capture.[30]

The quite distinct suggestion that utilitarianism does not have a substantive principle of justice that is independent of happiness, manifestly begs a central question.[31] Of course it does not; and why should it? For such a principle, if it is substantive and independent, would have to be of the type 'always treat people in such and such a way'. But it is the basic tenet of utilitarians that how people ought to be treated is entirely derivative on the question of what is necessary for the happiness of all in ideal circumstances. They deny independent status to values such as freedom, equality, and (in any substantive sense) justice, insisting that their moral value has to be ascertained by reference to consideration of happiness. Now in this claim they may be wrong. But, whether they are or not can only be determined by examining the full account of utilitarianism and the reasoning given for accepting it, and by a similar examination of competing theories. One needs an argument that convinces us that, say, certain freedoms just are morally good, and that pinpoints inadequacies in the rival utilitarian reasoning. One cannot simply assert that utilitarianism is self-evidently inadequate since it denies that freedom or justice in some specific substantive sense are in and of themselves morally good.[32]

We thus arrive at the view, according to utilitarianism, that a morally good society would be any society in which all persons were fully happy and acted in ways to maintain, and with a concern for maintaining, that happiness. The society might conceivably achieve this in a number of different ways, but that would make no moral difference: provided the conditions were met, each mode of social organization would be equally morally good. The inclusion of the stipulation 'with a concern for maintaining that happiness' is not logically necessary as a condition of right conduct; that is to say, one could do what is morally right and play one's part in maintaining the morally good state of affairs, without having any conscious concern for maintaining the community's happiness. But since to be a morally good person involves acting with a view to the good, it will be necessary if people are to deserve moral commendation. In addition, it is likely to be contingently necessary that people should have such concern, if the good state of affairs is to be maintained. A society in which people do not care to maintain happiness is not likely to succeed in doing so.

In response to a question of the type posed by Moore, such as 'would not a society which was perfectly happy, but which had in addition friendship, love, and beauty, be better?', we reply as follows. First, we should not confuse 'better' in some general sense with 'morally better'. The utilitarian may readily concede beauty, for instance, as a good, while denying it is a moral good. Thus he may overall prefer the society envisaged by Moore while maintaining that it is not morally superior. Second, an unnecessary polarization is being introduced. It may be that friendship, love, and even beauty will be shown to be necessary features of this society, people being what they are, as sources of happiness. Or, slightly differently, it may be that they contribute indirectly to the maintenance of happiness as, for example, one might suggest that, even if people did not particularly enjoy friendship, features of it such as obligation and loyalty might be means of ensuring happiness.

In the light of the foregoing, let us now consider to what extent certain well-worn objections to utilitarianism stand up. Sen and Williams, in their introduction to *Utilitarianism and Beyond*[33] refer to a number of familiar complaints. Some resent 'the uncompromising narrowness' of utilitarianism, while to others it is 'too comprehensive' or marked by too great a degree of 'ambition'.[34] Is it, they wonder, 'even needed'?[35] And surely it is to be registered as a defect in the theory that it neglects autonomy and 'a person's attachments and ties', to the point of ignoring persons as persons and betraying a lack of interest in 'a person's integrity'.[36] Commenting on the attempt of some philosophers to distinguish between the actual preferences that people may have and their 'true preferences', meaning essentially the preferences they would have if they had full knowledge, Sen and Williams question 'how ... allowance [should] be made for the fact that actual preferences will not be true preferences?'[37] They maintain that utilitarianism promises 'to resolve all moral issues by relying on one uniform ultimate criterion',[38] but feel there is a painful inadequacy in the fact that it 'lacks a psychology and politics'.[39] 'How could it be lived by anyone?', they inquire. 'Most human beings have needed, and assuredly will need, to use notions which utilitarianism can neither accommodate nor explain.'[40]

These comments and questions represent a very fair cross-section of standard worries about utilitarianism. Some of them deserve, and will receive in subsequent chapters, a fuller response than I can give here. But it is already clear, I hope, that none of them constitutes a serious challenge to the specific version of utilitarianism being advanced here. The question of whether the theory is too narrow, or too comprehensive, or too ambitious in scope seems in each case an inappropriate kind of question. They have a certain pertinency to economic utilitarianism in so far as that theory seeks to be a complete economic theory (and it must be acknowledged that many papers in the volume in question are concerned with economic utilitarianism). But one does not reasonably ask of an ethical theory that it measure up to some *a priori* standard of coverage. In one case, a theory might purport to explain everything down to what a person should do after dinner on Thursday. In another case, a theory might purport to do no more than establish a limited number of general principles. How far it goes, the degree of determinacy of action it provides, is largely a function of what the theory is, not of some pre-ordained rule about what ethical theories should provide. Having said that, it is not immediately apparent that this theory should offend those who look for either breadth or selectiveness. It is a relatively comprehensive theory in that it claims to explain the whole domain of moral activity, but it may also be seen as quite narrowly focused, either in that it is only concerned with what makes various actions morally right or morally justified, or in that it claims that the only thing that is good in itself is happiness. But the question is not whether, for instance, the latter is too narrow a perspective, but whether there is reason to suppose that it is true. Whether, in other words, the theory is plausible, regardless of its being in this sense narrow. As to whether it is 'needed', I confess that I can barely understand the question. If there is a better account of ethics available then it is not needed; if it is the most convincing we have, as I hope to suggest by the end of this book, then it is needed. One does not ask of any theory whether it is needed, save in the sense of whether it has been superseded by a more plausible theory.

Of course, if it were true that utilitarianism ignored things that we are agreed it should not ignore in relation to ethics, then in another specific sense it could be regarded as 'too narrow'. The phrase would then stand for the charge that it failed to convince, because it ignored moral considerations that are generally, and we therefore naturally presume, though not necessarily correctly, rightly accepted. Clearly, that is the thrust of the suggestion that the theory ignores persons as persons, rights, autonomy, integrity and the like. But if the claim is that the theory has no concern for persons as individual centres of consciousness, no place for individual rights, no interest in autonomy and no respect for integrity, it is plainly false. The theory is based on the assumption that all persons are equally deserving of respect in that they are persons: it is their personhood, for all that the salient characteristic of a person is said to be the capacity to experience happiness and misery, that makes them moral beings on this, as on many other accounts. Utilitarianism will generate rights, such as the right to free expression, as readily as any other theory. Once the appropriate rights and rules have been devised for a community, the theory insists on autonomy as a value, for it says that, from that point on, individuals must try to work out for themselves what is most conducive to the general happiness (regardless of the inadequacy of such a formula) and act accordingly. Integrity is a matter of adherence to moral principles, honesty and consistency, for the utilitarian as for anyone else, and no less important to him.[41] He too believes that 'a fair deal' may be important, even if a person does not specifically ' desire it'.[42] All that utilitarianism does is offer a particular account of the reasons why we should respect certain rights and value these qualities.[43]

If it be said that the point is that there are moral rights that individuals have regardless of their substantiation in utilitarian terms, or that autonomy is morally good in itself and should be the basis of all conduct (to the exclusion of utilitarian rules), or that there is something morally sacrosanct about personhood that owes nothing to the capacity to suffer or enjoy life, which is, one appreciates, the real objection, it is surely not too harsh to point out that the objection begs the question at issue. We know that we have an accumulated set of assumptions about moral rights, respect for persons and the like. Utilitarianism attempts to explain and justify some of these assumptions (and to dismiss others as ill-founded). To assert that they are not to be explained thus, because they are just there requiring no explanation, is to adopt an intuitionism which may conceivably be nearer the truth of the matter but, by the argument, cannot be shown to be so.[44]

The problem of distinguishing between actual and true preferences is a real one for some versions of utilitarianism, but not for this one. It will not be part of my thesis that we need to determine what people would prefer, if they had full knowledge. Instead I am arguing that we should determine what would be necessary for an ideally happy community (regardless of people's particular preferences) by consideration of what would be necessary to any conceivable happy society. For example, while many people may prefer to break promises, a society in which promise keeping was not taken seriously as an idea could not function, given features of social life that we have no reason to suppose we can radically escape from. If it could not function, it could scarcely approach the ideal of happiness for all as nearly as it might.

It is inaccurate to say of this version of utilitarianism that it 'promises to resolve all moral issues by relying on one uniform ultimate criterion' or by any other means. It does not promise to resolve all moral issues. Nor, given the state of the world, would it be wise for it or any other theory to suppose it could. What it does claim to do, which is different, is fully explain the nature of morality. This can be done without 'a psychology and politics', because an ethical theory remains on the level of an explanation of what right conduct ideally involves. To attempt to solve every particular moral issue that we encounter would perhaps require psychology and politics. It would certainly involve more than ethical theory alone.

'How could it be lived?' What, one wonders, does the question mean? On the face of it, it would be very easy to live as a utilitarian, nor, as has been explained, would to do so necessarily do violence to most of our everyday assumptions about rights, persons and integrity. The whole line of criticism involved in these objections is neatly summarized by the claim that there are 'notions which utilitarianism can neither accommodate nor explain'. That is simply not true. What is true is that we may not at first blush (or at second for that matter) like the way in which various moral notions that we presume, perhaps wrongly, have validity, are accommodated and explained. But that, again, is a different matter. Of course utilitarianism offends assumptions that are based on a non-utilitarian view. In itself that is not telling against the theory (although I shall have more to say on the relationship between an ethical theory and established moral sentiments in Chapter 10). The question is whether the theory expounded can be shown to be incoherent in some way or whether it can be 'bettered' by a more plausible theory.

In the same volume, Taylor makes some of the points that are summarized in the editors' introduction.[45] It is reasonable to observe, as he does, that utilitarianism may be the product of, and may lead to, an unjustified presumption that all morality can be scientifically explained; also that we do as a matter of fact tend to believe in qualitative distinctions, and that any theory by its particular nature may circumscribe the moral sphere more or less narrowly. But, as he himself sees, in relation to the last point, to get involved with argument in the abstract about how wide or narrow an ethical theory should be could amount to a purely terminological debate of little real interest. As I have already suggested, it is no concern of mine to argue that the moral domain begins and ends with, say, the establishment of certain rules on utilitarian grounds.[46] I am concerned only to argue that we ought to have certain rules of conduct, based on utilitarian criteria. This observation leads us back to Taylor's first point. Contingently, what he says may well be true. But whatever the presumptions of particular utilitarians may be, it is not the purpose of the theory to be scientific or to explain everything in a scientific manner.[47] Rather the purpose is to suggest that there is good reason to suppose that the theory constitutes a convincing explanation of what does make actions right. He is obviously correct, as we have already noted several times, to say that most of us believe in qualitative distinctions. One might of course respond by suggesting that our belief is ill-founded (and who is to say, in the absence of a convincing rival theory, that it is not?). But the utilitarian, on my account, does not in any case need to do this. As we shall see in Chapter 8, some of the qualitative distinctions to which Taylor refers may be classified as non-moral, and these the utilitarian may share. The ethical theory, for example, does not presume to cover the aesthetic value of beauty. Although I am inclined to suppose that, if following a certain moral rule conflicted with the desire to promote beauty, the utilitarian would give priority to the former, it might even be argued that aesthetic value was as important as moral value. But in either case, the value of beauty is not denied, it is merely beyond (or may be) the scope of an ethical theory.[46]

It is unlikely that the utilitarian would claim that certain other putative values mentioned by Taylor, such as integrity and honesty and various kinds of life, are beyond the moral sphere. But in arguing that these are only good because they contribute to happiness (which still seems a reasonable contention, for would one really value a world in which autonomy led to misery?), he is only explaining a coherent ground on which one could rationally defend such values, regardless of what people happen to believe. Integrity, in any case, is a formal quality involving elements that the utilitarian concedes, along with others, to be integral to moral responsibility: to be moral involves being principled and impartial, for example. Utilitarianism merely gives substance to the formal quality. Similarly, the utilitarian is as committed to rationality[49] as Taylor, partly because we appear to be so constituted as to respect the giving of good reasons for action, and partly because in discussing the merits of this or any other theory we are participating in a rational activity. That we attach a positive sentiment to these various values is not in dispute.[50] Our sense of their intrinsic worth is being explained, not denied, in so far as they are moral values, and left untouched in so far as they are not.[51]

We have now seen what in broad outline the utilitarian regards as an ideal world. And it is important to stress yet again that that is primarily what such a theory is concerned with: an account of what constitutes the good and, derived from that, an account of how ideally people ought to conduct themselves. Our actual duty, which is to say what we ought to do in various situations in our lives in the world as it is, may best be summarized as 'to strive towards the ideal', for that, on any ethical theory, is what moral persons do. On the grand scale, this means that we ought to devise and maintain institutions, social arrangements and rules of conduct calculated to promote and maintain the ideal. On a more personal level, it means that we ought to make particular decisions with a view to the ideal. This of course will in practice be extremely confused and difficult.[52] It would help if the theory could be developed in more specific terms. And, in certain circumstances, the next step on the writer's part would be an attempt to delineate more precisely what the rules of conduct might be, i.e., to consider whether such diverse things as promise keeping, free speech, matrimonial fidelity, and kindness are necessary to, or at least reliable ways of, promoting and maintaining the ideal, and hence to be classified as morally right ways of behaving. In fact, in common with many other writers on the subject, I shall not attempt to do that in any systematic way, although in the following pages much will be said that pertains directly or indirectly to the question. To provide any such account would take us well beyond the purely philosophical and involve claims about human nature and the physical world which I do not feel particularly qualified to make. But, in any case, the strictly philosophical argument is far from over. In clarifying somewhat, I hope, the way in which the utilitarian position needs to be understood, and in attempting to sweep away some of the more unreasonable objections that arise out of misunderstanding that position, I have merely, so to speak, set the stage. We still have to consider a number of seemingly reasonable questions that are designed to show that the innocent-sounding ideal outlined is either incoherent and hence unworkable even in theory, or that it is in any case inadequate as a truly moral theory, or both. The first of these questions is: what is happiness?

Notes

1. See R. Barrow, *Plato, Utilitarianism and Education* (1975) and J.D. Mabbot, 'Is Plato's Republic Utilitarian?' (1937). Mill would not have thought the thesis entirely absurd: 'The youth Socrates listened to the old Protagoras, and asserted ... the theory of Utilitarianism against the popular morality of the so-called sophist.' (*Utilitarianism*, p. 251)
2. F. Hutcheson, *Concerning Moral Good and Evil* (part 2 of the *Inquiry into the Original of Our Ideas of Beauty and Virtue*, 1973).
3. J. Bentham, *The Principles of Morals and Legislation* (1948), p. 1.
4. J.S. Mill, *Utilitarianism*, op. cit.
5. Ibid., p. 257.
6. It is worth noting that economic utilitarianism is the subject of much contemporary academic study. The recent volume edited by Sen and Williams, *Utilitarianism and Beyond* (1982) is, for example, heavily weighted towards essays on economic utilitarianism. Consequently, and unfortunately, an impression is given that utilitarianism is essentially a doctrine about the mechanics of high-level calculation concerning units of pleasure. The ethical doctrine I am concerned with is, by contrast, scarcely affected by consideration of such abstruse and complex minutiae.
7. To be precise we should distinguish between an economic utilitarianism that does not purport to be ethical and one that does. But neither is of concern to my argument.
8. See, e.g., G.E. Moore, *Principia Ethica* (1903), *Ethics* (1912), and *Philosophical Studies* (1960).
9. It is common these days to distinguish between utilitarianism as 'a theory of personal morality' and as 'a theory of public choice'. As will become apparent, this particular distinction is not very helpful to my purposes. I seek to elaborate an ethical theory that provides the criteria whereby we may determine that some particular moral rules, modes of conduct and institutionalized procedures are necessary. Beyond that, individual conduct should be informed by consideration of the criteria, but cannot, as I shall argue, be definitively regulated by them.
10. See below, Chapter 4.
11. See below, Chapter 8.
12. G.E. Moore, *Principia Ethica*, op. cit., Chapter 1.
13. MacIntyre, *After Virtue* (1981), p. 150: 'Just because enjoyment of a highly specific kind ... supervenes upon each different type of successfully achieved activity, the enjoyment of itself provides us with no good reason for embarking upon one type of activity rather than another'. True. But, as I hope is by now becoming clear, 'enjoyment' is not supposed to establish the reason for embarking on one type of action rather than another. The reason for action of a particular sort is to be found in the fact that the action promotes and consolidates a way of life that allows all to enjoy themselves in some way or another, equally.
14. J.S. Mill, *On Liberty* (in *Utilitarianism*, ed. M. Warnock, 1962). Quinton (*Utilitarian Ethics*) thinks that *'On Liberty* ... is only vestigially utilitarian'.
15. A distinction should be drawn here between valuing extrinsically in a logical sense and doing so in a psychological sense. It is possible, indeed quite common,

psychologically to regard something as being intrinsically valuable, while in fact, so far as logic goes, the value is extrinsic. See below, esp. Chapter 10.

16. See, e.g. *On Liberty*, op. cit., p. 136. 'It is proper to state that I forego any advantage which could be derived to my argument from the idea of abstract right, as a thing independent of utility. I regard utility as the ultimate appeal on all ethical questions; but it must be utility in the largest sense, grounded on the permanent interests of a man as a progressive being.'

17. R.J. Halliday, *John Stuart Mill* (1976) remarks that 'Readers of the essay [*On Liberty*] have never agreed either on what Mill's argument actually was, or on the relation of that argument to his intellectual history' (p. 114). As John Gray, *Mill on Liberty: a Defence* (1983) writes: 'it has long been the conventional view that [in *On Liberty*] Mill sets out to square the circle – to give a utilitarian defence of the priority of liberty over other values. What intellectual enterprise could be more misconceived, or more clearly doomed to failure?' (p. xi) Gray goes on to argue, with considerable conviction in my view, that, while it does not involve the equivalent of squaring the circle, Mill by and large succeeds. '*On Liberty* is not the folly that over a century of unsympathetic critics and interpreters have represented it as being, but rather the most important passage in a train of argument about liberty, utility and rights which Mill sustained over a number of his most weighty moral and political writings. Far from being the monument to Mill's inconsistency that his critics have caricatured, *On Liberty* is consistent almost to a fault, both in its own terms and in terms of a pattern of reasoning developed in Mill's other writings in which a utilitarian theory of conduct is applied to many questions in moral and political life. *On Liberty* contains a fragment of what I call Mill's Doctrine of Liberty in which a defence is given in utilitarian terms of the institution of a system of moral rights within which the right to liberty is accorded priority.' (p. xi).

18. MacIntyre (1981) p. 15, maintains that with at least some 'versions of utilitarianism ... no action is ever right or wrong *as such* [his emphasis]. Anything whatsoever may under certain circumstances be permitted'. At least on the view outlined in these pages the question of whether the first sentence is true depends upon the meaning of 'as such'. Certainly the utilitarian argues that no action is right or wrong merely by dint of being what it is. But the rule-utilitarian will argue that some are always wrong because they fall under a rule prohibiting them. In any event, the second sentence is not equivalent to the first and is not true of the species of utilitarianism I am concerned with. Promise breaking, for example, is always wrong on this view, and while, as on any theory, one might sometimes be inclined to condone a breaking of the rule, it is in no recognizable sense beyond that 'permitted'. See below.

19. Mill at one point 'defines' the utilitarian opinion in terms of 'the rules and precepts for human conduct, by the observance of which an existence such as has been described [in terms of exemption from pain and richness of enjoyment] might be, to the greatest extent possible, secured to all mankind; and not to them only, but, so far as the nature of things admits, to the whole sentient creation'. (*Utilitarianism*, p. 263.) Besides being further evidence that Mill was a rule-utilitarian, this passage comes close to a formulation in terms of ideal circumstances. It suggests that we focus on the question of what 'rules and precepts' would be sufficient for a community to enjoy happiness 'to the greatest extent possible' for all. If we presume that 'the greatest extent possible' could in principle amount to complete happiness, my position and Mill's would seem to be equivalent.

The same spirit is evident in this passage: 'As the means of making the nearest approach to this ideal, utility would enjoin, first, that laws and social arrangements should place the happiness ... of every individual, as nearly as possible in harmony with the interest of the whole; and secondly, that education and opinion, which have so vast a power over human character, should so use that power as to establish in the mind of every individual an indissoluble association between his own happiness and the good of the whole; especially between his own happiness and the practice of such modes of conduct ... as regard for the universal happiness prescribes.' (pp. 268, 269) In other words, Mill believes that one can devise a set of rules of life to ensure the happiness of all, provided all are willing to abide by them, and then bring people up in such a way as to ensure the latter condition.

20. See below, Chapter 9.

21. Hospers (1970) suggests the formula 'Do that act which produces the greater balance of happiness over unhappiness, or, if no act possible under the circumstances does this, do the one which produces the smallest balance of unhappiness over happiness.' This is preferable to many formulations, but is still to be resisted. As argued in the text, all these formulae seek to offer a principle for determining what to do in daily life. But utilitarianism does not seek to offer a sure-fire principle for solving all problems, let alone dilemmas, in imperfect conditions. The reason that the formulae are inadequate is that the task set is impossible. There is no fixed recipe for solving all moral problems in life. There may however be a coherent understanding of what conduct is actually right conduct, regardless of how difficult it may be to live up to it.

22. Anthony Quinton, *Utilitarian Ethics* (1973) summarizes three respects in which classic formulations of utilitarianism need clarification. 'First, there is the problem of deciding which consequences are relevant: *actual, intended* or *rationally expectable.* Secondly, there is the problem of deciding whether the consequences of an action should be assessed *absolutely* or *by comparison* with the consequence of available alternative. Thirdly, there is the problem of deciding whether obligation should be defined *positively,* in terms of the maximisation of happiness, or *negatively,* in terms of the minimisation of suffering.' (p. 4) Though more will be said pertaining to these issues throughout the book, it may be noted here that the shift to interpreting utilitarianism in ideal terms immediately reduces the problematic nature of these questions. What is relevant to determining what is morally right (and hence obligatory) conduct is the actual consequences that would obtain if all were to adopt such a rule of conduct. It is not a question of comparing alternatives, but of estimating what behaviour is necessary to allow of happiness.

23. See W.D. Ross, *The Right and the Good* (1930), and above, Chapter 2.

24. The standard view of utilitarianism (in any version, *mutatis mutandis*) has it that an action 'which, of the possible alternatives, maximises the good' is 'the right action'. 'If an agent does the right thing, he does the best of the alternatives available to him.' (The quotations here are from Bernard Williams, 'A Critique of Utilitarianism', 1973, pp. 85, 86, but they could be from virtually anybody.) The essence of my position is that this is incorrect (and the point here is not a purely verbal one): it is an action, or a rule, or a disposition that in concert with others is necessary or sufficient to allow of a situation in which all persons are equally and fully happy, that is a right action, a moral rule, or a virtuous disposition. An agent therefore does not necessarily do the right thing, if he does the best of alternatives available to him, or if he maximizes the good. He may simply be justified in doing what he does; he may do what is wrong. The more specific claim of Williams that 'making the best of a bad job is one of [utilitarianism's] maxims, and it will have something to say even on the difference between massacring seven million, and massacring seven million and one', (p. 93) therefore needs to be treated with caution. If the situation were in all other respects equivalent, the utilitarian, of whatever type, would indeed prefer to adopt the course of action that saved one life. But it is quite incorrect to see this reaction to this kind of situation as the focal point

of utilitarianism. Utilitarians do have a rule of thumb formula for making the best of a bad job, when a bad job is what they are faced with. But they do not claim to be able to do or say what is morally right in such situations, and their real concern is to establish what is right, so as to enable people to create a world in which such situations arise somewhat less often than they do at present, and decidedly less often then they do in the minds of philosophers.

25. '[The Greatest Happiness Principle] is a mere form of words without rational signification, unless one person's happiness, supposed equal in degree . . ., is counted for exactly as much as another's. Those conditions being supplied, Bentham's dictum, 'everybody to count for one, nobody for more than one,' might be written under the principle of utility as an explanatory commentary.' (J.S. Mill, *Utilitarianism*, p. 319)

26. J.S. Mill, *Utilitarianism*, Chapter 5.

27. As Hare (1982), p. 26, writes: It is 'sometimes alleged that justice has to be at odds with utility. But if we ask ... how are we to be just between the competing interests of different people, it seems hard to give any other answer than that it is by giving equal weight impartially to the equal interests of everybody. And this is precisely what yields the utility principle' .

28. J. Bentham (1948) op. cit., p. 311.

29. If we say, with Hampshire (1982), p. 154, that 'justice is the disposition to treat all men and women alike in certain respects, in recognition of their common humanity', then it is clear that utilitarianism embodies such a principle, for to focus on their capacity for suffering and happiness is merely to take a position on what element of their common humanity has moral significance.

30. Mill recognizes that 'in all ages of speculation, one of the strongest obstacles to the reception of the doctrine that Utility or Happiness is the criterion of right and wrong, has been drawn from the idea of Justice'. (*Utilitarianism*, p. 296) He equates justice with an innate sense of what is morally right. 'But though it is one thing to believe that we have natural feelings of justice, and another to acknowledge them as an ultimate criterion of conduct, these two opinions are very closely connected in point of fact. Mankind are always predisposed to believe that any subjective feeling, not otherwise accounted for, is a revelation of some objective reality. Our present object is to determine whether the reality, to which the feeling of justice corresponds, is one which needs any special revelation; whether the justice or injustice of an action is a thing intrinsically peculiar, and distinct from all its other qualities, or only a combination of certain of those qualities, presented under a peculiar aspect.' (pp. 296, 297) He then distinguishes justice in the sense of legal rights, moral rights, deserts, engagements or undertakings, partiality and equality. Common to all these types of justice, he suggests, is the idea of conformity to law as it ought to be. But, as he rightly observes, this account of justice 'contains ... nothing to distinguish that obligation from moral obligation in general'. (p. 303) He comes to the straightforward and unsurprising conclusion that, if justice is taken to refer to instinctive feelings of obligation 'not only have different nations and individuals different notions of justice, but in the mind of one and the same individual, justice is not some one rule, principle, or maxim, but many, which do not always coincide in their dictates, and in choosing between which, he is guided either by some extraneous standard, or by his own personal predilections'. (p. 311) Granting that, by definition, other ethical theories lead to alternative substantive conceptions of justice, he concludes 'while I dispute the pretensions of any theory which sets up an imaginary standard of justice not grounded on utility, I account the justice which is grounded on utility to be the chief part, and incomparably the most sacred and binding part, of all morality'. (p. 315)

31. As Anthony Quinton (*Utilitarian Ethics*, 1989) remarks: 'The most persistent objection to ... utilitarianism ... is that it fails to substantiate our unreflective convictions about justice ... There are principles of justice, it may be held, which are at once more certain or self-evident than the principle of utility and yet which are not compatible with it.' (p. 71) 'At the present time the alleged inadequacies of the utilitarian theory of justice is the main theme of the destructive criticism that is brought to bear on the doctrine.' (p. 81) Though Quinton himself modestly maintains that his discussion of the issue 'does not pretend to have resolved it', and concludes that 'what does seem clear is that justice is less easily accounted for by utilitarianism than Mill supposed', (p. 81) his argument suggests otherwise. He makes the point, for example, that 'what Bentham seems to have intended is that the criterion of value is the happiness of everyone affected. This does provide a minimal equality of treatment'. He continues by importantly and correctly dismissing the naive objection that 'the principle of utility supplies no ground for preferring an allocation of one unit [of utility] to each person over an allocation of the hundred units to one lucky man and of nothing at all to the other ninety nine'. As he says, we do not ever distribute units of fixed utility, but concrete things 'such as oranges ... which will have different utilities depending on the way in which they are distributed'. (p. 75) Notions such as particular needs and deserts also have to be taken into account, and will be presumed to be so when assessing the utility of distribution. Thus 'there are differences between the satisfaction-patterns of the individuals involved which, if the principle of utility is accepted, imply precisely the departures from strict, external equality that reflective moral intuition requires if just distribution is to be assured'. (p. 77) One can hardly say fairer than that!

32. Cf. T.M. Scanlon (1982), 'what a successful alternative to utilitarianism must do, first and foremost, is to sap [its] source of strength [the fact that it avoids the difficulty of establishing the foundations of rival views] by providing a clear account of the foundations of non-utilitarian moral reasoning'. (p. 103) He is right, I think, and courageous to face up to this point. However, I do not find his account of contractualism, in so far as it as odds with my account of utilitarianism, convincing.

33. A. Sen and B. Williams (eds), *Utilitarianism and Beyond* (1982).

34. Ibid., p. 1.

35. Ibid., p. 2.

36. Ibid., p. 5.

37. Ibid., p. 10.

38. Ibid., p. 16.

39. Ibid., p. 21.

40. Ibid., p. 21.

41. One of the most sustained criticisms of utilitarianism on the grounds that it 'cannot hope to make sense, at any serious level, of integrity' is provided by Bernard Williams, 'A Critique of Utilitarianism' (1973). See especially sections 3, 4 and 5. I have to say that I do not find his argument, in so far as I follow it, compelling. A major problem is that he conducts it by reference to two in themselves plausible and interesting examples of moral choice which are of the sort that my approach to ethics by way of the ideal is designed to avoid. Williams wants to expose the unacceptability of an attempt to calculate one's way out of a situation where to kill one individual would save several, or to accept a job doing research in chemical and biological warfare against one's conscience, perhaps with the consequence of slowing progress, on utilitarian terms; most particularly he wants to emphasize that it is important to consider who does things and not just the consequences of actions *qua* actions. But, as I have been at pains to bring out in the text, I do not believe that utilitarianism necessarily has a clear answer to give to the question 'what should the

individual do?' here. (Does any ethical theory?) It is not designed to answer such questions unequivocally and it should not be tested by reference to them. It is designed to establish such principles, perhaps, as 'one should never kill except in circumstances A and B' and 'one should not engage in chemical and biological warfare'. If it does establish such rules (as being necessary to a, though not necessarily the only, mode of existence that will allow of complete happiness for all), then those rules are moral rules. The agent ought to abide by them, save only if the circumstances of life lead to a clash between either of these clear rules and some other equally clear rule. If that is the case, as I fear it may be in Williams's detailed examples, deliberately designed, naturally enough, to seem problematic, then there is no right answer. In then resorting to an imperfect on-the-spot attempt to do what seems to have most utility, the utilitarian does not imagine that he is doing what is morally right, but doing the best he can.

42. Ibid., p. 6.
43. If space permitted, the subject of *Utility and Rights* (the title of a recent and significant collection of papers, edited by R. G. Frey) would receive more gracious treatment. Certainly one cannot hope to get away with Bentham's dismissive comment on the idea of certain fundamental natural rights as 'nonsense on stilts'. Nonetheless, it is legitimate to redress the balance of much recent argument by pointing out that the tendency to see utilitarianism as failing to account adequately for our presumptions about natural rights has no more self-evident appropriateness than the opposing view that talk of rights fails to account adequately for our presumptions about human welfare. Flew, for example, admittedly expressing himself within the confines of a dictionary entry, writes 'Mill considered rights to be grounded in general utility, but this seems radically confused: the function of assertions of rights (for example, to freedom of speech) seems to be precisely to *block* arguments for curtailment based on general expediency'. (*A Dictionary of Philosophy*, 1979, p. 285) The latter claim is, of course, true, but it pertains to a common function of rights assertion, rather than to any argument to justify or explain that function. The utilitarian view is that no adequate account has been given of the source or nature of these so called natural rights.
     Frey, in his introduction to the volume referred to, depicts the nature of the argument very plainly. Both classical and more recent preference utilitarianism are criticized in that their explanation of what is wrong with, e.g., killing, 'just does not seem to provide the intimate link to the destruction of individual, valuable, autonomous persons that, critics will urge, our intuitions demand'. (p. 15) So far so good, provided we recognize that 'our intuitions' refers to the intuitions of critics (and, no doubt, some of the uncommitted); nothing here to settle the issue of whether and, if so in what sense, the intuitions need to be taken seriously, or taken more seriously than they are by the utilitarian explanation of how they might be justified. But Frey concludes by saying: 'It seems natural, in other words, to see a person-relative theory as supplying over killing what a person-neutral theory with a consequentialist account of rightness arguably cannot, and so natural to see rights as suitable materials out of which to construct an adequate explanation of the wrongness of killing'. (p. 18) Seems natural to whom? Obviously not to utilitarians. 'Natural' in what sense other than 'coincides with our opinion'? On what grounds does it seem reasonable to see this as natural? The argument does not seem to be able to advance beyond the mere assertion by rights enthusiasts that there are certain natural rights, and the denial of those who do not agree. One may observe, however, that utilitarians at least offer a measure of argument and reason to support certain ascriptions of rights. Rights theorists do not, for the most part, advance beyond proclaiming the necessity to adopt a theory of rights divorced from any form of consequentialism.

See, in particular, L.W. Sumner, 'Rights Denaturalised' (1985), who argues convincingly that 'if we are to continue to take rights seriously we must contain them within the framework of an independently plausible moral theory', (p. 20) and proceeds to show that natural rights theory is not plausible: 'the very theories that have taken rights most seriously are incapable of showing that rights should be taken seriously'. (p. 39)

44. Bentham, of course, was not against rights nor of the opinion that talk of moral rights made no sense. What is at issue is whether and how particular claims to rights are logically grounded. He distinguished between fictional entities (such as, we might say, the imagination) and fabulous entities (such as, conceivably, giftedness). The former while not referring to any directly discernible element represent a comprehensible way of talking about a coherent notion (in Bentham's view they merely, generally, need to be more clearly articulated and firmly grounded); the latter purport to refer to an idea that is in fact chimerical. Legal rights were fictional entities, and as such in a sense quite real (while in another sense lacking real existence). It was natural rights that he regarded as fabulous entities. The utilitarian system, however, gives rise to *bona fide* moral rights (which are fictional entities). (All of which having been said, it should be noted that Bentham was capable of leaning heavily on the language of natural rights, when it suited his purpose. See, most particularly, 'A Plea for the Constitution' (*The works of Jeremy Bentham*, ed. John Bowing, 1838–43, vol. iv), where he condemns the practice of transportation as being contrary to 'natural justice'.)

45. C. Taylor, 'The Diversity of Goods' (1982).

46. Taylor, ibid., maintains that we value the citizen republic 'because we generally hold that the form of life in which men govern themselves, and decide their own fate through common deliberation, is higher than one in which they live as subjects of even an enlightened despotism'. (p. 143) Since 'the demands of utility and rights may diverge, [and] those of the citizen republic may conflict with both', he concludes that 'no single-criterion procedure ... can do justice to the diversity of goods we have to weigh together in normative political thinking'. (p. 143) But in the first place, the utilitarian may accept a diversity of goods, on the grounds that some are not moral goods. In the second place, the weight placed on the fact that we just do value the citizen republic (and certain rights) is extraordinary. Who are we? And on what reasonable grounds do we do so? The utilitarian at least has an answer to the latter question.

47. 'In the utilitarian perspective, one validated an ethical position by hard evidence ... Bluntly, we could calculate.' (Ibid., p. 129) Taylor goes on to suggest that the theory is 'but another example of the baleful effect of the classical epistemological model' and that 'the distortive conception [of epistemology] begins to shape our ethical thought itself'. To what extent it was the case that early utilitarians were inspired by a certain epistemological model does not concern me. Certainly we must distinguish the view that, in a sense, utilitarianism does involve hard evidence and calculation, from the view that it is *a priori* necessary that an ethical theory should do so. I, for one, do not hold the latter view. Furthermore, the sense in which utilitarianism, as I conceive it, is concerned with hard evidence and calculation is quite limited. We do not maintain that there is 'hard evidence' that happiness is the only thing that is good in itself, for example. Nor, as we shall see in Chapter 6, do we arrive at rules by precise quantification and calculation. We should recognize the danger of a 'distortive conception' [of epistemology] beginning 'to shape our ethical thought itself', but bear in mind that it need not do so.

48. In other words, it is not necessarily the case that 'languages of qualitative contrast ... get marginalised, or even expunged altogether, by the utilitarian ... reduction'. (Ibid., pp. 132,133) Personal integrity, Christian *agape*, and directing one's own

life, may have value, either moral or non-moral, for the utilitarian, and may legitimately call for a distinctive kind of commitment. There may also be the need, on utilitarian grounds, to recognize the plurality and incommensurability to which Taylor refers. Which way of life you choose is your business, provided only that you obey certain basic rules, and your personal commitment to something inherent in one way of life may be the decisive factor that justifies you in choosing it.

49. It is misleading to suggest that utilitarianism necessarily involves one in giving higher value to 'the rational man [who] has the courage of austerity: he is marked by his ability to adopt an objective stance to things'. (Ibid., p. 134) The emphasis on rationality is the product of the fact that we are engaged in philosophy, a species of rational activity. The philosopher in arguing for the theory should be rational. But utilitarianism does not maintain that one should always proceed in an austere rational manner. It maintains that one should abide by certain rules of conduct.

50. When it is said that 'it could be debated whether giving comfort to the dying is the highest utility producing activity possible in contemporary Calcutta. But, from another point of view, the dying are in an extremity that makes calculation irrelevant,' (p. 134) we respond, not for the first time, that that begs the question. Nonetheless, note that the utilitarian may agree. If he happens to share Taylor's sentiments he certainly will agree: there is no rule that says he should help the dying (see Chapter 9 on supererogation), but he just feels that he should. All that utilitarianism says is that, if you are looking for coherent grounds to support that feeling, you should consider that theory.

51. It is incorrect to say that 'one of the main points of utilitarianism' is to 'do away with' 'the qualitative contrast in our moral sensibility'. (Ibid., p. 139) Rather, it is to explain it.

52. As Harsanyi (1982) correctly observes, however, 'utilitarian theory does not involve the assumption that people are very good at making interpersonal utility comparisons. It involves only the assumption that, in many cases, people simply *have* to make such comparisons in order to make certain moral decisions'. (p. 50)

4. What is Happiness?

The utilitarian theory now to be examined from various points of view may be summarized thus: happiness is the only thing that is good in itself. (It and nothing else has the supervenient quality of goodness.) Morality is about the promotion of goodness. To behave morally is to do what is right for the sake of promoting the good. Our moral duty is therefore to perform whatever set of actions would be necessary and sufficient to ensure the happiness of all mankind.

It would be impossible in practice in an imperfect world for anyone consistently to make even a reasonable determination of what set of actions would ensure happiness in particular situations. Reliable calculations as to the happiness that would be consequent on particular actions would sometimes be not merely theoretically difficult, but practically impossible. Principles that are compatible in ideal circumstances might clash in practice. Above all, what clearly would promote happiness in an ideal world, or as part of a set of morally required actions, might not do so in the confused and corrupt circumstances of the real world. It therefore becomes morally incumbent on us to devise institutions, social arrangements, principles, rules and practices that seem ideally calculated, in concert, to promote and maintain the happiness of all. It is our moral duty then to abide by these rules. For utilitarianism is misrepresented (and implausible) as the theory that we should do whatever, at a given time, in a given situation, would promote happiness, even if we add (and understand what we mean by) a phrase such as 'maximally' or 'for the greatest number'. It is rather the theory that we ought to perform those acts that are as a matter of fact, taken together, necessary and sufficient for the happiness of the whole community, provided that all abide by them.

Thus the fact that, in the world as it is, killing some individual might increase the sum of human happiness does not make it acceptable, if it has been determined that in ideal circumstances one ought never to kill. Only in cases that are not covered by rules derived from consideration of the ideal, or in cases where the imperfections of the real world lead to clashes between rules or principles, does the utilitarian resort to working out what is morally justified, meaning that which he should do in that predicament.

As we have seen,[1] this account already contains an answer to two familiar complaints about utilitarianism: that it has no principle of justice and that the various distributive formulae that have been put forward are inadequate. The formulae are indeed inadequate, if seen as anything more than practical guidelines or rules of thumb (though one or other of them might come to be enshrined as a practical principle providing guidance towards one's moral obligations). A correct statement of the position is that ideally all persons should be fully and equally happy, and that plainly incorporates a principle of distributive justice. A principle of justice in any other sense is necessarily derivative on the theory itself, as in the case of any ethical theory. That is to say: a view of what justice demands or what it is just to do is parasitic on, or an alternative formulation of, a given theory.

There are, however, a number of other potential objections, criticisms and questions concerning utilitarianism still to be faced. The first of these is the point that, if we ought to be guiding our conduct to the end of ensuring that all are happy, we need to know what constitutes happiness. Incidentally, we should not confuse the correct observation that the theory would be useless without an adequate account of happiness, with the surely false point that people could not conform to this ideal without such understanding. It is entirely possible for people to aim at, recognize and experience happiness without being able to give a philosophical account of it. But it may be conceded that it would not be meaningful to assert the plausibility of utilitarianism without an adequate analysis of the concept. Accordingly, I shall now turn to that task.

Before discussing the concept of happiness itself, it is necessary to return to the theme of the nature of conceptual analysis in general.[2] For, just as it is part of my argument that much misplaced criticism of utilitarianism has arisen out of a confused idea of what an ethical theory is and purports to do, so it seems to me that a lot of objection to specific conceptual claims arises out of a confused idea of what analysis involves and may achieve. It is of course well known that there are divergent views amongst philosophers both as to how analysis should proceed and as to what it is actually trying to do. There is, for example, a considerable difference between the view, often attributed to Plato and his so-called 'essentialist' followers, that the philosopher seeks to locate, pin down and identify the characteristics that are a necessary part of concepts that have their own reality (rather as the lepidopterist captures and describes the features of a hitherto unclassified butterfly), and the view that the philosopher's task is to explore and tabulate linguistic usage, on the grounds that meaning is use.

I take it for granted that words and concepts, though very closely related, are distinct, and that strictly linguistic analysis can therefore be at best only a part of the philosopher's job. Of course it is a part, because it is a contingent fact that at least the majority of our concepts are symbolized verbally, and in many, if not all, cases a person's grasp of a concept will be co-extensive with their grasp of a certain vocabulary. Thus the way in which we use the word 'happiness' undoubtedly reveals something of what we think about happiness. To discuss the phenomenon of happiness, the idea or concept, without even acknowledging that a remark such as 'happy as an ant' seems peculiar, or that people tend not to describe those suffering from bereavement or physical pain as 'happy', would be extremely foolish.

But it seems clear that linguistic analysis can only be a part of our task, because our ultimate interest is not in a detailed analysis of how a word is used, which, apart from very possibly being confused even to the point of self-contradiction or incoherence, would tell us only what people think (which might or might not coincide with what is in fact the case). Without in any way committing ourselves to the allegedly Platonic view, we may acknowledge that our interest is in what it means to be happy, in the sense of what actually is involved in being happy, rather than in what, rightly or wrongly, people think is involved. A cow is a cow, whatever people's usage of the word 'cow' may suggest. Unicorns do not exist simply because at certain periods of history the populace believe and therefore talk as if they do. Of course, some concepts of abstract ideas such as democracy are far less securely bound by physical restraints than are concepts of physical creatures such as cows; but even in such a case we do not look for what is common to all actual uses of the word 'democracy' (the lowest common denominator, so to speak) to determine what shall count definitively as democracy. At the very least, we make demands of clarity and coherence on the concept, which may very well conflict with ordinary usage.

The situation therefore is comparable to that outlined in reference to the question of what an ethical theory is. We seek primarily a coherent account. It is sensible to start with some consideration of linguistic points, since how people in general use the word 'happiness' will help us to identify the broad area we are concerned with, the field in which we are operating. Language is our main mode of communication, and it would be foolish for me to set out to examine what I term 'happiness', without relating it in any way to what others term 'happiness'. But once we have done that, once we have ensured that we are talking about what, in the broad sense, English speakers would call 'happiness', as opposed to 'anger', 'having a cold', or 'riding a bike', our task is to ensure that we have an idea that is clear, internally coherent, sufficiently elaborate and consistent with our wider set of beliefs and assumptions. The philosopher's task is, taking his cue from everyday assumption as enshrined in ordinary language use, to formulate a conception that is meaningful and useful. I have argued elsewhere that the question of being correct or mistaken in one's analysis strictly speaking does not arise.[3] The question of whether a particular account of happiness represents what it truly is does not arise. The question is whether it is a coherent conception, in touch with, but not determined by, ordinary usage of the world.

Consequently, it is not my intention here to suggest that the reader necessarily means such-and-such by the word 'happiness', or that Mill or anybody else did, or that usage establishes the correctness of the account. Rather, I seek only to explicate what I mean by 'happiness', what I understand a happy person to be, and to do so in such a way that my account may be accepted as a clear and coherent conception which, while it may involve refinement, adjustment and even rejection of aspects of an everyday conception as enshrined in linguistic usage, nonetheless obviously bears relation to that everyday conception.

The view that I shall put forward is that happiness is a state of mind that may take many forms ranging from contentment to ecstasy, and that may or may not be accompanied by a variety of sensations. Thus a happy person may, in virtue of his happiness, experience a sensation of joy, a frisson of excitement, or a warm glow in the stomach; but one may be happy, perhaps in the form of contentment, in the absence of any specifically recognizable sensation. Happiness involves a sense of being at one with the world, of thinking or unreflectively feeling that things are as one would have them be. A completely happy man, by definition, would not have things otherwise. So far, I am doing no more than outlining what I take it to mean to say that someone is happy. I am suggesting that it would be contradictory to assert that someone was completely happy but didn't like certain features of their life, but that being happy should not be identified with any particular degree of emotional intensity or any specific physical sensation.[4]

But perhaps the most important claim that I want to make, in view of a popular sentiment which has been not infrequently endorsed by philosophers, is that the state of mind in question is not necessarily dependent on any particular material conditions in one's circumstances or psychological characteristics in oneself. In other words, while there are some states of mind which are logically incompatible with a happy state of mind, because they are defined in terms that involve a sense of being at odds with one's world, there are no other psychological traits such as, e.g., selfishness, good-humour or generosity, which are either necessary to or sufficient for experiencing happiness, and there are no material conditions at all that are either necessary or sufficient. Thus a person may conceivably be happy (or unhappy), whether mean, rich, poor, witty, kind, physically ill, the victim of rape or winner of the pools.[5] Unlikely in some cases, I grant, but conceivable. But on the other hand, in so far as a person is anxious, envious or frightened, then to that extent he cannot be happy, for these are concepts that are defined in terms of specific types of a lack of that enmeshment or harmony with one's situation that characterizes the happy person.

The above two paragraphs represent an account of what it is to be happy. They do not involve any attempt to break happiness down into its constituent parts, as one might define a certain disease; that is because I believe that happiness, like goodness, is a supervenient quality that cannot be broken down in that way. Two consequences of this view should be noted. The first is that the happiness that you and I experience may be different in texture, or experientially, while nonetheless being happiness in exactly the same sense, just as the beauty of one woman may differ from that of another, while being no more and no less an instance of beauty in the same sense of the word. We are making the same statement about each woman in calling her beautiful, yet each is distinct in her beauty. The second consequence is that different communities or, conceivably, different worlds might be happy in the same sense, perhaps in the same circumstances, but in different ways.[6]

Having set out my pitch, as one might say, let me now return to the beginning of a more extensive account, starting with some linguistic observations. First, I discount etymology entirely.[7] The derivation of the word 'happiness' is from the word 'hap', which implies chance, and it is of course a feature of much talk and thought about happiness that it is a matter of chance. But it really would be preposterous to assert that, because the word is etymologically tied to the idea of chance, and because traditionally or commonly people assume one's happiness to be a matter of luck rather than management, it must follow that it is so.[8] It would be comparable to the less dramatic but insistent presumption that only doctrines can be indoctrinated, or the absurd but, thankfully, as far as I know, untried argument that most of us are permanently dishevelled because we are without headdress,[9] or that our amusements must be deceptive since in its original fifteenth century sense 'to amuse' meant 'to delude'.

Furthermore, it is clear that, while many people often talk as if happiness is in the lap of the gods, and do so because they believe that to be true, even such ways of talking are not meant to suggest that 'happiness' means something chancy; they merely enshrine the popular view that as a matter of contingent fact happiness, whatever it is, is dependent on chance. It is therefore not even incompatible with ordinary usage to suggest that, whatever the truth about the extent to which chance governs our hopes of happiness, people may on occasion deserve and earn their happiness, or acquire it by a conscious attempt to do so. Certainly, the conception that I am elaborating has nothing necessarily to do with fate, luck or chance. I have no doubt that for many of us happiness may very often be at least partly a matter of chance; nonetheless to be happy does not mean to experience a serendipitous feeling of satisfaction, and it may not be a matter that has to be left to chance.[10]

Some of the more obvious characteristics of usage of the word 'happiness' that philosophers have drawn attention to include:

1. The point that there are clearly distinguishable uses of the word as, for example, between 'I am happy about the arrangements' and 'She is a happy woman'.[11]
2. The point that the word 'happiness' allows of degrees of intensity in a way that, for instance, the word 'contentment' does not. Thus, 'I am wildly happy' is acceptable, whereas 'I am wildly contented' is, to say the least, odd.
3. The point that it seems at best curious, at worst illegitimate, to use the word 'happiness' in relation to the satisfaction of trivial and/or isolated pleasures. Thus the ascription of happiness to a person on the grounds that they enjoy smoking or playing snooker all day seems to some a questionable or unusual usage.[12]
4. The point that it seems curious to describe various types of ne'er do well, rogue, or simpleton as 'happy'.

Each of these observations needs further comment.

Distinguishable Uses

There undoubtedly are different uses of the words 'happy', 'happiness', 'happily', etc. One could spend a great deal of time and energy distinguishing, first, the different parameters surrounding each distinct cognate of 'happiness' and, second, the range of uses available for any given one. But how important is it, for what purpose, to record that one may talk about a 'happy chance', but not the 'happiness' experienced by chance, or that Shakespeare's 'Happily (i.e. perchance), he may arrive forthwith' is to be distinguished from 'he arrived happily enough' (i.e. with a big grin on his face)? The question of importance for those who are concerned to examine what is involved in being happy or what happiness is, is whether any of these different uses involve different senses of the word, which is to say different conceptions and, if so, whether these different senses are of interest to one who is concerned with the question of being happy. Different usages that merely represent different connotations arising in different contexts, or that involve some clearly distinct meaning, are of no immediate significance. For example, 'I am happy with the arrangements' is clearly a usage of the word 'happy', roughly synonymous with 'I accept', that has no obvious relevance to the question of what it is to be happy. One would not, presumably, wish to argue that because one can be said to be happy with the arrangements, meaning no more than that one will go along with them, it follows that a person might be happy provided only that he did not object to anything. 'I am happy with the arrangements' is an idiomatic phrase meaning, more or less, 'it suits me'; it is very specific (it refers only to 'the arrangements'), and tells us nothing about the speaker's general state of mind. It is simply irrelevant to the issues at hand.

A locution such as 'he feels happy' is of more significance, for clearly the fact that we make such a remark is indicative of something about the way we think of happiness, and the question of the relationship between saying that and saying that 'he is happy' is a real one, and one that is germane to our inquiry. But it seems odd to infer, as some have done, that we need to distinguish between a feeling of happiness and happiness as a state of mind. Nor is there any obvious reason to see the existence of such phraseology as evidence of competing conceptions of happiness. To be sure, typically, we swing from talking about specific feelings of happiness to general states of mind, from happiness related to particular experiences to happiness overall, from short-lived sensations to long-lived ones, from shallow to intense degrees; but what happiness is – what is involved in being happy, what we mean by describing someone as happy – is no more affected by these considerations than the meaning of 'education' is affected by the fact that people talk frequently of 'moral education', 'education of the emotions', and 'life-long education'.

Degree of Intensity

It is debatable how true is the claim that 'happiness' allows of degrees of intensity in a way that 'contentment' does not. 'I am wildly contented' does indeed seem odd. But is this not, yet again, a linguistic point of the most banal sort (from the philosophical point of view)? After all, 'I am extremely contented' is not at all odd, so it does not even appear to be the case that usage consistently allows happiness, but not contentment, to be a matter of degree. I suppose that a fanatic for the nuances of usage might persist by maintaining that, at any rate, even if we talk naturally of degrees of contentment, we do not talk of varying intensities of contentment. But, in any case, what does it matter? Our concern is with what is involved in being happy. Whether and to what extent 'contentment' is a synonym for, or the name of a species of, or a subset of 'happiness', is of secondary importance. As far as that goes, it is appropriate to note that the way we talk clearly and emphatically allows of degrees of happiness, and that is an important consideration. It is part of our normal apprehension that being happy is no more an all-or-nothing affair than being educated or being healthy are. There are extremes in each case, and, as far as usage goes, we refer to relatively well educated, healthy, or happy people as 'educated', 'healthy', or 'happy', *simpliciter*. But we presume that one may be anywhere on a continuum from very slightly happy through to totally happy, with variations of both extent and intensity. This presumption, implicit in our usage, is not validated by that usage; but it is a presumption one sees no reason to challenge. Accordingly, I presume that we are concerned with a conception of a state of mind or an experience that allows of degree in this manner.

Closely related to this point is the observation that usage would seem to support the idea that happiness and misery are contraries, rather than contradictories, and that there is a continuum between the two. Certainly the two terms are mutually exclusive – one cannot be happy and miserable;[13] but they are by no means jointly exclusive: one may be neither happy nor miserable, but at various intervals along the way between them. So much is suggested by our usual way of talking but, more to the point, so much is surely part of the idea of happiness that we wish to explore and concern ourselves with. Our interest is not in an all-or-nothing, once for all, state of mind, call it what we will. It is in increasing the scope and degree of a state of mind that we regard as good in itself.

Trivial Pursuits

The claim that we do not ascribe happiness to people in respect of trivial or isolated wants is, again, questionable.[14] 'He's happy; he's playing snooker' seems a very common kind of observation to me. Nor is there any very obvious reason why a person should not be happy either while engaged in satisfying some isolated but obsessive want, or when living a life made up of satisfying what others might regard as trivial wants. In so far as there is any truth in the claim that happiness cannot arise from the satisfaction of trivial, isolated wants, I would suggest that it stems from a contingent fact about human psychology: that is to say, as a matter of fact we do not tend to find happiness in the satisfaction of a series of isolated, trivial interests such as, it may be, smoking cigarettes and watching horse races.[15] (Of course it is a matter of definition that one cannot be happy satisfying only wants that one regards as trivial oneself; for that is to say that one is not satisfied in respect of what one regards as important, and that is evidently incompatible with the idea of happiness as a satisfied state of mind.) But whatever the psychological facts, and whatever the implications of this or that usage, it is surely plain that the meaning of the term 'happiness' is such as to disallow relevance to distinctions between major and minor wants. To be happy is to be rid of unsatisfied desires, albeit in practice we will count ourselves happy and fortunate if we come only somewhere near to the ideal. But here again we see the importance of distinguishing between what an idea means to us and how in practice we speak about it. Usage, to be sure, suggests that happiness is a fleeting, unrealizable, lucky, half-formed creature. Usage may even reflect our experience of happiness as elusive and incomplete. But happiness – the meaning of it – is not to be confused either with our qualified success in attaining it or our view in relation to chances of achieving it.

Happy Fools

The final point that has sometimes been taken to emerge from usage is a very good example of the way in which too slavish a devotion to ordinary language may lead us astray, if such an example is still needed. For undoubtedly some people talk in such a way as to suggest that 'he is evil, but ever so happy', or 'he is foolish but happy', are self-contradictory statements. But it is surely obvious that to take this as evidence that such people cannot be happy is to place the cart before the horse. People do not necessarily say such things as a reflection of some truth; they may very likely say them as a consequence of a false belief. That this is so may be readily enough deduced from the fact that equally common are remarks of the type, 'the pure fool is the only person capable of true happiness', or 'the only path to happiness is by knavery'. To claim that 'happiness' means 'enjoying some state of mind consequent on virtue or wisdom' is plainly false, even by reference to such linguistic tests as etymology or usage, for, even those who believe it to be the case that only the virtuous can be happy, don't think that 'happiness' means that.[16] Indeed, it would undermine the core of their position if they did for, if happiness means that, there is no room to argue that people should strive to be good in order to win happiness as a reward, or that people should avoid wrong-doing for the sake of happiness. The essence of what we are concerned with is not the concept of virtue rewarded. We are concerned with the elucidation of a state of mind – how that state of mind may be attained is another and separate question.

Thus far I do not claim to have established anything beyond a few peripheral, though significant points, such as that usage will not take us far and that happiness cannot be defined in terms of virtue. I have merely outlined a conception of happiness and shown why appeals to usage are not going to deter me from upholding it. I shall now attempt to elaborate the concept I am concerned with in a more positive manner. I repeat that the question is not whether what I have to say is true, but whether it is a clear, coherent, sustainable account of something that people may experience, and that may reasonably be labelled 'happiness'. More than that cannot very obviously be done; and more than that is not necessary.

I take happiness to be a broad or general concept which, like love, beauty or sadness, may take many particular forms or encompass a variety of distinct species.[17] Happy individuals may thus be, variously, ecstatic, full of joy, quietly contented, positively cheerful, musingly satisfied, aggressively jolly or demurely aglow, just as friendship may take many forms and involve different degrees of excitement. In saying this I give notice that when I talk of 'happiness' I am not referring to a particular intensity of satisfaction: one might wish to talk of such a thing, but I know of no reason to suppose that 'happiness' should be reserved to label it, and when I (and I guess most other utilitarian-inclined persons) talk of such things as promoting happiness, it is not a hot-house of intense delight that I have in mind; nor, more generally, am I concerned to favour joy over contentment, loud good cheer over quiet delight: for it is happiness conceived as a general concept implying satisfied acceptance of one's circumstances that I am arguing we should promote.[18] At the risk of belabouring this crucial point, I must insist that it will therefore be no objection to this account of utilitarianism to say simply that I have an idiosyncratic view of happiness. For, provided that view is not incoherent or unclear, the question that matters is whether I can make a case for the ethical importance of what I choose to call 'happiness'. But as a matter of fact I do not think that my view is particularly idiosyncratic.

While people may experience more or less intensely, and may likewise assert or display their satisfaction more or less blatantly, without it necessarily affecting the question of whether they are happy or not, it is the case that, in order to be happy, a being must necessarily be self-conscious or self-aware. For, while being happy does not require the ability to articulate the fact, still less to understand the reasons why or the meaning of the term, it does require the ability to recognize or feel a sense of being at one with one's circumstances. It is, after all, a state of mind. A being that could not reflect upon itself could not be happy, by definition, and the question of which forms of life are capable of happiness is thus a question of which forms of life have self-awareness. It follows that new-born babies, for instance, cannot be happy or unhappy, strictly speaking, nor can certain extreme examples of the mental defective.[19] Conversely, certain species of non-human animal might well be capable of experiencing happiness or unhappiness.[20]

So it comes about that feeling and being happy are logically inextricable. To be happy it is necessary to recognize oneself as such, not in the superficial sense of being able to label oneself correctly as such, but in the sense of feeling oneself to be at one with the world. This is not a matter of contingent fact; it is not that the world is such that you won't find happiness, if you don't see yourself as happy. It is necessarily so for, if to be happy is to be in a state of mind that involves satisfaction with one's lot, one must sense oneself as being in that relation.[21] The notion that one might be happy without being aware of the fact is plainly nonsensical (unless that is taken to mean without being in a position, for whatever reason, to label oneself as 'happy'), and here, for once, we may note that usage to some extent supports us. Usage does not countenance first-person statements of the type 'I am happy, but I do not know it', nor third-person statements of the form 'Although he denies that he is happy, he is happy'. It is true that 'He is happy, but does not know it' is neither an unheard-of remark nor self-evidently contradictory. But it is surely incredible that one should imagine that a person, in so far as he does not consciously feel at one with his world, should nonetheless be described as 'happy', in that sense of the word that is predicated on such a feeling or sense. Such a remark has currency only because in general people have vague, unclear or simply different conceptions of happiness. Certainly a person can be 'happy' in the sense of 'fortunate' and not appreciate the fact, or have nothing to complain of objectively, but nonetheless bemoan his lot. But it is inconceivable that a person should be happy without being aware of it, if happiness is defined in terms of a conscious attitude towards one's situation.

Some have argued that while a person cannot be happy without feeling happy, one might feel happy without being happy.[22] One might be deluded, that is to say, perhaps by ignorance, drugs or hypnosis. But such an argument seems fairly obviously to hang upon an ambiguity in the word 'feel' which may mean either 'sense' or 'maintain'. One might mistakenly consider that one was happy, because one did not know what 'happiness' meant; and one might consider, maintain or claim that one's world could not be improved on, without a true appreciation of the possibilities. But, in so far as one feels, in the sense of 'has the experience of being' at one, then one is, whatever the actual circumstances, because 'being at one with the world' is itself, quite literally, a state of mind. Consequently, the test is the state of mind, not the world. Hypnosis, drugs and ignorance may in various ways be regrettable terms on which to find happiness (they tend, for example, to be precarious), but inasmuch as they may be the immediate cause of one's feeling at one with the world, it is clear that they may be the cause of happiness. To attempt to argue that one may feel happy thanks to drugs while not being truly happy is quite obviously to attempt to define happiness in terms of various views one may have about the value of finding happiness in one way rather than another.

Thus we may say that a person is completely happy if and only if they have self-awareness and they are conscious of no disharmony, no lack of fit, between the way the world is and the way they would like it to be.[23] Such a state of mind constitutes the happiness we are concerned with. Nothing is being said, yet, about the contingent facts of the matter – about the terms on which people may or may not find it, etc. – only that this is what is meant by calling someone 'happy'. The main importance of what has been said perhaps lies in the unequivocal statement that this is all that happiness is. We are making it plain, in other words, that utilitarianism is not concerned with promoting a specific type of happiness, such as bliss or exhilaration, rather than another, or with happiness defined by reference to various independent notions about what are and what are not acceptable terms on which to find happiness, or likely sources of it. Utilitarianism, as here advanced, is concerned with a broad state of mind. The conception is clear, coherent and in line with usage – but it is very general. Many forms and many ways of getting there may be found.

We return, inevitably, to the question of the status of this account. For there is no disputing the point that some people (including philosophers) will not call a person 'happy' if they are poor, in ill-health, drugged, divorced and so on. That is to say, the view has currency that there are various material and psychological conditions that are logically necessary to happiness.

An initial question here is whether those who advance such views actually mean what they say. I don't think it is unduly critical to suggest that at least some of them are guilty of confusing logical and psychological necessity (or even ethical necessity, if such there be). That is to say, it might be true that, just as a rich man will find it hard to get to heaven, so a poor man will find it hard to be happy; and it doesn't take much experience or imagination to conclude that, by and large, good health facilitates happiness. But none of this is of immediate relevance, since it amounts to a contingent claim about the chances of finding happiness in various ways (it obviously becomes relevant when we consider the viability of promoting happiness). But what of those who really do mean that it is logically impossible to be happy except on suchlike conditions? So that there shall be no misunderstanding, let us spell their position out. It must be that statements such as 'he is happy, but poor' or 'he is happy and on drugs' are self-contradictory for, if they are not self-contradictory, then it is logically conceivable that a person should be happy, though poor and drugged. And if that is logically conceivable, then it cannot be the case that we should never call a person 'happy' if he is poor or on drugs, as is being maintained.

It is difficult to know how to deal with such a view. Given my remarks above, I cannot reasonably make too much of the point that ordinary usage certainly doesn't seem to suggest that 'he is happy, but poor' is self-contradictory, though I shall take such support as I can from the point, and emphasize it: the onus would seem to be on those who maintain that it is self-contradictory to show that it is, and to explain away the evident fact that most people don't think that it is. Of course, in line with previous remarks, I must also concede that if some people insist that what they mean by 'happiness' is a state of mind that, among other things, does not depend on drugs and requires a certain material comfort or wealth, I, for one, am not going to waste my time arguing that they are incorrect. If that is their conception, so be it. But it can be said that not only is it an idiosyncratic conception (unless my sense of ordinary language is very amiss); it is also a problematic conception, and perhaps even perverse. It is problematic because it is based on value judgements that will not find universal assent and need some kind of supporting reasoning (which is not to say that such reasoning could not be provided). Happiness is obviously a normative concept, but that means only that it is something that we value; it does not mean that it has to be understood in terms that enshrine all our other values.[24] There is therefore no *a priori* justification for assuming that, even if we don't like the idea of people attaining a particular state of mind through drugs, we must therefore object to calling a drug-induced state of mind a happy one.

To take the easier example first, I am inclined to say that the idea that a person could not be happy while very poor, as a matter of conceptual truth, flies in the face of what most people think (as evidenced in their language), flies in the face of experience, for surely some poor people maintain that they are happy, and seem to be happy, in so far as we can intuitively judge these things without begging the question at issue, and flies in the face of one thing we do confidently assume about happiness – namely that different people find it in a quite astonishing variety of ways and circumstances. Hence I am tempted to regard it as a perverse piece of stipulation, and would certainly persist in asking for some good reason to adopt it, which, to my knowledge, has not so far been forthcoming.

The example of a drug-induced state of mind is undoubtedly more plausible, *prima facie*. This I attribute partly to the fact that we are generally more averse to people taking drugs than to their being poor, regarding the former as culpable in a way that the latter often is not, and partly to a vague idea that it is important for people's states of mind to be authentic. As far as these points go, I share the common presumptions. But one can easily enough argue that happiness found through drugs is to be resisted, because it is vulnerable, because it involves danger, because in the long run it may be self-defeating, and so forth, without trying to define it out of existence. Furthermore, the attempt to do the latter will require some deft footwork in respect of concepts such as authenticity. I would argue that it is far more clear-headed and satisfactory to recognize that drugs may be used precisely to alter one's state of mind and since few, if any, are going to deny that happiness is at least partly a state of mind, it seems reasonable to conclude that drugs may as easily be the cause of one's happiness as education, attitude adjustment, indoctrination, hypnosis, reasoning or a variety of other things, albeit one will have independent grounds for preferring some ways of finding happiness to others.

A similar argument surrounds the question of whether happiness is logically tied up with various psychological characteristics. For example, it has been maintained that one cannot be selfish and happy or, more generally, vicious, criminal, or immoral and happy. Conversely, it might be alleged that only truly caring, religious or reasonable people can be happy. Once again we must distinguish the contingent thesis that certain psychological characteristics as a matter of fact advance or retard one's chances of happiness from the logical thesis that they are conceptually linked. The former is not under consideration at the moment, and it is worth adding that all the contingent psychological data that some like to feed into the general debate must be to some extent suspect since, by and large, they have been gathered in the absence of a clear and agreed conception of happiness. For example, we cannot take on trust the conclusion of empirical research to the effect that married people are happier than single people,[25] if the conception of happiness employed by the researchers is not one that we share or if, as is too often the case, it is unclear, confused, or incoherent in some way. The view that it makes no logical sense to suppose that a person could be selfish and happy, or criminal and happy, or that only those who care about other people can experience true happiness is, as far as I can see, without any visible foundation. Criminal, selfish, uncaring persons have maintained that they were happy and shown all outward signs of being happy. On what conceivable grounds could we maintain that what they experienced, their state of mind, was not of the same order as that enjoyed by Jesus Christ or Socrates? And if we cannot with good reason say that, what would we be doing other than issuing a fiat that persons whose satisfied state of mind is gained in what are to us offensive ways shall not be accounted 'happy'? They may not be morally commendable, even, be it remembered, on the utilitarian account. But what has that got to do with whether they are happy?

But, in the end, the important question is not the meaningless one of whose conception is right, but what are the implications of adopting either one. My conception of happiness begs very few further value questions; it allows us to unite in seeing the importance of happiness while holding various different things dear. It also allows us to distinguish clearly between the question of what 'happiness' means, and contingent questions such as how it may most easily and effectively be promoted, or what means of attaining it are morally acceptable.[26] A conception that already ties in the value of, say, avoiding drugs, being unselfish, being married or having some wealth, is by no means obviously a good we all wish to promote. I am therefore content to say, in summary, that

- it does not seem to be the case that usage sanctions these various more specific conceptions which, on my own account, is not to say that they are unacceptable, but is to say that they are idiosyncratic, possibly ideological, confusing and unlikely to gain general assent;
- there seems to be no argument to support the contention that the specific should be linked with the general; for example, if it is not disputed that happiness is at least partly a state of mind, on what grounds would one add 'provided it is attained on such-and-such terms'?
- happiness in my sense is indisputably good; that is not the case with any more specific conception;
- finally, it makes little difference to my overall argument, for I seek to show that we should be concerned about happiness in my sense.

By contrast, whereas it is clear that claims about there being certain specific material or psychological conditions that are logically necessary for happiness are open to serious dispute, I am aware of no one who thinks that it would make sense to juxtapose happiness and certain other general terms referring to certain other, some of them more specific, states of mind. It seems indisputable, for instance, that 'he is happy but anxious', 'he is happy, but envious', 'he is happy, but lonely', and 'he is happy, but frustrated', are contradictions in a way that 'he is happy, but poor' or 'he is happy, but on drugs' have not been shown to be. In my view, this confirms the plausibility, the soundness, of my analysis. For what characterizes all the terms that do seem to be logically incompatible with happiness (and I make no attempt to offer an exhaustive list) is that they are terms that refer to a state of mind that, whatever its particular intensity or sensation, about which we neither necessarily know nor need to know, is at odds with one of various kinds of aspect of the individual's world. If a person's happiness can be equally well vitiated by the very possibly distinct kinds of sensation involved in wishing that one's immediate future was more predictable, resenting one's neighbour's success, feeling thwarted by circumstance, and regretting that one is alone, that surely confirms the idea that 'happiness' and 'unhappiness' are general terms. They may take many forms and be occasioned by a variety of different situations. What defines them is not any particular circumstance, but the individual's attitude to them – his state of mind. It is not that being alone necessarily makes one unhappy, but that some people, at odds with their loneliness, are thus, by definition, unhappy. And this seems correct: being alone, having friends who are more successful etc., are not necessarily incompatible with happiness; but if you feel about these situations in a certain way, which may be generically summarized as 'not being at one with them', you cannot be happy. This, as I say, surely confirms the idea that happiness is logically bound up with acceptance of one's situation and the claim that what can be accepted is a matter of psychology and contingency, not a matter of definition or universal law.

At any rate, as I have been at pains to stress, while I believe that my conception is a reasonable one to adopt, the more important point is that that is the one I am adopting. Only if it were unclear, incoherent or quite out of touch with the way in which people generally use the term 'happiness' (and hence, we may suppose, tend to conceive it), would it be reasonable to object to it. I hope and believe that none of these claims can legitimately be made about the account I have given.

Three further points do need to be touched on in this chapter, however. The first is the question of the relationship between 'happiness' and 'contentment',[27] the second the relationship between 'happiness' and 'pleasure', and the third the ethical value of happiness.

The first issue I take to be one of no more than verbal significance. Some people would undoubtedly maintain that, at best, I have offered an account of contentment rather than happiness. I think myself that it is quite true that the state of mind I am referring to could reasonably be labelled 'contentment'. This is not particularly surprising, since many thesauruses would list 'happiness' and 'contentment' as synonyms, indicating precisely that in general usage the words are frequently interchangeable. Nor would it be of any concern to me, if it were suggested that we should use the latter term, and say that utilitarianism is being presented as a thesis founded on the premiss that only content-ment is morally good in and of itself. The ideal of a world of fully contented persons, if that means people who are completely at one with their circumstances, remains the concern. It has not been disputed that the word 'happiness' is sometimes used to mean something more specific, such as 'a sense of vibrant joy' or 'ecstasy'. All that has been argued is that that is certainly not its only meaning, and that the ideal we are concerned with is not that of a world of permanently ecstatic individuals. I might add that some usage involves making 'contentment' a little more specific than the concept I wish to focus on. For if 'contentment' is defined in terms of passive acceptance as opposed to positive enthusiasm (not that I think that distinction quite so straightforward as the polarization suggests), then it is not the right word for my purposes. I am not arguing for a specifically passive acceptance; I am arguing for a harmonious state of mind, a sense of being at one, whether it takes the form of passive acceptance or positive enthusiasm. It seems to me a contingent likelihood that the ideal world, i.e. one in which all are fully at one or enmeshed with their situation, would in fact involve both. But my point here is simply to meet verbal knock with verbal response: there is a case for saying that, judging by usage, my choice of 'happiness' is preferable to 'contentment'.

The connection between happiness and pleasure is not merely a verbal question and is in itself altogether more philosophically interesting.[28] However, despite the fact that the more prominent utilitarians, such as Bentham and Mill, often talked in terms of pleasures and pains, and may be criticized for having failed to work out a very lucid account of their relationship to happiness, it is not, I think, necessary for my purposes to pursue that question here.[29] It may be possible to rewrite the happiness thesis in terms of pleasure and pain, but it may not be; and, even if it is, it is not apparent why that would be an improvement on the statement that utilitarians regard happiness, conceived of in the manner outlined, as the only thing that is good in itself.[30]

Finally, I have re-iterated throughout this chapter that happiness, thus conceived, is self-evidently and indisputably good. Nobody, I take it, could reasonably claim that he saw no value in happiness for, while one may argue about whether it is worth being happy on certain terms, or whether other things do not have equal value, to say 'I see no value in being at one with my world in general' is contradictory. To feel at one with one's world, to be satisfied with circumstances is, by definition, to take a positive evaluative position. Now, of course, in principle one can denigrate the value of enmeshing with certain particular situations, and one can logically maintain that some other value should have precedence over happiness. But the latter will require some argument to support the contention, in a way that placing a value on happiness does not, for surely no other value, though many are widely held, has this quality of being self-evidently valuable. The reader cannot (and does not, I am sure) expect the whole utilitarian thesis to be established at one and the same time. The argument here is that happiness self-evidently has value in and of itself, and that nothing else does. On that platform the utilitarian theory will be based. The base can only be shaken by denying the value of happiness or by establishing the value, in and of itself, of something else – something that, in common with many people, I do not think has ever been entirely successfully done. The point that one may denigrate the value of particular experiences of happiness is not a problem for the utilitarian, for he may do so too. It should not need saying that it is not the utilitarian thesis that, wherever someone is happy, that is an acceptable state of affairs. He will very often say, notwithstanding the intrinsic goodness of happiness, that it is deplorable that certain people are happy in certain circumstances. For the theory, as opposed to the premiss, is about the distribution of happiness and, by extension, about right and wrong ways of acquiring happiness.

Nonetheless the shade of Mill's notorious claim that happiness is the only thing that is desired as an end in itself,[31] thus it is the only thing that is desirable in itself, and hence, playing on the ambiguity of 'desirable', it is the only thing that ought to be desired as an end in itself, may seem to hang over these remarks; for, may it not be said that I have made the point that happiness has value, but not that it has specifically ethical value? In my view, it may. I do not claim that it is self-evident to a degree that brooks no contradiction that happiness is morally good, although I believe that it is and do maintain that there is something *prima facie* slightly odd about denying it. (One might compare here the view that it is better in some sense, not necessarily moral, to be healthy than to be sick; that seems to me to be fairly obviously true, but not in fact a logically necessary truth.)

However, three considerations may strongly incline us to the view that it is reasonable to suppose that happiness is a moral good, in a way that it is not so clearly reasonable to regard other things, such as freedom, as obviously morally good. First, though many people do not believe that happiness is the only thing that is morally good in itself, and explicitly maintain that sometimes it should be sacrificed for another good, few if any specifically deny moral value to happiness. Certainly some people sometimes seem to do so. But it is part of my wider argument that such denials are based on a misunderstanding of what is at issue. As we have seen, people may and do deny that happiness is the only thing morally good in itself, or that any action is right so long as it makes for much happiness, or that telling the truth is only morally incumbent on us when it pleases people to hear it. But these and suchlike claims are not our current concern and, indeed, are not claims that the fully articulated theory of utilitarianism would endorse. The question is only whether we do see some moral good in itself in people being happy; and the answer to that, I am suggesting, is that we do. No trickery is intended here. This is to say merely that we do attribute moral value to happiness. Of course it does not follow that we are correct to do so, or that it logically follows that it has such value. But we perhaps tend to underestimate the significance of our fundamental convictions in an area such as ethics. While it may not please the academic side of us or satisfy our desire for certainty and precision to give weight to widespread intuitions, if we are perforce dealing with a matter that does not seem to allow of the degree and kind of unequivocal demonstration or proof that other matters do, then it is surely more reasonable and convincing to appeal to such common sentiments, than to ignore them in favour of more idiosyncratic convictions.[32]

Second, it is also a matter of common experience that while certain individuals do proclaim various other moral values and may in strict logic deny such value to happiness, they do not, when pushed to extremes, consistently ignore the claims of happiness or some similar term such as 'well-being'. That is, an advocate of freedom is not prepared to say 'I don't care whether every individual on earth is thoroughly miserable and suffers unspeakably as a consequence; people ought nonetheless be left entirely free.' Again, I do not suggest that it would be self-contradictory or otherwise incoherent to take such a position, but I do suggest that some considerable weight should be given to the fact that by and large people do not take it. It is decidedly not irrelevant to the ethical debate that we feel it impossible to ignore the claims of happiness as a moral consideration and continually query the claims of other values by reference to happiness, in the final analysis.[33]

Finally there is a consideration that approaches more nearly the status of a logical argument. To regard something as morally good is by definition to be drawn strongly towards it, to recognize it as having, not simply spasmodic attraction, but strong and permanent drawing power, so to speak. I do not refer here to what may pass for moral demands at any given time, since clearly we are not necessarily drawn to specific injunctions such as 'Do not steal'. I refer to what is moral, and hence in practice to what the individual truly recognizes as moral. To believe sincerely that it is morally right to keep promises is, among other things, to believe that promise keeping has to be; it involves psychological awareness of and response to the drawing power of the injunction, for all that one will sometimes not be moved by it. Now the point of psychological hedonism, the doctrine that 'nature has placed mankind under the governance of two sovereign masters, pleasure and pain',[34] or, in weaker form, that human beings are strongly motivated by consideration of what does and does not fundamentally satisfy them, is to emphasize the scarcely deniable fact that we do not simply like happiness, but rather are necessarily and strongly drawn towards it. Certain individuals may conceivably be equally or more strongly psychologically drawn to other things, but they stand in need of an argument to convince others who do not share their predilection that they ought to – whereas nobody could deny the drawing power of happiness. This drawing power or attraction is, of course, not a sufficient condition of a moral good, but it is, as we have seen, a necessary condition. And happiness is the only putative moral good that undeniably meets this necessary condition.

The argument of the previous paragraph is far from being as clear and compelling as I would like it to be, which is why I have also drawn attention to the previous two considerations. It seems inevitable that we should see moral good in happiness, and we do so as a matter of fact, and admit as much when arguing *in extremis*. It would still be coherent to some degree to deny it, but one must ask why, given these points, we should think it reasonable to do so. Furthermore, we are guilty of bad faith, when we suggest without convincing argument that we should not see happiness as morally good, when in fact psychologically we do so.

As I have suggested throughout, the resistance to the utilitarian theory and its premiss that happiness is the only thing that is morally good in itself seems to stem largely, if not entirely, from the capacity that people have to misunderstand and caricature what the theory involves and leads to. The main purpose of these opening chapters has been to introduce the theory in such a way as to enable me to point out the misconceptions involved in traditional criticisms of utilitarianism, so that the reader may conclude: 'the premiss is as plausible as any I can think of, and the theory that derives from it turns out to be intuitively convincing, and its implications far from the counter-intuitive set of prescriptions and practices that have popularly been supposed to follow from it.' Such a conclusion may be all that we can expect by way of proof in respect of an ethical theory. But we would do well to heed the warning of Aristotle: 'In studying this subject we must be content if we attain as high a degree

of certainty as the matter of it admits ... it is a mark of the educated man
and a proof of his culture that in every subject he looks only for so much
precision as its nature admits.'[35]

Notes

1. See above, Chapter 3, pp. 49–51.
2. See above, Chapter 2, pp. 31–33.
3. See, in particular, 'Does the question "what is education?" make sense?', *Educational Theory*, 33 (1983).
4. On this point, see further R. Barrow, *Happiness* (1980); also *Plato, Utilitarianism and Education* (1975). Cf. E. Telfer, *Happiness* (1980).
5. To be contrasted with the views of, e.g., Brian Barry (1965), who denies that one who lives a vicious life could be happy, Jean Austin (1968), who finds it inconceivable that the unkind should be happy, Robert Simpson (1975) and Irwin Goldstein (1973), who emphasize the necessity of friendship and wealth. R.M. Hare's (1963) contention that we could not regard the mental defective as happy is slightly different. Happiness does presuppose a certain level of consciousness to which a mental defective might in some cases conceivably not attain.
6. See below, Chapter 5.
7. Cf. J.S. Mill, *Utilitarianism*, p. 302. 'I am not committing the fallacy ... of assuming that a word must still continue to mean what it originally meant. Etymology is slight evidence of what the idea now signified is, but the very best evidence of how it sprang up.'
8. As J. Wilson (1968) succinctly points out: 'You can be happy without being ... fortunate.'
9. 'Dishevelled' 'without head-dress XV; (of the hair) unconfined XVI; fig. disorderly XIV.' *The Oxford Dictionary of English Etymology*.
10. There is a popular opinion to the effect that one will not achieve happiness by consciously striving for it. There may be some truth in this, but it would seem to be a contingent point. One can certainly organize one's life in a deliberate way with a view to happiness, and may succeed in one's ultimate aim.
11. D.A. Lloyd Thomas (1968), for example, refers to four different 'uses' of the word 'happy'. Robert Dearden (1972) similarly refers to three different 'senses' of the word.
12. Eg., R. Dearden, op. cit.
13. In respect of the same thing.
14. See, for example, Stephen K. Bailey (1976), who obliquely suggests that 'an endless series of beers guzzled in front of the television set carrying an endless series of organised thuds and punitive bangs is not as much evidence of happiness as rich patrons sitting in their box seats watching Tristan and Isolde through pearl-covered opera glasses'. (p. 42) He continues: 'Even with the twentieth century's massive depreciation of Victorian rhetoric, millions of people have continued to find nourishment of the free self in fulfillment of perceived obligations and in the performance of voluntary service.' (p. 45) 'Few human experiences can match in sheer exhilaration the rewards of the cultivated mind at play and at work along the frontiers of its capacity.' (p. 46) Stirring stuff, but any truth that it may have would seem to be at the level of contingent generalization.
15. See, on this topic, John Wilson's (1968) distinction between first and second order wants.
16. See note 5. See also K. Graham (1977) on the limits of ordinary language.
17. In other words I see the strength of the concept precisely where, e.g., MacIntyre (1981) sees its weakness. He is at great pains to stress that 'the notion of human

happiness is *not* [his emphasis] a unitary, simple notion' (p. 61) and concludes, rather too rapidly, that 'to have understood the polymorphous character of happiness is of course to have rendered [that] concept useless for utilitarian purposes'. (p. 62) 'If someone suggests to us, in the spirit of Bentham and Mill, that we should guide our own choices by the prospects of our future ... happiness, the appropriate retort is to enquire: "But ... which happiness ought to guide me?" For there are too many different kinds of enjoyable activity, too many different modes in which happiness is achieved. And pleasure or happiness are not states of mind for the production of which these activities and modes are merely alternative means. The pleasure-of-drinking-Guinness is not the pleasure-of-swimming, and the swimming and the drinking are not two different means for providing the same end state. The happiness which belongs peculiarly to the way of life of the cloister is not the same happiness as that which belongs peculiarly to the military life. For different pleasures and different happinesses are to a large degree incommensurable: there are no scales of quality or quantity on which to weigh them. Consequently appeal to the criteria of pleasure will not tell me whether to drink or swim and appeal to those of happiness cannot decide for me between the life of a monk and that of a soldier'. (pp. 61, 62)

It is true that happiness is polymorphous, though it is also, at another level, a unitary notion. It is a general term, embracing a number of species. But we do not ask 'which species of happiness ought to guide me?' (even assuming that it would be correct to say that the utilitarian should be guided by his happiness which, of course, it is not). It does not matter in itself which species of happiness is enjoyed. The utilitarian is saying that it does not matter what people take happiness in, provided that it is in ways that allow all to be happy. We then realize that there are certain contingent and necessary conditions of common happiness; they provide the criteria for selecting ways to behave and live. It is precisely the polymorphous nature of happiness that makes utilitarianism plausible.

John Gray, *Mill on Liberty: a Defence* (1983) refers to the same passage from MacIntyre and remarks, more cautiously than I, 'I trust that the arguments of the previous chapter show MacIntyre's claim to be exaggerated. The abstractness and complexity of Mill's conception of happiness represents the attempt in a spirit of psychological realism to come to grips with the diversity and variety of human purposes and to identify happiness with the successful pursuit of self-chosen goals rather than with the having of any sort of sensation'. (pp. 125, 126) On the issue of whether it is logically impossible for men to desire pleasure or not, I do not see any need to add to Quinton, *Utilitarian Ethics* (1973). There is the view that 'What is desired is always some specific thing: a glass of wine, a good looking woman, a peerage. The achievement of these objects is no doubt attended with pleasure, but it is the objects and not the pleasure that is desired'. But, asks Quinton, 'why should it be supposed that the desire for some specific thing is not a desire for the pleasure that the thing can provide? After all what is desired is the thing in circumstances in which it will give pleasure. Suppose I have a desire for a glass of wine. More explicitly what I desire is to drink it. But that is not quite explicit enough. I shall not be satisfied if I am rendered unconscious and the wine is poured into my mouth and got down my throat while I am in that state'. (p. 61)

18.   'How much more there is to aim at when we see that happiness may coexist with being stationary and does not require us to keep moving.' John Stuart Mill, 'Notes for a speech on Wordsworth delivered at the London Debating Society', 1829, quoted by Karl Britton, 'J.S. Mill: A Debating Speech on Wordsworth, 1829,' *Cambridge Review*, vol. LXXIX, March, 1958, p. 420.

'If by happiness be meant a continuity of highly pleasurable excitement, it is evident enough that [a life of permanent happiness] is impossible ... [But the happiness utilitarians refer to is] not a life of rapture; but moments of such, in an existence made up of few and transitory pains, many and various pleasures, with a decided predominance of the active over the passive and having as the foundation of the whole, not to expect more from life than it is capable of bestowing ... The main constituents of a satisfied life appear to be two ... tranquility and excitement.' (John Stuart Mill, *Utilitarianism*, p. 264) While these remarks of Mill do not purport to present an analysis of the concept, it will be apparent that my account of happiness is entirely in accord with the spirit of his perception of it as a general state of mind that may take many particular forms.

19.   See R.M. Hare (1963).
20.   See, e.g., P. Singer (1977) and (1979).
21.   Cf. G.H. Von Wright (1963) 'to be happy is to be in a certain relationship ... to one's circumstances of life, [but] happiness is not in the circumstances ... but springs into being with the relationship'.
22.   See, e.g., J. McPeck (1978) on being and feeling happy, and Jean Austin, op. cit., on drugs and happiness.
23.   Bertrand Russell (1975) maintained that 'to be without some of the things you want is an indispensable part of happiness' and the view dies hard. But if it is true, as it may be, it is surely contingently true, and true only because human beings are not happy 'with nothing whatever to grumble at', because their expectations are often disappointed, and so on. In other words, while it may be true that if everything turned out tomorrow to be the way we said we wanted it to be, we could be rapidly disenchanted, it does not follow that to be happy is not to be understood in terms of such harmony. A similar argument can be deployed in reference to such ideas as, e.g., divine discontent. See Barrow (1975).
24.   J.J.C. Smart, *An Outline of a System of Utilitarian Ethics* (1973, pp. 18–27) depicts 'a world made safe for electrode operators' in which individuals stimulate sensations of pleasure electronically. 'Should we say that the electrode operator was really happy? ... whether we should call [him] "happy" or not, there is no doubt a) that he would be contented, and b) that he would be enjoying himself.' Smart then proceeds, not entirely clearly in my view, to suggest that we would not call him happy because 'to call a person "happy" is to say more than that he is contented for most of the time, or even that he frequently enjoys himself and is rarely discontented or in pain. It is, I think, in part to express a favourable attitude to the idea of such a form of contentment and enjoyment ... That is, "happy" is a word which is mainly descriptive ... but which is also partly evaluative'. (p. 22) I do not see any warrant for the latter assertion; nor am I clear where such a warrant could come from. It is no doubt true that we do not judge people to be happy in cases where we cannot believe that they would be, and such cases might conceivably include those where we think it would be improper or unworthy for them to be happy. But far from showing that people logically could not be happy in situations where they ought not to be, they imply the opposite. The plain fact is, I submit, that to say 'He is happy' is *not* to say 'he is contented and enjoying himself in ways that I can approve of'. 'He finds his happiness in immoral ways' is perfectly intelligible. I agree, however, that one has some initial doubt about describing the electrode operator as happy. Smart himself provides one possible explanation of our doubt, when he points out that there is a distinction between what would please us, and what pleases us in prospect. Thus we might be uneasy at the idea of calling such a person happy, because we are not disposed to imagine we should feel happy in such circumstances. But I should also emphasize the points that a stimulated sensation of pleasure is not the same thing as a state of mind, so that one would no more call the person contented than happy (either word only being applicable with reference to the agent's conscious awareness of the pleasure), and that to be happy (or contented) the agent has to be

satisfied in respect of the main features of his life (e.g. work, friendship, ambition) which are left unconsidered in the example.

Bernard Williams ('A Critique of Utilitarianism' 1973, p. 114) rightly asks of Smart's claim 'that "happy" is a partly evaluative term, in the sense that we call "happiness" those kinds of satisfaction which, as things are, we approve of ... by what standard is this surplus element of approval supposed, from a utilitarian point of view, to be allocated? There is no source for it, on a strictly utilitarian view, except further degrees of satisfaction, but there are none of those available, or the problem would not arise'.

25. See, for example, *The Institute for Social Research Newsletter* (1974), which cites two studies that claim to show that 'marriage and family life are the most satisfying parts of most people's lives and being married is one of the most important determinants of being satisfied with life.' (p. 3) Robinson and Shaver (1978) summarize: 'all studies indicate married people to be significantly happier than unmarried people'.

26. J. McPeck, 'Can Robin Barrow be happy and not know it?', *Proceedings of the American Philosophy of Education Society* (1978) has also described it as 'maximally tolerant'.

27. On 'contentment' and 'happiness', see, in particular, Theodore Benditt (1974) and Roger Montague (1966–7). The latter establishes that the two words are not synonymous but not, I think, that happiness cannot be adequately characterized in terms of contentment.

28. Related to this topic are J. Wilson (1968), R.M. Hare (1982), J.C. Harsanyi (1982), M.A. Bertman (1972), and R.N. Bronaugh (1974).

29. We should note MacIntyre's (1981) point that 'not all pleasure is the enjoyment supervening on achieved activity' (p. 184) and as such internal. There are also external pleasures such as those of the palate. This is a useful distinction, but of no direct relevance to the concept of happiness.

30. I incline to the view that happiness is to be distinguished from the sum of pleasures and that it is important to conceive of utilitarianism in terms of the former. Harsanyi (1984), for example, is correct to observe that 'it is by no means obvious that all we do we do only in order to attain pleasure and avoid pain. It is at least arguable that in many cases we are more interested in achieving some objective state of affairs than we are interested in our own subjective feelings of pleasure and pain that may result from achieving it'. (p. 54) Such a consideration is telling against a traditional interpretation of hedonistic utilitarianism in terms of pain and pleasure, but not against the view put forward here in terms of happiness. Certainly, it is arguable that we are often more interested in 'achieving some objective state of affairs than ... in our own subjective feelings of pleasure', but that is not to say that our interest in achieving the state of affairs may not constitute a source of happiness. (Besides which, as has been emphasized in the text, utilitarianism does not suggest that our interest or motive is always directed towards our happiness, let alone our pleasure.)

Relevant to this issue is the evidence that some individuals cannot experience physical pain, and the research of E.A. Kaplan ('Hypnosis and Pain', 1960), and Ernest Hilgard (*Divided Consciousness*, 1977), which suggests that, under hypnosis, an individual can experience pain in a specific part of the body (say, the left hand), write about the pain with the right hand, yet orally deny any experience of pain. Just what we should make of this and similar evidence that suggests that our conscious self not only organizes but to some extent filters and controls another level and wider range of experience is unclear. But to me it suggests, first, that the adage that it is 'all in the mind' gains considerably in plausibility, and second, that happiness, at least, is the consequence more of how one sees one's situation (perceives, interprets, etc.) than of the sensations of pain and pleasure that one experiences. To be noted in respect of this issue are Bernard Williams's remark 'I shall ... assume, along with most modern writers in philosophy ... that in talking of happiness ... one is talking about people's ... getting what they want or prefer, rather than about some sensation of pleasure or happiness' (*A Critique of Utilitarianism*, 1973, p. 80) and Quinton's observation that [The failure of Bentham's attempt to define happiness as a sum of pleasures] 'does not mean that happiness has to be conceived as some mysterious and unanalysable state, logically unrelated to pleasure. A man is happy to the extent that his more persistent and deep-seated desires are either satisfied or are known by him to be readily satisfiable. No aggregation of intense bodily delights can compensate for the frustration of long-term and serious desires for more than a short time. Nevertheless pleasure, in the inclusive sense of the word, remains the essential ingredient of happiness.' (A. Quinton, *Utilitarian Ethics*, 1973, p. 45)

31. J.S. Mill, *Utilitarianism*, pp. 288 ff.
32. As even Taylor (1982) concedes, 'No one seems very ready to challenge the view that, other things being equal, it is better that men's desires be fulfilled than that they be frustrated, that they be happy rather than miserable'. (p. 139) And Kant, for example, acknowledged that men have a 'universal inclination to happiness.' (*Foundations of the Metaphysics of Morals*, trans. Lewis White Beck, 1959, p. 15)
33. Cf. Mary Warnock, *Ethics Since 1900* (1960), 'Is it after all perhaps not so self-evident that empirical considerations about what does people good and what does them harm are irrelevant to deciding what is a moral principle and what is not?' (p. 139)
34. J. Bentham, *The Principles of Morals and Legislation* (1948), p. 1.
35. Aristotle, *Ethics* (1. vii). For Aristotle's view on happiness, see *Nicomachean Ethics*, 1, viii. 3–8. 'If there be some one thing which alone is a final end, this thing ... will be the good which we are seeking ... Now happiness above all else appears to be absolutely final in this sense, since we always choose it for its own sake and never as a means to something else ... The same conclusion also appears to follow from a consideration of the self-sufficiency of happiness – for it is felt that the final good must be a thing sufficient in itself. . . Moreover, we think happiness the most desirable of all good things without being itself reckoned as one among the rest ... Happiness, therefore, being found to be something final and self-sufficient, is the End at which all action aims.' (Trans. H. Rackam, Loeb Library, Heinemann, 1926) Many have worried whether Aristotle (and Bentham and Mill after him) was not guilty of denuding the thesis that happiness (or pleasure) is the only end of any force, by maintaining as a matter of definition that anything that motivates a person is a happiness consideration (or a pleasure). But to point out, for example, that an individual may do something for the sake of honour because, whether he recognizes it or not, he is moved by considerations of honour in the sense that he would not be happy to ignore the claims of honour, seems to me a significant thesis.

5   Is Utilitarianism Necessarily Conservative?

In the previous chapter, it was argued that happiness may take very many different forms; that is to say, the precise nature of the state of mind of a happy individual may vary from person to person along a continuum that we mark by terms such as 'ecstatic', 'pleased', and 'contented'.

There does not seem to be any logical warrant, or indeed a vestige of reason, to insist that happiness ought to be exclusively associated with a particular state of mind or type of sensation; and, if we were to make such an assumption, it would seem to follow that our judgements and pronouncements about happiness are even more arbitrary and speculative than we generally believe to be the case. For, what do you know about my state of mind in respect of the type of satisfaction I experience when I claim that I am happy? And how could I begin to establish whether the happiness that certain women experience on giving birth is indeed happiness, i.e., the specific state of mind allegedly necessary to happiness?

I may reasonably classify myself as 'happy', if the term is understood as referring to a state of mind, whatever its specific form, which involves satisfaction with a certain identifiable set of circumstances. Similarly, I may reasonably claim that there is some objectivity to my belief that my brother is happy in this sense, if it is based on reasoning to the effect that he is not anxious, not depressed and not lonely. (I may make these latter judgements by reference to observable facts and relatively uncontentious statements on his part as to whether the facts trouble him or not, again without reference to any specific account of the nature of the mood he is experiencing.) But I could not reasonably make judgements about my happiness, or any one else's, if I were presumed to be commenting on a shared or common type of sensation. To this day, philosophy and neurophysiological evidence notwithstanding, it remains something of a mystery as to precisely what our neighbour experiences when he falls in love. But there is no mystery (or need not be) about what he means by saying he has fallen in love.

It follows from this conception of happiness that, since what makes various people happy is to some large extent a contingent matter, it is entirely conceivable that different individuals or, by the same token, differently ordered societies, may find their happiness in different ways, precisely by virtue of their differences, and yet be equally happy. According to our overall argument, distinct but equally happy societies will also be equally good. Just as totally different kinds of landscape may be equally beautiful, or transparently distinct types of relationship equally full of love, so, in principle, quite different social arrangements may equally provide happiness. One is not, of course, necessarily maintaining that various different social arrangements would be equally acceptable to all people as a matter of contingent fact. On the contrary, building on the manifest fact of human variety, the point is that some people will find happiness in some situations, others in another. And this point, which is a logical consequence of the way in which happiness is defined combined with an undisputed contingent fact about human beings, is one that can be observed to be the case every day of the week: who is not aware of the fact that some of what makes his neighbour happy means nothing at all to him?

This feature of happiness, crudely that one man's meat is another man's poison, has sometimes been levelled against utilitarianism as an objection.[1] That is rather curious, for it is surely part of the strength of utilitarian theory that, in the first place, it recognizes a manifest truth (that different circumstances make different people happy), and that, in the second place, it allows of a degree of diversity in morally acceptable conduct (and can in principle explain that diversity), without descending to the incoherence of extreme relativism.

By 'extreme relativism' I mean any view that regards ethical judgements as merely a matter of taste and, therefore, given human diversity, relative to time and place. Few of us these days deny that, from a wide variety of different ethical perspectives, differing circumstances may make a difference to the appropriateness of particular substantive judgements. For instance, while people may argue about whether there is some universal principle of fair dealing, few will dispute that what constitutes fair dealing may vary between societies. But it is one thing to maintain that what constitutes moral conduct at the level of specific practices may vary between societies to the point where there is no directly discernible connection between them. It is quite another to maintain that there are no overarching moral principles that help to determine what different practices are morally acceptable in different circumstances. In the course of my overall argument, in explicating utilitarianism, I am implicitly seeking to refute the latter claim, by establishing that the theory is universally applicable. But at this point I need only convince readers of the wild implausibility of the specific and extreme claim that there is nothing objective about morality and that moral rules are based only on cultural preference – a view that, despite its to me self-evident absurdity, has its devotees, at least nominally.[2]

We need to be clear about what is, and what is not, being claimed by those who deny any objectivity to ethics. Those who argue for a cultural preference view may be quick to point out that this does not mean they are saying that moral codes are arbitrary: cultures may have, and generally are thought to have, reasons of various sorts that explain why they approve this practice rather than that. So much is common ground. The disagreement is not about whether there are reasons for adopting certain rules in particular societies, but about whether there can be objective moral reasons for adopting them. It is about whether there is any grounding to support an argument of the type, 'it is morally right for this society to approve X and Y, given their circumstances'.

Now it seems to me plain, and well brought out by the way in which the question is here raised, that to adopt such a cultural preference view is not to put forward an ethical theory at all, but to put forward a view that denies that there is such a thing as morality. It is a version of Thrasymachus' argument, referred to above,[3] that right is might, meaning that what passes for moral probity is no more than behaviour sanctioned by those in power, presumably in their own self-interest, rather than to Callicles' claim[4] that might is right, meaning that it is morally justifiable for the strong to control the weak. There is, I freely admit, no necessary reason why people should not deny morality. But it is important that it be recognized when that is what is being done. For Thrasymachus' view, unlike Callicles', immediately gives rise to the question of whether we can in good faith adopt such a position. And the answer is, surely, that we cannot.

Never mind the argument for the view, never mind the possibility that it be true, never mind the fact that people do profess it; one cannot consistently deny morality and exhibit moral sensibility. Yet we do continue to exhibit moral sensibility. Like it or leave it, we experience outrage at the sight of wanton cruelty, for instance, that is not merely deeper in intensity than our outrage at the erection of yet another ugly building, but that is different in kind. It is outrage that is bound up with a belief to the effect that this kind of behaviour is simply not to be

engaged in. This just ought not to be. We may happen to be extraordi-
narily indignant about some architectural monstrosity, but our objection
is of a different order from our objection to savage and aimless mutilation
of other people. It really doesn't matter for my present purposes what the
psychological or cultural explanation of such a phenomenon may be, nor
even that it may prove impossible to explain why people should feel this
way, let alone to justify the feeling. The fact is that we do feel this way.
So long as that is the case, we cannot sincerely maintain that we do not
believe in the very idea of morality. Any theory that requires that we see
keeping promises, for example, as no more and no less a convention than
driving on the left hand side of the road, if it is to be sincerely adopted,
requires that the individual sets aside his instinctive recognition that they
are different in kind. Perhaps some people can do that in respect of the
example of keeping promises – but can any reader sincerely do it in
respect of the very idea of moral obligation and duty? Assuming that you
cannot; assuming, that is to say, that you are familiar with the feeling of
a distinctively moral response to something, no matter what, you, like
me, may consider but cannot embrace the view that there is no such thing
as morality, and that what are taken to be moral rules are all necessarily
merely social conventions of one kind or another.[5]

It should be noted that the above line of argument does not necessarily
involve commitment to some notion of a supranatural basis for morality.
Talk of overriding principles and obligations that transcend cultures does
not depend on some religious backdrop, or some Platonic world of ideas.
One might believe, for example, as I am inclined to do, though I present
no argument for it, that morality is quite literally man-made. That is, one
might believe that the very idea of moral obligation is something that has
been thought out and imposed on his world by man, rather than something discovered or recognized by man. On this view, our moral understanding would correspond more to, say, our understanding of poetry
than to our scientific understanding. In the latter case we think that we are
coming to see how the natural world does in fact work; in the former case
we come to understand a form of activity that mankind invented and
developed. But this is of no material consequence to the present debate.
There may be no sense that can be given to the idea of a transcendental
justification for adopting a moral attitude. The fact remains that we have
a moral sense, and in trying to understand or make sense of it, it is absurd
to evolve an account that denies that we have it. One might reasonably
deny that there is any good reason to adopt a particular moral theory or
code; but one cannot reasonably say 'I see no reason to be moral', unless

it is the case that one has no moral sense at all. Such people may exist, but they do not seem to include moral philosophers, even, so far as I know, those who profess extreme relativism.

Many other arguments might be entertained concerning relativism, but enough has been said to make it clear that, on the one hand, the point that moral judgements are in many respects and to various degrees affected by local conditions is conceded but that, on the other hand, the notion that there is nothing supracultural about moral judgements is a denial that there is reason for the specifically moral sentiment, which can only be convincingly maintained by those who have truly rid themselves of it.

It is surely a plus, therefore, rather than an objection, that utilitarianism is an account of morality that accommodates the manifest fact of cultural variation and divergent moral rules, while staunchly maintaining that there is something, some linchpin, that holds the whole works together, and defines what we are talking about. For if 'morality', even as a man-made concept akin to 'unicorn', means something, it must have defining characteristics. It is the nature of these defining characteristics that an ethical theory seeks to elucidate, just as aesthetic theory seeks to define the nature of the aesthetic experience. But since few philosophers these days accept dogmatic, exclusive and specific moral theories, it is to the credit of utilitarianism that its account necessitates the conclusion that substantive overriding moral principles are few and far between. We do not need to go into the many objections to moral theories that maintain that there is a large number of specific principles of the type 'one should never lie', 'one should always be kind', 'one should always return what is entrusted to one', still less those that even more specifically enjoin us to refrain from adultery and coveting our neighbour's ass. It was in reaction to the incoherence, implausibility and inutility of such theories that relativistic arguments were first devised. But while the idea of a lengthy and detailed list of prescriptions for behaviour is hard to justify in objective and transcultural terms, so, equally, is it hard, if not impossible, to justify the other extreme, which proclaims that there is no such thing as a universally valid moral principle. As we have seen, and as so often, the truth lies in the mean.

I regard it as a distinctively attractive feature of utilitarianism that it involves acceptance of the idea of a degree of objectivity, as a truly moral theory must, while recognizing that a great variety of behaviour may be justified in varying circumstances, as a theory that is not to fly in the face of established argument and findings must. But I do not argue that we should accept the view that happiness may be found in many different ways because it renders the utilitarian theory attractive in this way. I do not argue for it at all. I merely observe that it is so: happiness may be achieved in a variety of ways, and those different ways may be equally acceptable, the resultant happiness equally good.

This is not to say that any way of achieving happiness is all right.[6] We need to recall that utilitarianism, being an ethical theory, is concerned with all human beings; it is not concerned simply with individual happiness; it is concerned with the happiness of all, happiness being a good. Therefore, what is being said is that any way of achieving complete happiness for all is morally acceptable – or, in more realistic terms, different ways of achieving an equal amount of happiness for all (or for as many as possible) are equally morally acceptable. Objection to various particular social arrangements thus becomes largely a matter of argument about what will and will not contribute to the desired end. To indoctrinate people in order to make them happy, for example, assuming it to be logically possible, is objectionable, in so far as it is, not because it is written in the heaven that thou shalt not indoctrinate, nor because it is necessarily morally repugnant to indoctrinate, but because, or so it may be argued, it won't work. In other words, if there were a process of indoctrination that would ensure the happiness of all for all time, the utilitarian would embrace it. But it is implausible in the extreme to suggest that there is one. Actual attempts to engineer happiness in this way in totalitarian states have incontestably led to massive misery. Theoretical arguments and imaginative utopias have to resort to such a degree of fanciful conditions as to render them wish-fulfilling to the point of embarrassment. In the absence of any remotely convincing argument to show that we could ensure the complete happiness of all by indoctrination, the utilitarian is as entitled to deplore the practice of indoctrination as anyone else. But his moral repugnance is based on the inutility of the practice. (It is incidentally important to note that we are not referring here to the injection of soma, or other such *Brave New World* fantasies. Happiness, as has been said, presupposes the conscious mind: a mind that can judge things to be as required. In theory, this might be achieved by feeding into the mind one set of beliefs rather than another, but by definition it could not be achieved by drugging the individual into a non-reflective state. As a matter of logic, the individual has to have various beliefs and to be capable of conceiving of things being otherwise, in order to experience happiness.)

There is, however, a most interesting objection to utilitarianism, raised some years ago by MacIntyre, that needs to be considered in this context. MacIntyre argued that 'utilitarianism is necessarily interpreted in the light of ... dominant beliefs and attitudes'.[7] He went on to suggest, in essence, that not only is that equivalent to saying that it is necessarily conservative, but also that it follows that an evil society might be justified by utilitarianism. For in an evil society, which is, by definition, characterized by people choosing to behave in various objectionable ways, the attempt to apply utilitarianism will involve seeking to satisfy those various objectionable wants, needs and desires. He specifically suggests that various objectionable features of our society can, for example, be justified on utilitarian grounds (because we *are* a competitive, materialistic, class-conscious, etc., type of people). But, while this line of reasoning is well worth examining, it is curious too and, I believe, plainly and importantly incorrect, as may be inferred straightaway from the fact that no utilitarian philosopher would necessarily regard our society as morally well ordered, and I am not aware of any who in fact think that it is.

I shall ignore the point that MacIntyre's argument somewhat begs the question by taking it for granted that certain features of our society, such as its materialism and class structure, are self-evidently objectionable, because I share his sentiment. But it should be stressed that, on the face of it, sentiment is what we are dealing with. There is no argument provided by MacIntyre to show that this moral objection to aspects of our society is justified. But, as was argued in Chapter 3, the question of whether utilitarianism is true cannot be determined simply by reference to our current moral sentiments, which have very possibly been formed in the light of other incorrect or incoherent theories. Our sentiments could be misconceived: it might be that we ought to be competitive and materialistic, and that utilitarianism establishes that this is so. However, I have argued that, while current sentiment cannot dictate moral theory, we should nonetheless take some account of it, so, in consistency, I will do so, and accept MacIntyre's view that utilitarianism, if it is to be plausible, ought not to justify certain current social arrangements. (And, incidentally, he may well be correct in opining that some people do try to justify contemporary social organization on utilitarian grounds, whether they should or not, despite my observation that no philosopher with a proper understanding of the theory would do so.)

What then is the truth regarding this matter? Does utilitarianism necessarily justify the *status quo,* and logically prevent one from making radical criticism of contemporary practice? It plainly follows from the characterization of happiness given that, at any given moment, what will make members of a society happy is at least partly dependent on their current beliefs, wants, needs and so forth – in general terms, their aspirations. (Indeed, I might observe that MacIntyre's line of argument implicitly entails some support for an analysis of happiness along my lines.) It is, in other words, true that, at least to some extent, what will make people happy is 'necessarily' related to 'dominant beliefs and attitudes'.

But MacIntyre then mistakenly equates 'interpreting utilitarianism' with 'establishing what makes people happy'. Utilitarianism is not simply the doctrine that each individual should do whatever makes him happy nor, as we have seen, is it adequately summarized as the view that we should provide the greatest happiness for the greatest number, or such-like. Interpreting the theory is not simply a matter of giving people *panem et circenses* or the contemporary cultural equivalent. The importance of Chapter 2 should now be apparent, for there it was pointed out that utilitarianism is only adequately characterized as the view that our ideal is a society in which all can be fully and equally happy. When we add that people are capable of finding happiness in different circumstances, this characterization of utilitarianism does allow the possibility of there being distinct but equally good sets of social arrangements. But it plainly does not lead to the moral endorsement of any society that could be improved on in terms of its aspiration to the ideal, and it plainly requires us to object to practices that, while they provide some happiness, do so at considerable cost, also in terms of happiness. We have yet to give direct consideration to the question of what factors are relevant to estimating the sum of happiness that various practices may lead to, but we can nonetheless make the general point here: as an ethical theory, utilitarianism is not concerned simply to ensure that what we do leads to an appreciable gain in happiness; it maintains that we ought to do those things that, taken together, will ensure the complete happiness of all. It is true that it is immaterial to the utilitarian whether the happiness of a society derives from pushpin or poetry, provided that the quantity of happiness provided by either is equal. But neither pursuit would be acceptable, notwithstanding the happiness they provided, if in some way they militated against the ideal of complete happiness for all. And if, for example, it happened to be the case that pleasure in pushpin would be short-lived, it could be rejected as a morally desirable pursuit on those grounds alone. Still more could one say that a community that evolves a mode of happy existence involving competition, material greed and selfishness, notwithstanding the fact that people come to accept it, is bound to cause a great deal of unhappiness, and on those very grounds can be condemned as self-defeating. One can learn to live with competition, even classify oneself as competitive. But given the nature of the competitive spirit, it is a necessary truth that some disappointment will accompany a competitive system.

The above paragraph makes two points: the logical one that a society that squares practice and belief will not necessarily be justified by utilitarianism – for it has to be squared in a way that is not self-defeating, that takes account of the long term, etc.; and the contingent one that our society could not really satisfy a utilitarian, since it incorporates a number of features that make it necessary that we should fall short of the ideal, not to mention those that as a matter of contingent fact fairly obviously do so. Let us concentrate on the general rather than the particular.

A society might exist in which torturing every third child at the age of twelve gave happiness to the community generally. People, we will presume, have been brought up to think this practice acceptable, and to take pleasure in it, as some have taken pleasure in cock fights or snuff movies.[8] Alternatively, it might be tied up with certain religious beliefs. In asking whether this behaviour is justified, a utilitarian will look to the question of what people enjoy and, *a fortiori,* take some account of how they are as a matter of fact currently constituted. This will to some extent at least be a product of the *status quo.* We must concede that a utilitarian will not have the option of saying *a priori* 'this simply won't do; you ought not to take pleasure in this practice. It is morally objectionable'. Nor can he maintain that, though a source of happiness, this practice is a source of inferior happiness to some alternative practice, if the phrase 'inferior happiness' is taken to mean 'intrinsically less worthy'. (The question of in what sense, if any, there can be different qualities of pleasure or happiness will be discussed in Chapter 8. Here it is sufficient to say that I forego any advantage to my case that might be derived from arguing that there are different qualities of pleasure.)

But while this society's predilections are in themselves a factor to be taken account of, and while they cannot be dismissed as necessarily objectionable, the utilitarian is not governed by them. For it is plain, even without reference to Bentham's felicific calculus,[9] that anyone whose moral view is predicated on an ideal state of affair respecting happiness, must consider the advantages and disadvantages, in terms of the ideal, of pursuing happiness in one way rather than another. In this case, the utilitarian has to consider the wisdom and efficacy, in terms of happiness, of an arrangement whereby a great deal of happiness is derived from torturing every third child rather than, say, from playing bingo. The calculation or estimate will not be in terms of alleged intrinsic quality, as we have said, but in terms of viability.

Whatever we presume about this society, if we take some account of reasonable generalizations about human beings, it seems likely that this practice will involve some pain for the parents. I do not dispute that a society might conceivably give rise to parents who are relatively unconcerned about, and certainly accepting of, the practice of torturing every third child, perhaps as a result of imbibing some tale about it being necessary for the greater glory of God, or to ward off divine wrath; but even in such a society one may imagine that there would be some little twinges of sorrow and dissatisfaction to reckon with. More certainly and obviously, the victims are not going to enjoy being tortured as much as they might have enjoyed alternative pastimes, and it is undeniably the case that this practice cuts short the sum of their happiness. All of this the utilitarian will consider. And he will remember that what he is looking for is a set of ways of behaving that allows all equally to be assured of full and continued happiness. He does not need to be a mathematician, let alone a rigorous and mindless interpreter of Bentham, to recognize that this isn't a very smart way to proceed. While it is conceivable that a society should gain some happiness from this arrangement, and it is possible that its discontinuation would in the short term diminish the sum of happiness, it seems clear that it could be improved on in terms of happiness. As such it is not satisfactory to the utilitarian. One may add that contingently the case against such a practice would in all probability be a great deal stronger: in fact, people are likely, at best, sadly to believe that it is required, rather than to derive great happiness from it. But for present purposes it is sufficient to observe that, even if that were not so, the practice would not recommend itself to the utilitarian.

Those who are sceptical about utilitarianism will no doubt be concerned about the tenor of the previous paragraph. They will feel that, while it shows that the utilitarian would not be forced into countenancing such torture by the mere fact that it is psychologically acceptable to a society, and that in reality it is somewhat absurd to suggest that he would countenance it at all, it also reveals how amoral, or out of touch with morality as we understand it, utilitarianism is. They will wish that I would recognize that moral people simply throw up their hands in horror at the very idea of torture, and that I would do likewise. But we need to distinguish between what our ingrained moral sentiments happen to be, what they should be, and the manner in which they are in fact to be justified. It is worth pointing out that some societies have come close to adopting a practice such as I have envisaged, and thought it morally acceptable, which serves to remind us that what is self-evident to us today has not in all instances been self-evident to others. I repeat that we cannot reasonably conduct an inquiry into ethics with a closed mind on the rightness and wrongness of certain acts. But, having said that, it should be stressed that my actual moral sentiment on this issue is, in all likelihood, no different from that of non-utilitarians. I too have moral revulsion to the idea of torturing every third child. The parting of the ways comes only when we try to justify or explain the logical, as opposed to the psychological, grounds for this revulsion. The utilitarian suggests that the only plausible way to explain the wrongness of this behaviour is ultimately in terms of human happiness. He therefore goes on to maintain that while many of us share this revulsion for a wide variety of different reasons, the grounds for justifying it, as opposed to explaining it, can only be found in considerations of happiness. The moral revulsion, which we might feel as a straightforward consequence of being brought up to regard torture as repugnant, is justified by the recognition that it is, on the face of it, a blatant contribution to human suffering. But this view, and the detached tone that it is necessary to adopt in discussing the matter, in no way implies that the utilitarian feels any less morally indignant about it than anyone else.

The immediate point is that the utilitarian would not condone such a practice.

In other words the point is established that, *contra* MacIntyre, a utilitarian is quite at liberty to make radical criticism (on moral grounds) of his society; for he can criticize the way in which people are pursuing happiness, without necessarily denying that they do gain some happiness and that the society is to that extent good. The further charge that that is not enough, and that we ought to condemn certain practices regardless of considerations of happiness (which was not MacIntyre's explicit claim, although his argument gains some momentum from the implication), is to be resisted by pointing out that it begs the question. Its seeming plausibility derives from our current sentiments, but these cannot be treated as sacrosanct, and they might, in any case, be explained on utilitarian terms.[10] Only if a society were completely happy and inescapably set to remain so, would a utilitarian have no case against it; and even then he could reasonably pose alternatives, though he would have no moral motive for so doing.

Turning now to substantive and more realistic examples, we may acknowledge that many people would derive a certain amount of pleasure from, for example, taunting Pakistanis, queer bashing, kangaroo hunting, getting rich at the expense of others or mugging old ladies. But it in no way necessarily follows that, on the utilitarian account, they are thereby justified or that, as members of a society that enjoys such pursuits, we cannot as utilitarians raise moral objection. In so far as such activities involve pain and suffering, as they manifestly do to some extent, they are to be deplored. If we are concerned with our duty, what we ideally and therefore in fact, if we can, ought to do, then we should refrain from such activities. They are, on utilitarian terms, wrong for, while they bring some happiness to some, they are calculated to bring some unhappiness to others, and hence are antithetical to the ideal of a world so organized that all are enabled to be equally and fully happy.

If it were the case, *mirabile dictu,* that no alternative set of activities could conceivably result in anything nearer the ideal in the real world, or produce the same overall amount of happiness, then the utilitarian would have to accept this set of activities as preferable to alternatives. But we have now moved from consideration of what we ought to do, from consideration of our duty, to consideration of what may be justified, which is to say consideration of making choices circumscribed by reality. Furthermore, we are doing so in the context of a most implausible hypothesis. It is true that a utilitarian, like most other people, does in daily life have to make difficult and imperfect decisions as to what is justified in the situation in which he finds himself, as opposed to what is unambiguously right conduct. But it is only in the context of theoretical arguments like this that the poor fellow has to take seriously the idea that the odd bit of mugging, though emphatically not morally right, might be justified. And it is vital here to emphasize the nature of the hypothetical situation, rather than simply to exclaim: 'There you are – utilitarians accept that in theory Pakistani bashing might be moral.' Only if we lived in a world in which any other form of activity that might be engaged in by potential Pakistani bashers was, on balance, productive of even more unhappiness, would a utilitarian condone it. And even then, it would be a matter of condoning or accepting it, rather than a matter of believing it morally right behaviour. The utilitarian would reluctantly see it as the lesser of various evils, and in such an absurd hypothetical situation what other theory has any more convincing suggestion to make? If human happiness were to all practical intents and purposes dependent on a particular activity, notwithstanding that it also produced some suffering, it is not self-evident that it should nonetheless be avoided.[11]

Such hypothetical circumstances need detain us no longer. They have been introduced to remind us that the only circumstance in which a utilitarian would accept pain-provoking behaviour as justified is when all alternatives are worse. Even then, justification should not be confused with moral duty. In point of fact, there is no difficulty at all in thinking of literally thousands of activities that would satisfy such persons, even in the world as it is, and cause less harm to others. That is what football matches, soap operas, consumer goods, rock music and pubs are for, one might say. Furthermore, the criticism in question presupposes that people are irredeemably what they are. We know that that is not the case: people are extremely malleable in all sorts of ways and, in particular, can be re-educated or socialized.[12] Not only is it not the case that people necessarily find, say, drinking heavily or stealing more pleasurable than walking or going to the cinema, but even those people who do find the former more enjoyable can be brought to take equal pleasure in the latter. A utilitarian never loses sight of the fact that the ideal is complete happiness for all. In that sense he keeps his eye on the Idea of the Good and judges human activity in the light of it. In the light of the ideal, a community in which some persons gain happiness at the expense of the suffering of others, and in which the fear of potential victims, and the tension and repulsion in the air generally, have to be added to the victims' suffering, is obviously unacceptable. The utilitarian will say that this is not a way in which people ought to behave; they should be brought to find their happiness in other pursuits.[13]

In short it is simply not the case that one cannot make radical criticism of the *status quo* from a utilitarian perspective; rather, one is obliged to do so on occasion. It may be the case that it is psychologically difficult for us to conceive of alternative ways of living that would yield equal satisfaction to us, at less expense in terms of the unhappiness of others. But here again there is no necessary or otherwise unyielding truth to yield to. It is possible for human beings to display sufficient imagination to conceive of alternatives. For example, I do not naturally think of a caste system or of apartheid as likely to promote happiness, and no doubt many Indians and South Africans do not naturally think of the class society of Britain as potentially congenial. But any of us are capable of considering such alternatives, recognizing possibilities, trying alternatives out and adapting to them. Indeed, philosophers in particular would seem to make something of a living out of imagining other worlds.

At the risk of repetition inspiring boredom in the reader, I will conclude by emphasizing the key and irritatingly wrong-headed characteristic of much criticism of utilitarianism. This is the mistake of assuming that all that utilitarians care about is happiness and that, therefore, provided a state of affairs makes most people happy, it is morally acceptable. Such a view is simply mistaken.

In the first place, happiness is not the only thing that utilitarians care about. They care about a just distribution of happiness, and about every individual being fully happy. They care about the ideal. Their premiss that happiness is the only thing that is morally good in itself is not to be confused with the doctrine that whatever makes someone happy is morally right, or even justified. The latter is not the utilitarian view. Not only is the theory concerned with the just provision of happiness but, in addition, contingently, utilitarians come to care about a host of other things and, within the system, one may say with good reason: thus I care about kindness because I have reason to think it a desirable quality in terms of promoting the ideal. The fact that being kind is not accorded the status of an independent absolute moral principle – a status that no ethical theory has successfully substantiated, though some have tried – in no way implies that kindness is of less concern, less inclined to evoke moral sentiment, or less of a moral duty for the utilitarian than for others.

In the second place, it does not follow from the premiss that happiness is the only thing that is good in itself that the utilitarian would, for example, regard the Roman habit of watching people being torn to death in the amphitheatre as morally acceptable, since they seem to have thoroughly enjoyed it. Rather, it follows that the utilitarian will only regard as morally right what he believes to be reasonable ways to achieve the ideal of a happy community all told. The view that the practice of gladiatorial contests is one such way being less than convincing, we may deduce that no Roman utilitarian would have borne such a spectacle with equanimity. Nor is the utilitarian downcast by the observation that, as things are, the pursuit of happiness by individuals would often seem to involve the diminution of the happiness of others. His optimism is largely born of his recognition that the ideal can be more nearly approached both by changing features of our world and by changing ourselves. Far from being necessarily conservative, it is a theory that allows of and actually demands a great deal of radical criticism of the way things are.

Notes

1. Consider again, for example, MacIntyre's (1981) resounding statement: 'To have understood the polymorphous character of pleasure and happiness is of course to have rendered those concepts useless for utilitarian purposes.' This is the reverse of the truth.

2. Of course a major difficulty in ethics, as in many other branches of inquiry but not all, is that propositions that have nominal assent do not in fact do so, because different people mean different things by them. An hour's serious discussion with a group of reasonable graduate students should generally suffice to illustrate that nominal agreement on issues such as the objectivity, subjectivity, relativity, arbitrariness, conventionality and truth of moral judgements represents very little in the way of substantive agreement.

3. See Plato, *Republic*, Book 1. See above, Chapter 2.

4. See Plato, *Gorgias*.

5. Note, in other words, that I do not necessarily deny that the origin of our distinctively moral feelings might lie in deliberate or accidental social engineering or influence. But, even if it is our social context that has developed a distinctive type of feeling, so long as we have it, we cannot consistently pretend that it means nothing to us. We cannot argue away what we actually do experience. Compare the idea of denying that there is such a thing as a distinctively aesthetic response, on the grounds that our experience of it is the product of our cultural setting.

6. Hampshire (1982) remarks: 'The one unnatural, and impossible, cry is the consequentialist's: "Away with convention: anything goes provided that it does not interfere with welfare or with principles of justice".' (p. 156) I hope that it is clear from the text that I accept Hampshire's distinction between convergent moral claims that refer to universal human needs and reasonable calculations that should be the same everywhere, and those moral claims that may be equally binding but are culturally specific; indeed, I am offering an explanation of just such a distinction. Hampshire writes: 'At all times and in all places there has to be a sexual morality which is recognised; but it does not have to be the same sexual morality with the same restraints and prescription. The rational requirement is the negative one: that the rules and conventions should not cause evident and avoidable unhappiness or offend accepted principles of fairness.' (p. 154) Precisely so. Utilitarianism, as here portrayed, proclaims that there are some rules that are necessary for the happiness of any community, and they are the moral rules that constitute right conduct. It is equally necessary to have other moral prescriptions, but their form may reasonably vary from culture to culture.

   Cf. here Scanlon's view (1982): 'If it is important for us to have *some* duty of a given kind (some duty of fidelity to agreements, or some duty of mutual aid) of which there are many morally acceptable forms, then one of these forms needs to be established by convention. In a setting in which one of these forms *is* conventionally established, acts disallowed by it will be wrong in the sense of the definition given. For, given the need for such conventions, one thing that could not be generally agreed to would be a set of principles allowing one to disregard conventionally established (and morally acceptable) definitions of important duties. This dependence on convention introduces a degree of cultural relativity into contractualist morality.' (p. 112) And likewise into the species of utilitarianism here advanced.

7. A. MacIntyre, 'Against Utilitarianism' in *Aims in Education: the philosophical approach*, ed. T.H.B. Hollins (1964), p. 4.

8. For of course we accept MacIntyre's (op. cit.) point that 'we *learn* to want things'. (p. 8) Though attention should be paid to the question of the limits, logical and physical, that there may be on what we could 'learn to want'.

9. See J. Bentham, *The Principles of Morals and Legislation* (1948), Chapter 4.
10. See below, especially Chapter 9.
11. For further discussion of the suggestion that the utilitarian has some awkward problems to deal with concerning innocent victims, scapegoats, etc., see below, Chapter 9. Worth noting here is Hare's (1982) comment: 'Fantastic hypothetical cases can no doubt be invented in which they would have to favour [extreme inequalities of distribution]; but ... this is an illegitimate form of argument.' (p. 27) My reasons for so concluding are not identical to those given by Hare, but we are in agreement that the fact that situations can be conceived in which the utilitarian theory does not provide a clear and intuitively acceptable prescription cannot count as an objection to it without the addition of considerable further argument. Note also Frey's (1984) comment: 'Critics, of course try to assist this process by artificially devising cases, often of a bizarre or fantastic nature, in which these generalisations are wholly inappropriate,' in reference to the propensity for argument exploring the contingent possibilities surrounding acts of killing. (p. 7)
12. J. Elster (1982), in common with a number of other contemporary philosophers, is concerned about the problem of distinguishing various levels of want (desire, preference). He has an interesting discussion of 'adaptive preferences' (for example, the fox adopts the view that the grapes are sour because he knows that he is not going to get them). He usefully categorizes various ways in which preferences may be manipulated, acquired, modified, etc. On certain traditional views of utilitarianism such inquiry could be of considerable importance. But the undoubted fact that preferences can be arrived at in various ways is of no direct concern to the species of utilitarianism being adumbrated here. Our focus is on what, if anything, all persons would seem to have a need for as a feature of a society that will allow all equally to be happy. Utilitarians are not in the business of trying to determine what wants people do have, still less how they came by them. They are in the business of trying to establish what are sufficient sets of requirements of happiness (of the satisfaction of wants, preferences, etc., perhaps), having made the claim that a situation in which all are fully and equally happy cannot be morally improved on.
13. John Gray, *Mill on Liberty: a Defence* (1983), while pursuing a somewhat different thesis in a somewhat different way, nonetheless seems to interpret Mill in a way not dissimilar to the view of utilitarianism (which I think is close to Mill in spirit) that I am expounding. Gray suggests that 'Mill's indirect utilitarianism consists in the thesis that ... the direct appeal to utility to settle practical questions is typically self-defeating. This self-defeatingness of direct utilitarianism is supported partly by reference to the distinctive characteristics of human happiness, and partly by claims about the necessary conditions of stable social co-operation'. (pp. 46, 47) He goes on, in an important passage that is too long to quote in full, to mention and respond to a consideration that echo's MacIntyre's: 'the boundaries of the self-regarding domain will be determined by the currently dominant conceptions of interests ... Such relativism can be avoided, however, without making interests wholly invariant socially and historically. Men's interests might be, and indeed must be shaped by the standards and circumstances of their time and culture, but to say this is not to say that men's interests wholly depend upon or are entirely constituted by recognition by society'. (pp. 50, 51)

6. Rule- or Act-Utilitarianism?

Perhaps the single most important question to be considered in this discussion is whether rule- or act-utilitarianism constitutes a more plausible thesis. Its importance lies partly in the fact that the account I have so far given already implies commitment to rule-utilitarianism, as I shall explain, so that a failure to convince on this issue must lead to rejection of the overall thesis. In addition, as I shall argue, act-utilitarianism is indeed open to some of the standard objections raised against utilitarianism, so that, if we see no good reason to adopt rule-utilitarianism, we do not have adequate grounds for embracing utilitarianism at all. This, then, is something of a make or break issue, and one is a little daunted at the outset by the recognition that some of the more prominent utilitarians of our own time, such as J.J.C. Smart, have argued robustly for act-utilitarianism.[1]

The view that I am putting forward is predicated on the claim that happiness is the only thing that is morally good in itself. From that premiss we have enunciated a theory to the effect that one ought to act in ways that would promote the happiness of all equally and fully since, if happiness is the only thing that is good in itself, an ideal world must be one in which all people are completely happy. (The 'equally' derives from the universality of what we understand as ethical principles.) But this must imply some form of rule-utilitarianism. For if our concern is ultimately to achieve an ideal state of affairs, we have to evolve a harmonious set of rules that contributes to the ideal, rather than concentrate on the maximization of happiness on particular occasions. The ideal is not simply that I shall be very happy on Tuesday, or that what I do on Wednesday shall produce more happiness all-told than what I might have done. The ideal is a world in which matters are so ordered that everybody is perfectly happy. What we ought to do is what is conducive to that ideal. That ideal could not possibly be served without formulation of and adherence to a number of rules of conduct. An ideal state of affairs can only be consciously and consistently striven for, when there is a degree of predictability and foreknowledge. Given that people differ in their wants, needs and interests, and given that in practice individuals cannot have complete understanding of the consequences of various particular acts, it is barely credible that a community of independent agents should be able to do what is right (i.e. what does contribute to the ideal) in the absence of certain regulative rules. In just the same way a society would be extremely unlikely to realize its ideal of road safety in the absence of rules, and could not conceivably do so except on the assumption that individuals have the inclination and the capacity to anticipate the behaviour of each other. What the rules should be may to some extent be arbitrary. For instance, we may drive on the right hand side of the road or the left. But, nonetheless, we need a rule if we are serious about the ideal.

Conversely, if we were to accept act-utilitarianism, a standard objection such as that the utilitarian might condone a seemingly vicious act is plainly correct. If, that is to say, the issue is simply whether this act that I am about to perform will generate more happiness than any alternatives open to me, it is clear that circumstances could be such that it is better for me to steal, lie, cheat on my wife, or even kill an innocent person, than to do anything else. As I shall argue below, utilitarianism, properly understood, does not justify or even tolerate the elimination of an innocent scapegoat, as has sometimes been supposed. But it is the case, and it is something that partly explains why utilitarianism has been rejected, that straightforward act-utilitarianism may justify such an act. For, if it is truly the case that I ought to do that which, of available options, would produce the most happiness, one would have to be startlingly unimaginative not to be able to conceive of situations where one might have to sacrifice an innocent victim. One can fend off such a conclusion for a while, by stressing such points as that long-term effects have to be taken into account, and that effects may be indirect and should be taken to include such things as the coarsening effect of an action on the nature of the agent; but, in the end, it is undeniably true that human beings may be placed in situations where, say, a murder would lead to greater happiness than any alternative.[2]

The above paragraph does not in itself settle the issue of whether we should adopt rule- or act-utilitarianism. One might, for example, stand by act-utilitarianism and argue that it is only our sentiment, itself the product of culture and upbringing which might have been different, that causes us to feel that stealing or murder are necessarily wrong. The whole point of utilitarianism, it might be said, is to explain that, for example, sometimes murder is not wrong. Second, it might be said (and correctly as far as it goes) that life sometimes places us in dilemmas, i.e., in situations where there is no clearly right way to proceed. Thus nobody, not even the act-utilitarian, need maintain that killing an innocent person is sometimes morally right – merely that on occasion it is the lesser of two evils. Third, the act-utilitarian might try to avoid the unpalatable conclusion that his thesis allows that it may be justifiable to kill an innocent person by denying what I have referred to as undeniable: contingently, taking a subtle and long-term look, it is inconceivable, he might assert, that more happiness would ever ultimately be generated by such an act than could be generated by some alternative act.

But, while the above arguments have to be taken seriously, and while act-utilitarianism is therefore not altogether discredited, the view that an act is morally right if, of those available, it will produce the most happiness, clearly does lead to the logical possibility of acts that we in fact feel to be morally wrong not being so. That, I repeat, is not decisive in terms of rejecting the view. But it does mean that such a version of utilitarianism is open to what many have regarded as a very strong objection.

A similar argument could be gone through in respect of trivial versus worthwhile pursuits. The act-utilitarian may find ways of defending himself from the charge that he would see nothing wrong with a world that was ineffably trivial. He could, for instance, deny that what is conventionally regarded as trivial is in fact so, arguing that part of his point is that the prejudice that sees poetry as intrinsically superior to pushpin is without foundation. Or he could try to maintain that human beings are so constituted that in fact they would sooner or later get bored with trivia. But he could not deny, with any plausibility, that it is conceivable that a community's happiness might be entirely based on pursuits that would generally be classified as trivial. In this case, however, there is a further point to be made. Whatever the objection to triviality, and it is of course a pejorative term, it is far from clear that it is morally objectionable. Philosophers seem sometimes to move rather too rapidly, and altogether unconsciously, from moral theory to moralizing. On the face of it, while serious-minded chaps like philosophers are bound to deplore a world of popular culture, and may even find some good reasons for doing so, they have no business treating trivial interests as though they were inherently immoral. And, indeed, there is a case for saying that trivial pursuits have at least the merit of being innocent, as a matter of definition. Playing bingo cannot both be trivial and inherently morally bad, because if it is the latter it can hardly be dismissed as trivial. Moral objection to it would have to be related to extrinsic factors. But while, therefore, the view that utilitarianism might promote trivial activity is not self-evidently a strike against it as an ethical theory, it is true that the act-utilitarian might have to defend himself against it.

Let us now look in more detail at what is involved in the two alternative types of utilitarianism.[3] Act-utilitarianism maintains that every individual act should be judged in terms of its consequences in respect of happiness. What one ought to do always depends on who one is, where one is, who is affected and so forth. If it is generally true that one should not lie or steal, that is contingently so. It is because as a matter of fact telling a lie or stealing will generally cause more unhappiness than any alternative action; but it is always conceivable that the facts might have been otherwise. (Theoretically there might be a type of action that invariably involved an intolerable and avoidable quantity of unhappiness. In such a case the act-utilitarian would consistently condemn it, but he would still be considering each occasion on its own merits. In point of fact, of course, it is difficult to discern a type of action that is always, in any circumstances, productive of insupportable levels of unhappiness.)

Act-utilitarianism is far from self-evidently preposterous. The fact that human nature, for all its diversity, seems to have a number of more or less constant features, particularly within the context of a particular culture or society, means that calculating the likely consequences of an act is by no means always a hopeless task. There is a *prima facie* plausibility about the suggestion that, if happiness is what really matters, then the sum of happiness on every particular occasion ought to be our concern. And, while in the abstract it may seem that the theory will inevitably be giving approval to some individual acts of theft, deceit and murder, because one can imagine situations in which such acts would be productive of more happiness than any alternative, in fact it is unlikely to do so. Given that nobody enjoys being murdered, for instance, given that a murderer will have to pay for his crime or live in fear of doing so (for the law is not likely to change simply because the agent subscribes to this ethical theory), given that the victim's family and friends will suffer, and given that the entire populace will suffer increased anxiety when a murder is committed, it is difficult to conclude that the act-utilitarian would very often be likely to regard murder as morally right.[4]

Similarly, any competent act-utilitarian could establish that 99 per cent of the time one ought not to mug, and add that, if there were a situation in which one might legitimately do so, the situation would, by definition, be so dire as to make it far from self-evident that one should not. Nonetheless, act-utilitarianism is the thesis that the rightness or wrongness of an act depends solely on the consequences of that particular action. (I should say in passing that I do not classify Mill as an act-utilitarian. His unclear phrasing concerning the tendency of acts seems to me to imply that his concern was with classes of acts: thus he wants to know not what this murder will achieve, but what murders of this type will achieve. To classify a number of individual acts as being of a type, and to take a position in relation to that type is to operate in terms of a rule. One ceases to ask what the consequences of each particular act may be, and instead acts in the light of a preconceived judgement relating to acts of this type.)[5]

Rule-utilitarianism is the view that one should be governed by rules relating to the promotion of happiness, and that every individual rule should be judged in terms of its consequences, in respect of happiness.

Thus the essential difference between the two positions lies in their answer to the question of whether there should be any rules. The rule-utilitarian is not necessarily committed either to the view that everything should be subject to rules or to the view that, where there is no rule, anything goes. The position is rather this: utilitarianism entails the possibility that there should be some rules. For, if the ideal is a world of complete happiness, it is evident that some rules of conduct may be necessary to achieving that end. The question is whether, in terms of happiness, it is better to leave people to make decisions or lay down some ground rules. But where there is no case for a rule, the rule-utilitarian is, naturally, what is termed an act-utilitarian: for, always, the consideration is what is conducive to happiness. If happiness is a moral good, it is always morally desirable to promote it rather than diminish it. The question is purely and simply whether there is a utilitarian case for formulating some rules.[6]

I should have thought that the answer was very obviously that there is. First, there is the issue of the reliability of individual judgement. If we do not have any rules, we leave every decision as to what ought to be done to the individual. Very often, individuals will make mistaken decisions, because they are weak-willed, perhaps, because they are selfish or angry, or because they are simply not equipped to make sound predictions about the consequences of their actions. The result will be a great deal of unhappiness. The point is purely contingent, but none the less significant for that. Second, there is the issue of cohesion. A great deal of our happiness is largely dependent on our acting in ways that are consistent and predictable. There may be many types of personal relations that would afford happiness, for example, but it is important that two people in a relationship should want and expect one of the same kind. Similarly, some cultures may derive happiness from private property, others might not have such a concept; but within a culture the happiness of all is to some extent tied up with a uniform attitude to property. Thus, we need rules to order and regulate the community in such a way as to ensure this cohesion of interest and attitude. Third, there is the issue of confidence or certainty. Although particular individuals can happily live with varying degrees of security and predictability, happiness, as we have seen, is logically incompatible with certain states of mind such as anxiety, frustration, lack of confidence, and insecurity. There is evidence that, in general, people cannot cope with too much freedom.[7] Concepts such as anxiety only have application in contexts where there is uncertainty. Thus, again contingently, an absence of rules sets the stage for, and is likely to lead to, increased anxiety and frustration, and hence unhappiness, by dint of removing security.

In other words, if a large and psychologically varied number of persons is to have a chance of happiness, it is likely that we would be better off having certain rules. It does not matter if we leave people to make up their own minds about, say, whether they should make contributions to charity; but the chances are that, if individuals are left to decide for themselves whether the world will be happier rid of their particular enemies, there will be many mistaken calculations of major consequence. Though people can come to cope with varying degrees of uncertainty, most of us gain some considerable degree of happiness from feeling that it is safe to walk down the street, sharing similar values, being able to predict each other's behaviour, having an identity of outlook, and so on. Thus the argument for rule-utilitarianism is straightforwardly utilitarian and strong. It concludes that the world will be happier for having certain rules, what rules those should be being determined by reference to human nature and the context of particular societies. One will certainly have to face further argument concerning what the rules should be, but hardly on the point that some rules are required.

It seems to me so plain and so crucial to recognize that rule-utilitarianism is the logical refinement of utilitarianism, that we must pause to consider certain well known arguments against it. A curious, but standard objection maintains that there is in fact no difference between the two forms of the theory, because rule-utilitarianism inevitably collapses into act-utilitarianism. The claim here is that, since a rule-utilitarian would dispense with a rule that was not generally productive in terms of happiness, he should in consistency calculate on any given occasion whether it is productive to abide by it.[8] But this reasoning is fallacious. The argument was not that abiding by the rule will invariably prove beneficial on each particular occasion. It was that it is beneficial to adopt the rule (and of course abide by it, since that is what rules are for), even though on occasion adherence to the rule will not promote happiness. It is true that one determines to adopt a rule such as 'thou shalt not kill' on the grounds that, while an act of killing might indeed be beneficial on a particular occasion, on balance having the rule is more beneficial. But it does not follow, and is in fact self-defeating to assume, that therefore one should ignore the rule, whenever it seems beneficial to do so. The utilitarian advantage lies precisely in the fact of it being a rule. One might reasonably and correctly calculate that on a particular occasion it would be more productive to kill a certain person than to abide by the rule prohibiting the act, but then one is obliged to recollect that it was always known that such cases would arise; the argument was that on balance the benefits of having a rule, which is obeyed as such, outweigh the benefits (in terms of happiness) of deciding each case on its merits. So, the fact that one assesses the advantage of having a rule exactly as one assesses the advantages of performing an act, does not entail that one rejects it on the occasion that it is not productive. Far from it being the case that rule-utilitarian collapses into act-utilitarianism, to proceed as if that were so, by dispensing with the rule when it seems beneficial to do so, is to ignore the essence of rule-utilitarianism. A rule that one ignores when it is judged appropriate to do so, is not, on any theory, a rule.[9]

Similarly, it is confusion that leads people to suggest that adding qualifications to a rule, which is a common practice amongst utilitarians, is somehow tantamount to embracing act-utilitarianism. A rule-utilitarian, let us suppose, might not argue for a simple rule against killing, but instead argue for a qualified rule such as, perhaps, a rule against killing except in self defence, or against killing except when fighting for one's country. According to some critics that is equivalent to saying that one should not kill, except when the sum of happiness will be increased by doing so, because, they argue, the grounds for excluding self-defence or war from the prohibition were presumably that killing in self-defence or war were in some way judged to promote rather than diminish happiness overall.[10]

The critics are right to presume that the decision to qualify the rule must have been based on consideration of happiness in some way, if it is to count as utilitarian at all. It would be inconsistent with any form of hedonistic utilitarianism to appeal to other considerations such as the alleged self-evident right to defend oneself, or the moral value of patriotism. But in all other respects this argument is incorrect. The qualification in question is a qualification to the scope of the rule, not to the terms of its application. It serves to define more narrowly the type of action that is prohibited, rather than to weaken the prohibition. Though the prohibition now only applies to a limited class of killings, it remains an absolute rule. The previous formulation said that one should never perform any act of killing; the new formulation says that one should never perform certain types of killing. The critics are therefore wrong to suggest that the new formulation introduces the idea that one should judge each case on its merits. There is a very clear difference between saying 'One should always perform a certain type of action', however much the type of action may be qualified, and saying 'one should sometimes perform a certain type of action'. In this case the rule-utilitarian is not saying that one should sometimes, but not always, refrain from killing of any sort. He is saying one should always refrain from killing of particular sorts. Nor in all probability (though it could conceivably be otherwise) is he suggesting that the qualification should be added because killing in self-defence will invariably be justified on utilitarian terms. It is far more likely that he would argue that while some acts of killing in self-defence would not be justified on utilitarian terms in themselves, nonetheless, on balance, a utilitarian case can be made for leaving the decision to individuals to make in particular situations.

The defining characteristic of an act-utilitarian is that he believes that the individual should decide each case on its merits; the defining characteristic of the rule-utilitarian is that he believes that, in the interests of happiness, there should be certain rules that are to be followed in all circumstances. It does not matter how much the substance of a rule is modified or qualified; so long as one maintains that, as qualified, it is to be followed as a rule, the distinction remains, and one is proceeding as a rule-utilitarian. To say 'Never kill except in self-defence' is not equivalent to saying 'Never kill except when it will promote happiness to do so', even if the grounds for excluding self-defence from the prohibition were related exclusively to considerations of happiness. Only if the argument happened to have taken the form 'There should be a rule against killing, excluding killing in self-defence, purely and simply because killing in self-defence always is morally justified and other types of killing never justified', would it begin to make sense to argue that this is a species of act-utilitarianism. For in this case, it might be argued, we are not really formulating a rule of conduct, so much as emphasizing a contingent fact about various acts: killing in self-defence is always beneficial; other types of killing never are. But that is not the claim, it is not the manner of the argument, and it is not likely to be anyone's view. The argument has consistently been that there is utilitarian advantage in adopting a rule, however it is qualified, and regardless of the fact that sometimes to abide by the rule will in itself cause unhappiness.

It has also been argued that rule-utilitarians are not truly utilitarians at all. When all is said and done, they do not, it is suggested, determine what they ought to do by reference to promoting happiness, which is the essence of utilitarianism. They follow rules, even when it is manifest that to do so will generate unhappiness. If happiness is truly the only moral good, how can it be morally acceptable, let alone right, to do things that evidently cause great unhappiness? How can one call oneself a utilitarian in such circumstances?

Here we need to recall the argument of Chapter 3, where some important general points were made about the nature of utilitarianism. It is true that, for the utilitarian, happiness is the only thing that is morally good in itself, and therefore that his ultimate criterion in estimating the rightness and wrongness of actions is happiness. But it is not true that it follows, or that the utilitarian thesis is, that one should always do whatever, of available options, will promote most happiness. The utilitarian, in common with proponents of any other ethical theory, is concerned with the ideal. He maintains that we should strive for a world in which all are fully happy. We therefore have to consider what social arrangements are most likely to bring us near to the ideal, allowing for the constraints of human nature and material circumstance. The argument for adopting certain rules has been conducted on these terms: it is in the overall interests of happiness that we should abide by certain rules. To say, therefore, that in following a rule one is turning one's back on utilitarianism, is false, even when application of a rule in a particular context does militate against happiness. It is simply a question of the rule-utilitarian taking a wider and longer-term perspective in respect of happiness. And that, it has been argued, is what he should do, on utilitarian grounds. For if happiness is what matters, it can scarcely be satisfactory to act in ways that bring immediate gratification, even at the cost of an ultimate overall diminution of happiness. In fact, as should by now be apparent, it is act-utilitarianism, not rule-utilitarianism, that may be charged with not being truly utilitarian, precisely because the argument for adopting rule-utilitarianism is itself a utilitarian one.

So far I have argued that there are strong grounds for adopting rule-utilitarianism on utilitarian grounds, and assumed that the grounds will be contingent.[11] It is because of various facts (that might conceivably have been otherwise) about human nature and physical circumstance that we are led to adopt certain rules in the interests of happiness. Nothing said so far suggests that it would be inconceivable that there should be an entirely happy community in the absence of rules of conduct, only, that it seems most unlikely, as people are. But some rules may be a matter of logical necessity. For example, while it is logically conceivable that people might be of such a sort that decisions as to when killing was morally justified could safely be left to individual judgement, it is arguable that there must necessarily be a rule enjoining us to keep promises (or, more likely, a qualified rule enjoining the keeping of certain types of promise).[12]

It is difficult to conceive of a world in which people could be happy without some notion of the need to keep promises. A world in which no one could be relied on to keep a promise would be a world in which there could be no meaningful undertaking, no reliable predictions in respect of conduct that is not determined in some way, no assurance. Certain individuals might be happy in such a world, although it is a fair bet that contingently most would not. But it is questionable whether a society as a whole could conceivably function, let alone function happily, in such circumstances. To say this is obviously to fall short of any strict logical necessity. Trying to imagine a world in which no undertaking is meaningful, but which is nonetheless viable, is not like trying to imagine a square circle. Nonetheless, it remains hard to conceive, in a way that a society in which killing is accepted as a part of life does not. Similarly, while different people may have different interests, the concept of happiness would seem to be such that in order to be happy one must develop an interest in something, so that a utilitarian society would have to have some concern for developing interests. And, rather more obviously, once that is conceded, there are various interests that are logically incompatible, and consequently a society would necessarily have to find some way of regulating them. One rule which is indisputably a logical necessity is that one should always refrain from acts that cause gratuitous suffering to others. For, although the agent might derive satisfaction from such acts, and even maintain that it outweighs the unhappiness of others, it is self-evident that the ideal cannot be achieved in this way.

I shall not pursue this matter any further, since whether or not certain types of action are logically necessary for a happy society makes no difference to the question of whether utilitarianism is a plausible theory. But we may note that it is possible that some rules will be logically necessary, that some will be necessary in any society because of contingent but universal truths about mankind and nature, and that some will be necessary to particular societies only, because of the particular nature of the people and circumstance of those societies. It is, in addition, quite straightforwardly possible that different societies will have an equal need of certain types of rule on the formal level, but have good reason to interpret them differently at the substantive level. In practice it is likely that all societies will need rules to govern social relations, but the form those rules take may legitimately vary from society to society.[13]

We have seen that rule-utilitarianism cannot be reduced to act-utilitarianism. The fact that in devising and framing rules we look to the consequences in terms of happiness, and that we do likewise in qualifying them or making them more explicit and particular, is not to be identified with judging every individual act on its merits. We have seen also that, on utilitarian grounds, we are obliged to adopt rule-utilitarianism. The case is largely, if not entirely, contingent, but is no less compelling for that. Because of the nature of happiness, the nature of a human society, and seemingly universal characteristics of humans beings, combined, we see that if we wish to approach the ideal of a world of fully happy individuals, we have to adopt certain rules. They are rules relating to actions where there is more to be gained in terms of happiness from certainty, predictability, uniformity and consistency, than will be lost in terms of individual predilection and particular cases. Rules that are thus justified are to be followed absolutely: action in accordance with them is morally right, and it is our duty to perform such actions.

This leaves the question of what we should do in those cases that are not governed by rules. Formally, the answer is clearly that we should do that which, of available options, will promote most happiness. We are not here concerned with the idea that at any given moment we should be trying to do that which would most contribute to the sum of human happiness; such acts of supererogation will be considered below.[14] The question here is how one should behave within situations in which one finds oneself. Thus, assuming that there is no moral obligation for me to leave my comfortable job and pleasant circle of friends and acquaintances, in order to make a greater contribution to the sum of human happiness by helping the poor in Ethiopia, how ought I to conduct myself at work, within the bosom of my family, and in relation to my friends, neighbours, acquaintances and so forth?

At this level, I should proceed as an act-utilitarian. I should conduct myself with a view to maintaining and contributing to people's happiness, my own included, but counting for no more than anyone else's. Assuming my friends appreciate phone calls, invitations, meetings in the pub and gossip, I should provide these things, assuming too that they are not particularly burdensome activities to me. If they are, I have to determine whether their appreciation outweighs my disenchantment, or whether we would not all be better off if we drifted apart. What would in fact be best in terms of happiness may here also be referred to as what is morally right or my duty. But, of course, in such daily dealings I will never be sure what is truly for the best. So what I ought to do, this now being what is morally intentioned, is what I sincerely believe is for the best. In doing what is morally intentioned, I may not be doing what is actually morally right, but that I cannot help. At least I am acting in a way that entitles me to moral commendation.

Likewise, when it comes to the thornier ground of personal relations between lovers. One might try to argue on utilitarian grounds for certain rules to cover such relationships, such as that one should only have sexual intercourse in marriage, that one should never get divorced, or never separate when there are children involved. I confess that I cannot see any plausibility in such arguments, and I consequently do not believe that any moral rules should govern such relationships, beyond those rules that govern all conduct as, for example, rules relating to promise keeping. If you can and do sincerely promise to love and obey someone for all time, then you should do so, perhaps. But it might be wiser not to make such a promise and, in any case, I would argue that the nature of promising is such that this avowal cannot seriously be regarded as a promise. If you believe (as I do not) that there is a case on utilitarian grounds for a rule to the effect that one should always tell the truth, then you must do so, even if it severely embarrasses you. But when it comes to questions such as whether an extra-marital affair is morally justified or whether a couple should be divorced, the answer is in either case that we do not know for certain what is right, and that what we ought to do is therefore what we sincerely believe will be most productive of happiness, taking all persons affected into consideration. The very obvious fact that such counsel gives very little specific practical guidance is neither here nor there. If the utilitarian theory is plausible, and hence taken to be correct, it follows that this is the way we should proceed. That we will make mistakes, or find it literally impossible to estimate consequences in terms of happiness, is nothing to the point. Our moral obligation, in such situations, is to do what we sincerely believe most likely to promote happiness. If we really cannot tell, then though what we do undoubtedly may make a material difference to the sum of good in the world, it nonetheless does not matter, from the point of view of moral justification, what we do.

At this point, it will be convenient to summarize not only this chapter but the overall argument so far.

Moral goodness is, in Ross's phrase, 'a supervenient quality' and it is indefinable, in the way that Moore maintained. We have a shared understanding of this quality, in the sense that we know something about its significance – it is to be sought; it represents our aspirations – but we cannot literally see it, nor provide a definition or a synonym for it. It is the word that represents the goal. The utilitarian thesis is not the thesis that happiness alone is in and of itself morally good, but that is the premiss on which the thesis is based. This premiss is not to be confused with the assertion that 'good' means 'happiness producing'; it does not. Nor is it being said that provided people are happy all is right with the world. Rather it is being asserted that while friendship, truth telling, generosity, etc., may be very desirable things, while it may be good to engage in them, while it may be our duty to do so, they are not in and of themselves good. It makes sense to ask whether friendship is good, in a way that it does not of happiness. Thus, other things may be good, but they are not by their nature good. (Moore's question concerning two worlds, one of which has friendship and one of which does not, does not discredit the point. It might be better in various ways, but it is not self-evident that a world without friendship is morally bad in the way that a world without happiness is.)

To the perception that happiness is the only thing that is good in itself is added the formal distributive principle that all persons *qua* persons are of equal significance and the contingent observation that happiness may arise in a wide variety of circumstances. From this is deduced the observation that a morally acceptable society would be any social arrangement in which all people were equally and fully happy. Our moral duty is therefore to strive for such a society. What people ought to do is behave in ways that are conducive to the ideal.

It has now been suggested that from what we know of human beings certainly, and in the light of what is conceivable possibly, certain rules of conduct need to be formulated. These rules may be qualified rules, in the sense that they narrow a generic type of behaviour by listing specific exceptions, but they are to be obeyed without qualification. They are adopted on utilitarian grounds, that is to say on the grounds that their adoption will itself promote happiness in the long run. The fact that on a specific occasion to break such a rule would increase the happiness of all concerned is neither here nor there. A prior calculation has taken such a possibility into account and concluded that notwithstanding such occasions the rule should obtain. (This is of course to be distinguished from a case in which we recalculate and reject the rule for all time, on the grounds that having the rule does not outweigh the unhappiness caused by having to obey it on certain occasions.)

The ethical theory of utilitarianism is thus that human beings ought to devise those rules absolute adherence to which would promote happiness maximally and equally, and in other respects seek to do that which of alternatives would promote most happiness. The individual's moral duty is to adhere to the rules absolutely, and in situations that are not covered by rules to do that which he sincerely believes will be most productive of happiness, taking all persons affected into account. In the latter case, what he does may or may not be morally justified, depending on whether it is in fact more productive of happiness than alternative ways of proceeding. But whether it is morally justified or not (and often we will not be in a position to say whether it is), it will be a morally intentioned act and, as such, will entitle the agent to moral commendation. (A similar situation may arise where circumstances make it impossible for the agent to abide by one rule without infringing another.)

Such a theory has intuitive plausibility, does not do violence to our sentiments, explains things well, and can be rationally defended.

Notes

1. J.J.C. Smart, 'An outline of a system of utilitarian ethics' in *Utilitarianism: For and Against* (1973). See also Smart's entry under 'Utilitarianism' in *The Encyclopedia of Philosophy*, ed. P. Edwards (1967).

   Recently, versions of rule-utilitarianism seem to be more widely favoured. See, e.g., R.B. Brandt *A Theory of the Good and the Right* (1979).
2. See below, Chapter 9.
3. Brandt appears to have been the first person to introduce the 'act' and 'rule' terminology. R.F. Harrod (1936) was the first explicitly to point out the advantages of rule-utilitarianism, though, in my judgement, J.S. Mill certainly, and Bentham essentially, were both rule-utilitarians by understanding, if not by unambiguous expression.
4. I think, therefore, that Harsanyi (1982) overstates the case when he says 'prior to the emergence of rule-utilitarian theory, utilitarians could not convincingly defend themselves against the accusation that they were advocating a super-Machiavellistic morality, which permitted infringement of all individual rights and all institutional obligations in the name of some narrowly defined social utility'. (p. 41) But certainly, such has often been taken to be the case.
5. J.S. Mill, *Utilitarianism*, chapter 2. E.g., 'actions are right in proportion as they tend to promote happiness'. (p. 257) 'We feel that the violation, for a present advantage,

of a rule of such transcendant expediency, is not expedient.' (p. 274) 'But to consider the rules of morality as improvable, is one thing; to pass over the intermediate generalisation entirely, and endeavour to test each individual action directly by the first principle, is another.' (p. 276) 'Mankind have been learning by experience the tendencies of actions.' (p. 275) Commenting on this latter passage, Anthony Quinton, *Utilitarian Ethics* (1973), writes 'This is one of two clear pieces of evidence that Mill was a rule-utilitarian and not an act-utilitarian'. (p. 47) Bentham similarly uses the term 'tendency': 'an action then may be said to be conformable to the principle of utility ... when the tendency it has to augment the happiness of the community is greater than any it has to diminish it.' (*Principles of Morals and Legislation*, (1948), p. 3)

John Gray, (*Mill on Liberty: a Defence*, 1983, p. 29) denies the claim, made most notably by J. O. Urmson ('The interpretation of the Moral Philosophy of J. S. Mill', *Philosophical Quarterly*, 1953, pp. 33–39), that talk of the tendencies of acts is 'conclusive evidence in support of a rule-utilitarian interpretation of his moral theory'. But Gray, while preferring to classify Mill's view as a species of indirect utilitarianism (following Bernard Williams, though not quite in the direction the latter might have hoped), does concede that such language indicates that Mill is not an act-utilitarian. I concur with the view, incidentally, that 'rule-utilitarianism' is an inadequate label if it is interpreted too narrowly to cover only legal or formal social rules. I construe the term more widely to cover, for example, the dictates of conscience. The issue, though important in itself, is not crucial to the overall argument in the text.

6.   As Harsanyi (1982) observes: the question is simply 'which version of utilitarianism will maximise social utility?' (p. 56) He also sees that the same criterion must be used to determine whether a rule needs qualification: 'in other words, rule-utilitarianism not only enables us to make a rational choice among alternative possible general rules for defining morally desirable behaviour. Rather, it also provides a rational test for determining the exceptions to be permitted from these rules'. (p. 59) See further below. Abraham Tucker, *Light of Nature Pursued* (1768), was one of the first to point out that there are good utilitarian reasons for guiding action by general rules.

7.   See, e.g. E. Fromm, *Fear of Freedom* (1942).

8.   For a succinct statement of one version of this kind of objection, see Smart (1973) op. cit. The objections 'boil down to the accusation of rule worship: the rule-utilitarian presumably advocates his principle because he is ultimately concerned with human happiness: why then should he advocate abiding by a rule when he knows that it will not in the present case be most beneficial to abide by it?' (p. 10) I believe that Smart's question, and other related but distinct concerns raised by, e.g., D. Lyons, in *The Forms and Limits of Utilitarianism* (1965) and R.M. Hare, in *Freedom and Reason* (1963), are sufficiently answered in the text.

9.   Smart (1973), op. cit., suggests that the claim 'that in most cases it is most beneficial to abide by the rule seems irrelevant. And so is the reply that it would be better that everybody should abide by the rule than that nobody should'. (p. 10) Neither, it will be noted, represents the claim I have made which is rather that the benefit lies in there being a rule. Bernard Williams, 'A Critique of Utilitaranism' (1973), correctly suggests that if we are 'sensible' we will agree 'that the utility of acts that follow on the obtaining of a rule is not to be equated with the utility of acts that consist in obeying the rule'. (p. 122) However, he goes on to say that 'to equate the utility of a rule's obtaining with the utility of it being followed is not the mark of any utilitarian doctrine, direct or indirect – it is just a sign of simple mindedness'. One sees his point, and it is true of traditional views of utilitarianism, but it does not quite work with reference to the view I have presented. For, in working out what

is right by reference to the ideal, one is indeed saying the utility of this rule lies in its being always followed by all. That is why obedience to it is morally right even granted that in real life the action remains right notwithstanding the fact that the rule is not uniformly adhered to. One would not make a rule, on my view, covering an action that one could not conceive of being universally adhered to.

10. See, for example, D. Lyons (1965 op. cit.). Smart (1973, op. cit., p. 42) argues that 'the act-utilitarian will, however, regard these rules as mere rules of thumb, and will use them only as rough guides'. Smart is an act-utilitarian who sees the value of rules of thumb to guide action when there is no time for reflection. I am a rule-utilitarian who allows that there are some (many) actions not well covered by a rule. It is true that the decision to break a rule when it suits one does not necessarily make the rule pointless. There may be some rules of thumb on my view. But some rules must be binding rules, because they are not there for reasons of convenience or the difficulty of calculation and so forth, but because we benefit from an absolute ban injunction in relation to some types of act.

11. Bernard Williams ('A Critique of Utilitarianism', 1973) suggests that 'forms of utilitarianism which help themselves too liberally to the resources of indirectness lose their utilitarian rationale and end up as vanishingly forms of utilitarianism at all. Whether that is so is not just a question of nomenclature or classification ... It is a question of the point of utilitarianism'. (p. 81) It is true that too many qualifications and concessions to the traditional or classical view of utilitarianism may change it so radically as to not only make it unhelpful to call it by the same name, but also to change its nature in a significant way. But it is not entirely clear to me how one establishes unequivocally what its true nature or its essential point is, given that we are engaged in a debate about its precise nature that has been continuous, in a very overt way, since the time of Bentham. Certainly the qualifications and modifications to alternative conceptions that I introduce here, most especially the insistence on rule-utilitarianism (a species of what Williams refers to as 'indirect' utilitarianism), do not in my view conflict with the 'point' of classical utilitarianism. Indeed, I would claim that at times critics such as Williams seem to have a rather limited understanding of the point of it, which partly explains their feeling that the theory is characterized by 'a great simple-mindedness'. (p. 149) But, in any case, even if, in some sense and to some degree, my account of utilitarianism gets away from what Williams thinks was the point of, say, Mill's version of utilitarianism, I should remain unperturbed: my main concern is to suggest that the ethical theory I articulate is highly plausible. Given that, whether it should be called a utilitarian theory or not really is 'a question of nomenclature or classification ... in itself ... of no interest at all'. (p. 81)

12. Act-utilitarianism, by contrast, 'would greatly reduce the social benefits associated with the making of promises as an institution. It would make it rather uncertain in most cases whether any given promise would be kept. People would be less able to form definite expectations about each other's future behaviour and would have a general feeling of insecurity about the future'. (Harsanyi, 1982, p. 58)

13. Hare's (1982) distinction between Level 1 and Level 2 principles, though introduced in a different context and though distinguishable from my distinction between what is morally right and what is morally justified, is pertinent here. When he remarks 'To educate oneself and other men in level 1 principles *is* [his emphasis] for the best, and only the crudest of act-utilitarians fail to see this', (p. 35) he comes close to saying that there are utilitarian grounds for adopting certain rules or principles. His distinction is between the level of intuitive application in practice of accepted principles, and the level of detached critical reflection on the adequacy of such principles. In my terms, Hare's critical level of reflection yields rules that enshrine

right conduct, leaving us to intuitively (or reasonably) determine what is justified when the rules do not clearly determine conduct.

14. See Chapter 9.

7. Quantity or Quality of Happiness?

Traditionally, the argument that I am concerned with in this chapter has centred on the question of whether there are different qualities of pleasure, rather than on the question of whether there are different qualities of happiness. However, I shall treat it in the latter terms, notwithstanding the fact that reference will be made to Mill whose argument is couched in terms of pleasure. I stated above[1] that, given that there are distinctions to be drawn between pleasure and happiness, utilitarianism as I understand it is better understood in terms of the provision of the latter.

Happiness may take many forms, but can be clearly understood as a general concept which represents our goal, regardless of the specific form it takes.[2] By contrast, pleasures seem to be of many very different kinds and not readily to lend themselves to classification under a broad heading of pleasure in a generic sense. This point, if it is correct at all, is of course only a point about usage: we do not tend to talk of people enjoying pleasure without specifying the types of pleasure they experience. Even if we refer to someone as pursuing a life of pleasure, we tend to think in terms of a series of distinct pleasures, rather than an overall state of mind. I do not want to make too much of this, since I see nothing outrageous in the suggestion that we might choose more often to talk of a generic pleasurable state. But there does seem to be some sense in the way we generally talk here. Happy states of mind may vary in intensity and feel, but pleasures are surely subject to a much more wide-reaching and precise categorization. There are intellectual pleasures, physical pleasures, aesthetic pleasures and sentimental pleasures, for example, whereas it does not seem appropriate to talk of an intellectual or aesthetic happiness. There are specific sensations of pleasure associated with, say, sexual activity, smoking, playing cricket and contemplating a sunrise, in a way that specific sensations of happiness are not naturally associated with these pastimes.

But not only is there a *prima facie* case for saying that, if we are concerned with an ideal state of mind, 'happiness' is a more appropriate term than 'pleasure'; there are also grounds for saying that one cannot do justice to the utilitarian theory in terms of pleasure alone. One can, for instance, experience pleasure without being happy, most obviously because the pleasure one is experiencing does not occupy one's whole mind. My pleasure in smoking may be accompanied by feelings of guilt and self-loathing, which are incompatible with a happy state of mind, or it may involve concurrent unpleasant side effects, such as a dry throat and a nasty smell. Conversely, one may delight in pain. It is not only the blatantly masochistic who may be so constituted as to find happiness in a way of life that nonetheless causes them to moan and groan about circumstances. Whatever one does at a superficial level, if one in fact is the sort of person who would not know what to do without something to grumble at, one who fundamentally enmeshes with a situation that affords the opportunity for continued low-key complaint, then one is happy. Such a person might possibly, though unidiomatically, be said to be taking pleasure in life, but it would be confusing to suggest that that life was one of pleasure. Pleasure and pain are not co-extensive with acceptance of and rejection of a situation, as happiness is. To be happy is to accept one's situation without reservation, in ideal terms; to be unhappy necessarily involves an impetus to reject it. But one can take pleasure in an activity or a series of activities, without being satisfied or accepting the state of affairs. One can live happily with pain. One can be unhappy leading a life of pleasure.

The above comments do not purport to do more than indicate why I prefer to focus on the term 'happiness' rather than 'pleasure'. While, for practical purposes, the utilitarian may very often be able to examine issues in terms of whether people experience pleasure or pain, it should be remembered that the ideal is not to provide a series of pleasurable experiences, nor even an absence of painful ones, unless such provision would lead to the desired happy state of mind, which, on the face of it, it surely might not.

In any event, the question of concern to us is now whether, when we are estimating the likely consequences of an action or rule, in respect of the utilitarian criterion of happiness, we should take into account alleged differences in quality or worth between various states of happiness, in addition to, and as distinct from, such factors as the number of people involved and the duration of their happiness.

It may be noted in passing that the phrase 'quality of happiness' does not, perhaps, come as naturally as 'quality of pleasure'. This I attribute partly to the relative familiarity of the latter. But the *prima facie* oddity of the idea of varying qualities of happiness, which strikes us because familiarity has not dulled our senses, may indicate that in fact both formulations are misleading. And that is the conclusion to which I shall argue: strictly speaking, a pleasure cannot itself vary in point of quality, any more than a pain or a spasm can; it is not the pain itself that may differ, but its length, its intensity and, of course, its occasion. It seems clear to me that talk of quality of pleasure is in fact talk about such characteristics as these or, more specifically, about the worth of its source. The question 'was it a particularly good quality pleasure that you experienced?', if we discount intensity, duration, etc., is as meaningless as 'was it a particularly good beauty that you enjoyed?'

Thus, when people debate the issue of whether the pleasure derived from pushpin is of the same quality as that derived from poetry, if they are not confusing quality with quantity, they are in fact debating the question of whether the pursuit of pushpin is as worthwhile an activity as that of poetry, and not whether the pleasure experienced somehow differs in quality. Indeed, the latter would seem to be an absurd debate to engage in, even if it made sense, since common experience tells us that one may get more out of a trivial pursuit than a serious or complex one on occasion, and philosophers remind us that we do not and cannot have direct experience of other people's feelings. Given, then, that we assume that we know that two people each have the same quantity of pleasure, one from pushpin and one from poetry, what do we imagine ourselves to be debating? If quality is determined by reference to some 'feel' distinct from quantity, then we cannot talk about it, and we know that it need not be the case that the feel of poetry is superior. The quality of anything else is tied up with various specific attributes; why should the case be any different here? Superior quality wine is not wine that, in addition to having a flavour, a bouquet, body, or what have you, also has something called quality. Its quality lies in its meeting certain specifiable criteria relating to wine. One might expect the same to be true of pleasure: its quality is one and the same thing as its meeting the sort of criteria appropriate to a good experience of pleasure. And these criteria are, for example, those of intensity and duration.

Famously, John Stuart Mill has often been interpreted as maintaining that there are distinctions of quality to be made between pleasures.[3] Nor is it an altogether wayward interpretation.[4] After all, he introduces the topic in the context of defending himself against the charge of propounding 'a doctrine worthy only of swine', refers explicitly to taking 'the higher ground' of arguing for 'the superiority of mental over bodily pleasures' in terms of 'their intrinsic nature', and states bluntly that 'it is quite compatible with the principle of utility to recognise the fact, that some *kinds* of pleasure are more desirable and more valuable than others. It would be absurd that while, in estimating all other things, quality is considered as well as quantity, the estimation of pleasures should be supposed to depend on quantity alone'.[5] The reference to 'kinds of pleasure' is generally taken to imply that, in Mill's view, the pleasure of, e.g., poetry, is more desirable than that of pushpin, regardless of quantity.

At one stage, I was inclined to argue that Mill has accidentally misled us as regards his own position, inasmuch as, while we infer that he did indeed mean that the happiness of a Socrates dissatisfied was superior to that of a fool satisfied, regardless of intensity, duration, etc., in fact what he was offering was a more sophisticated understanding of the idea of quantity. To estimate quantity properly, we have to do rather more than simply count how many people are affected, for how long, and how intensely. However, I now think that, for once, I have overestimated Mill. He was seriously confused on this matter.

It has often been remarked that his argument to establish the superiority of certain pleasures is, to put it mildly, weak. He maintains that competent judges prefer 'the pleasures of the intellect, of the feelings and imagination, and of the moral sentiments', the so-called higher pleasures, 'to those of mere sensation', the lower pleasures such as sexual gratification or those of the appetite.[6] Since they alone are capable of experiencing both kinds of pleasure, their verdict must stand. This clearly will not do as the final word on the subject. It is true, perhaps, that those who are incapable of appreciating the higher pleasures are *ipso facto* ruled out as judges of the issue. But it is not the case that even the unanimous verdict of those who can appreciate the so-called 'higher pleasures' would establish their superiority, even if we charitably, and possibly with good reason, suggest that it would be a significant point. For example, we might feel that it is sensible to be swayed by the judgement of those who enjoy both poetry and detective fiction that the former is superior, but we could not reasonably assert that that judgement in itself proves the superiority. Furthermore, it is highly questionable whether the premiss is correct. In general terms, beings who have intellectual interests are by definition going to find some satisfaction in indulging them and, therefore, one might say, beings who are essentially or preternaturally contemplative are going to rank the 'higher pleasures' above the 'lower pleasures'. But when this general, definitional, point is converted into specific examples, it seems far from clear that those who are well educated and intelligent necessarily prefer intellectual and cultivated pursuits to others, let alone that they regard them as intrinsically superior.

The main problems here are what Mill means by a competent judge and what he means by a 'more valuable' pleasure. As to the first point, there is an obvious danger of circularity in the argument. For it might be felt that what Mill means by a competent judge is no more than a person who is not only capable of experiencing, but is actually inclined towards, the pleasures of the intellect. As we have just seen, if he presumes that capacity to experience both types of pleasure makes one a competent judge, then he has confused a necessary with a sufficient condition of competence. If he does not, then the argument requires a clear definition of competence, and some evidence that judges of competence in that sense do invariably prefer the higher pleasures.

But the second point is more important, since Mill points out, this time with greater plausibility, that, although those who know both types of pleasures can fairly readily make a case for the superiority of the higher pleasures in terms of their 'greater permanency, safety, uncostliness, etc.', that is not what he is trying to do. So what is he trying to do? What does he mean by 'a more valuable' pleasure? He says, 'If I am asked what I mean by a difference of quality in pleasures, or what makes one pleasure more valuable than another, merely as pleasure, except its being greater in amount, there is but one possible answer. Of two pleasures, if there be one to which all or almost all who have experience of both give a decided preference ... that is the more desirable pleasure.'[7] Again, this could be interpreted as the claim that if most people of wide experience value one thing more than another, then it is more valuable. But that, as we have said, is not necessarily true. The alternative interpretation would be to assume that Mill is defining 'more valuable' as 'what is more popular with those who have experience'. But that is not what 'more valuable' means in anyone's vocabulary. So we are left wondering in what sense he maintains that some pleasures are of superior quality to others.

The matter becomes slightly clearer, when he continues:

If one of the two (pleasures) is, by those who are competently acquainted with both, placed so far above the other that they prefer it, even though knowing it to be attended with a greater amount of discontent, and would not resign it for any quantity of the other pleasure which their nature is capable of, we are justified in ascribing to the preferred enjoyment a superiority in quality, so far outweighing quantity as to render it, in comparison, of small account.[8]

From the point of view of the account of utilitarianism that I am advancing in this book, Mill's reference to 'discontent' in this passage is very important, for it reminds us that he will go on to say that his critics have confused happiness with contentment.[9] I have already argued, however, for a view of happiness that treats the two as more or less synonymous, and that in itself, at least in Mill's view, disassociates the thesis being put forward generally in these pages from the problem that he is grappling with. For, he concedes, correctly, that if one were concerned with making everyone happy in a sense that allowed it to be sometimes indistinguishable from contentment, rather than, say, in a sense that equated it with ecstasy, the case would be different. He does not apparently believe, as well might he not, that intellectuals are necessarily more happy, in the sense of contented, pleased with their lot, or prone to enjoy life, than non-intellectuals.

But, to return to his problems, he is at pains to rebut the idea that utilitarians are just swine, intent on the gratification of the charmingly entitled 'baser instincts'. In order to resist the idea, he has got it into his head that he must establish that 'it is better to be a human being dissatisfied than a pig satisfied.'[10] Now, it is possible that in some non-moral sense of 'better' this is true. One might be able to give sense to the idea of a hierarchy of species, in terms of their complexity, capacities and so forth, and conclude that, just as a flawed sonnet may be more worthy of our attention than a perfect limerick, so a dissatisfied human might be more worthy than a satisfied pig. And one could obviously argue (how convincingly is another matter) that, if you are a human being, you would in some non-moral way be better off acting as one, however unsatisfactorily, than emulating the life-style of the pig.[11]

But the insistent question remains: does the quotation above concerning those who are 'competently acquainted with both' types of pleasure, does anything Mill writes, help us to understand what is meant by a 'superiority in quality' of pleasure? It seems not. If a person prefers poetry to sex, 'even though knowing it to be attended with a greater amount of discontent',[12] then one must surely suppose either that, despite a greater quantity of discontent in some respects, the intensity (or, more generally, amount) of the pleasure derived from poetry outweighs it, or that the pursuit of poetry is regarded as more worthwhile, regardless of the question of the pleasure derived from the pursuit. Thus, either the quality of a pleasure is identified with its intensity (or some other criterion of quantity), or another criterion of moral worth has been implicitly introduced. As was mentioned at the beginning of this chapter, the only other sense that one can give to the idea of the quality of a pleasure is its distinctive feel or sensation, analogously to the taste of a wine; and that will not help us, partly because we do not know, and do not have much reason to believe, that the 'feel' of a specific pleasure such as that of reading poetry is invariably the same, and partly because even if it were, to classify one 'feel' as superior to another, if it is not done in terms of aspects of the amount of pleasure in some way, involves introducing a new criterion of worth. In exactly the same way, if Beethoven is musically superior to Elgar, this must be either because he is more musical (i.e., there is more of what we look for in music), or because, when all is said and done, we judge music to some extent by extra-musical criteria.

In my view, Mill probably believes, at some deep, unconscious level both that the pleasures of contemplation are more intense than those of the body, and that they are intrinsically superior, regardless of pleasure considerations. But he has confusedly and confusingly, and I presume still unconsciously, lumped the two together, labelled the two combined a 'superiority in quality', and incorrectly concluded that he is still taking pleasure as the sole criterion of moral worth.[13] In some of his argument on this issue, his position is of course quite understandable and tenable. He is correct in saying that utilitarians need not be, and conspicuously were not in the case of his own circle, Philistines and swine. (Indeed, ironically, the danger is that they may be seen as prigs and pedants rather than pigs and beasts.) It is reasonable to point out that repeated and consistent testimony from those who know both kinds of pleasure would be significant (although not conclusive). And in fact his view that the so-called higher pleasures are superior is, in many cases, correct. But not for the reason given. Not because it is better on utilitarian terms to be a Socrates dissatisfied than a fool satisfied, period. But for the reason that Mill acknowledges, but tries to improve on: because the fool will not be satisfied for long. If we bring into play the ever-important consideration that Mill did not perceive, namely that we must interpret the theory in terms of the ideal, it is easy to see that, while contingently, in the world as it is, many fools may be happy, in the long term and in the round, so to speak, a community of fools will not be able to remain happy. For fools, by definition, do foolish things, which is to say inappropriate things in terms of their own goals. People who want to be happy and know how to be happy, cannot be called 'fools'.

Mill has failed to appreciate how much the Benthamite calculus covers or how powerful it is.[14] He has not recognized that quantity, as conceived by Bentham, incorporates at least some of what at an everyday level we are referring to, when we talk of quality. Specifically, I think, he has effectively ignored or miscalculated the power of the intensity dimension. For, it is differences in intensity, as far as personal experience can tell, which largely makes the pleasures of, say, poetry 'feel' distinct and seem to be almost of a different order from those of the soccer game. I may truthfully claim to enjoy the latter more; but even if that is so, it may be conceded that it is pleasure of a different order, without introducing some non-quantitative criterion. Its being of a different order might make it intrinsically inferior in terms of quantity of pleasure, while it remains extrinsically superior in terms of quantity, for me. If the word 'intensity' seems to some to carry too much weight here, we might substitute reference to the 'luminosity' of various pleasures. Such a term would still refer to an intrinsic aspect of pleasure, which would not involve reference to some other criterion of value, yet which could be taken account of in quantitative assessments.

I am aware, incidentally, that Mill expressly denies this way out. He says, 'When therefore, those feelings and judgment (of the experienced) declare the pleasures derived from the higher faculties to be preferable in kind, apart from the question of intensity, ... they are entitled ... to the same regard.'[15] But it will not be the first time that a great mind has been shown to be confused by a lesser one. One can only re-iterate that he neither makes his case, nor makes it clear.

I turn now to the more important observation that, regardless of what Mill thought he was doing, utilitarianism cannot consistently admit to the idea of degrees of quality in happiness. If there are such degrees, in a sense other than the sort of sense I have referred to, then I confess that utilitarianism is untenable. It is not disputed that there are degrees of happiness, nor that there are different species of happiness, nor that different pursuits may yield varying amounts of happiness. It is denied that we can give independent sense to the idea of different qualities of happiness and, at the same time, maintain the utilitarian thesis.

The reason for this is quite straightforward and, I believe, incontestable. If happiness is the only thing that is good in itself, there is no criterion of moral worth in existence to allow of a distinction between experiences of happiness in terms of their quality, in the sense of intrinsic moral worth. If I claim that the happiness to be derived from philosophy is superior to that to be derived from football, and I do not mean that it is more durable, more productive, more intense, etc., then I am clearly saying that there is some other criterion of moral worth besides that of happiness.

Incidentally, this point should not be confused with the incorrect assumption that utilitarians have no other values, which will be discussed in the next chapter. They certainly may, and do, have both other moral values (e.g. freedom of speech) and non-moral values (e.g. beauty). But what they obviously cannot have is commitment to some other ultimate criterion of moral value. One cannot say, as Mill appears to, both that 'the sole criterion of the moral worth of an action is its happiness potential' and also that 'this action, though rich in happiness potential, is swinish and therefore of relatively little moral worth'.

But what utilitarianism can do, as the foregoing discussion has shown, is have a more or less sophisticated understanding of how the happiness potential of an activity can be affected by quantitative considerations. Here, naturally enough, we turn to Bentham and his felicific calculus.

The extent to which Bentham's intentions have been traduced by literal-minded responses to his calculus, and the consequent incalculable amount of damage to the image of utilitarianism this has led to, seem to me quite extraordinary.[16] Nonetheless, I do not think the misapprehensions are worth more than passing notice. Here, if ever, to state is to refute. Despite the admittedly schematic tenor of Bentham's writing (and life) it is clear that the calculus is not intended to provide a means of precise measurement: more, it is clear that Bentham did not expect precise measurement by any means. If there be any doubt about this, let us pass at once to the more important considerations that utilitarianism cannot expect precision and is absolutely unaffected by the fact that it won't have it.[17] All those criticisms that depend on the claim that precise calculation is impossible can therefore be dismissed in the spirit that Mill showed when he remarked in such a context that any system would work ill 'if we suppose universal idiocy to be conjoined with it'.[18] To be sure, people will not always, if ever, have the time to make intricate calculation of consequences prior to action; people cannot in many cases be sure of what the consequences will be; people will not be able to acquire some of the necessary data, such as how intense the pleasure of others will be. All such fretful responses (perhaps the more to be guarded against in an age dominated by the scientific paradigm) are simply beside the point in assessing the plausibility of utilitarianism.

The point of Bentham's calculus, well understood by a few commentators such as Quinton and Stace,[19] but not by enough, is simply to establish the considerations that need to be taken into account in estimating whether one action is preferable to another. The word 'calculus' is of course most unfortunate, given its close association with the rather exact science of mathematics. But the importance of the calculus lies in its listing the considerations that need to be taken into account, in its formulating the relevant criteria for forming a judgement, rather than in the forlorn hope that it might function as a means for solving all our problems with certainty and exactitude. Where Bentham showed more perspicacity than Mill was in seeing that utilitarianism's plausibility is partly dependent on a sophisticated and subtle understanding of the many dimensions that there are to the idea of quantity of pleasure.

I have to decide, let us suppose, whether to reveal a secret entrusted to me (or, we have to consider whether a rule should be established concerning such actions). Everybody is by now aware that a utilitarian does not simply ask 'will it make me happy?' We know that utilitarianism is concerned not with doing what makes the agent happy, but with doing what most enhances the ideal. So, at the very least I must consider who else is affected (what Bentham calls the 'extent of happiness'). But, if I want to know whether on balance the interests of happiness are served by an action or a rule, that is clearly not enough. I need to know of each of the persons affected, how long their happiness will last ('duration') and how 'intense' it will be. A rather more subtle, but no less important, consideration is how likely it is that those potentially affected will in fact gain happiness for, while the idea that one has to know precisely and certainly what will happen is absurd and unnecessary, it clearly is the case that some consequences in terms of people's happiness are more predictable than others and, when that is so, it should be taken into account ('certainty'). Closely related to that is the question of whether the happiness in view is likely to be an immediate or a long term consequence ('propinquity'). And then there are 'fecundity' and 'purity', the former referring to the relative likelihood of the experience of happiness leading to further similar experiences, and the latter to the relative likelihood of its not being followed by experience of unhappiness. (I would prefer to run these two together, and talk simply of 'implications'.[20])

Thus by listing extent, duration, intensity, certainty, propinquity and implications (or fecundity and purity), Bentham has helped us to appreciate the complexity of a quantitative assessment, and shown us what we need to take into account. In addition, as I have stressed, we do not make such an estimate on every occasion we need to act; rather, we have to estimate what rules would be necessary to allowing of full happiness for all, taking these factors into account. And how does one make use of this so-called calculus? One simply imbibes this understanding, and when it comes to deciding on a rule, or making a decision about one's obligations, one draws on that understanding. The point that the agent will not have time to preface his action with due consideration is, as Mill said, as irrelevant as the fact that the Christian does not have time to review the Bible prior to action. In the first place, one internalizes one's knowledge in either case and, mysterious as it may be, it is a fact of experience that both the Christian and the utilitarian can make instantaneous and well founded decisions in the light of that knowledge. In the second place, the establishment of rules (by reference to these considerations) makes calculation unnecessary on most particular occasions. But third, and considerably more to the immediate point, an ethical theory is not a species of survival kit or a type of *vade mecum*, still less is to be assessed in terms of its 'user-friendliness'. The point of utilitarianism is to tell us that these are the appropriate criteria for determining right conduct. If it so happens that, as a consequence of this theory, it is time-consuming, difficult or actually not possible in some cases to determine what we ought to do, that is not in itself an objection. It would merely show that on this view the moral life may not be easy to lead. And why should that not be the case? Similarly, it is specifically the case that I cannot know how intense an experience of pleasure will be for you, but that does not alter the fact that it is a relevant consideration.

The general question that we have to ask in respect of the plausibility of any ethical theory is whether it is coherent, clear and satisfactorily in touch with our basic understanding of the nature of morality, and whether we have considered all aspects of the matter. The particular question to which we have to revert in the case of this theory, and in the context of this chapter, is whether an assessment of the beneficence of a rule or action by these criteria is sufficient to account for what we are pleased to call the relative quality of experiences of happiness. Can we, that is to say, plausibly maintain that considerations of duration, intensity, certainty, propinquity, fecundity and purity (extent being irrelevant here) are sufficient to explain our sense of differing qualities of happiness? Or are we to be forced into conceding that there remains a distinctive element of qualitative difference, in which case we must either establish how it is to be recognized as a property of happiness itself, or else see it as a property independent of happiness, and hence, since *ipso facto* we are introducing a new criterion of worth, acknowledge that utilitarianism is an untenable doctrine?

As has been indicated throughout this chapter, I am at a loss to make sense of the idea of a distinctive element that represents the quality of happiness, if it is neither to be assessed in terms of some independent criterion of worth nor in terms of quantity of happiness. It may be a very common response to say that there is something that may variously be called the 'feel', the 'taste', the 'flavour' or what have you, of a pleasure or an experience of happiness, and that it is there that its quality is to be found. But the frequency of a response does not guarantee its coherence. Mill suggested that, since in estimating the worth of most things we make reference to quality, we should do so in the case of pleasure. But surely (and this should particularly have recommended itself to a utilitarian such as Mill) in judging the quality of an opera, an ice cream or a poem, we are precisely referring to our degree of satisfaction (when we are not simply using 'quality' as a generic term to encompass the criteria that go to make a good opera, ice cream or poem). An ice cream of quality is either an ice cream made of superior ingredients (in the straightforward sense of, for example, creamier milk), or one that more fully meets the criteria of a good ice cream (for example, a creamier texture), or it is one that we prefer (one that more nearly corresponds to our ideal so far as eating it goes).

Quality is not a property of things; it is another supervenient concept. Reference to the quality of a pleasure cannot imply 'superior ingredients', because the analogy does not hold at this point: pleasure is not the product of various particular elements being conjoined, and by the same token it cannot meaningfully be said to refer to pleasures that more fully meet the criteria of a good pleasure (save only if one adopts a specific theory about the terms on which it is appropriate to feel pleasure. Clearly, sexual pleasure is bad, if it can be substantiated that one ought not to engage in sexual activity for enjoyment). One opera might be regarded as qualitatively superior to another on the grounds that it is, in the final analysis, as a consequence of the way in which it has been constructed, more satisfying. But a pleasure cannot be rated superior to another in this way, unless 'more satisfying' is interpreted quantitatively. Certainly, different pleasures and experiences of happiness may have a distinctive feel about them, but this can be entirely accounted for by varying sources and causes, and the notion of varying intensity. Whereas, conversely, the notion of the 'feel' being something distinct is barely intelligible and, if it were, it is still not clear why the 'feel' should be identified with the quality.

In short, to upset the utilitarian thesis at this juncture, what is required is a case for saying that one experience of happiness may be qualitatively superior to another by reference to some other criterion of moral worth. For all that we have said in this chapter, it may be possible to establish some other criterion of moral worth, but it will not be possible to maintain that this criterion is also a part of the definition of some happy states of mind and not others. That is to say, one might, in principle, argue that the happy state of mind of a fool is not admirable, or one might argue that it lacks richness. But in the first case one would need either to establish that being foolish offends against some independent moral requirement or that it is not truly productive in terms of happiness, all told; in the second case, one would need to show why richness matters intrinsically, as opposed to as a factor in assessing the overall quantity of the happiness.

I shall conclude by observing that I am unembarrassed, as was Mill,[21] by the charge that utilitarianism is brutish because, notwithstanding the argument about quality, it is evident that while a 'fools' paradise' is conceivable for a short time, it is not conceivable in the long term. A happy society that was primarily interested in the lower rather than the higher pleasures is quite conceivable. And naturally, if there were such a society, truly happy on those terms, the utilitarian would morally approve it. But in point of fact it is most unlikely that the ideal could be approached without drawing on the higher pleasures. In the first place, unless one can protect oneself against all change, one needs the wherewithal, intellectual and imaginative, to cope with, control and adapt to change. In the second place, people who can do so, by and large, seem to prefer poetry to pushpin. In the third place the quantity of pleasure all told in respect of pushpin and poetry is seldom if ever equal. That was rather Bentham's point when he made the conditional statement that 'quantity of pleasure being equal, pushpin is as good as poetry',[22] and, more particularly, when he classified the six considerations that may between them render one experience of happiness superior to another, without needing to bring in reference to some mysterious notion of quality as an independent criterion.

Notes

1. See above, Chapter 4.
2. Cf. Alexander Pope, *An Essay on Man*, Ep. IV, 1:

   'O happiness, our being's end and aim
   Good pleasure, ease, content, whate'er thy name
   That something still which prompts the eternal sigh
   For which we bear to live or dare to die.'

3. J.S. Mill, *Utilitarianism*, pp. 258, 259.
4. Anthony Quinton, *Utilitarian Ethics* (1973): 'He seems to say that a non-bodily pleasure is more valuable than a bodily pleasure that is its quantitative equal, or even superior, in pleasantness. This, at any rate, is what he has been generally taken to mean and with good cause'. (p. 42)
5. Ibid., pp. 258, 259.
6. Ibid., p. 258.
7. Ibid., p. 259.
8. Ibid., p. 259.
9. Ibid., p. 260, 'confounds the two very different ideas of happiness and content.'
10. Ibid., p. 260.
11. One might also risk the wrath of anti-naturalists and try to argue that human beings ought to develop peculiarly human characteristics, because they are human characteristics.
12. Ibid., p. 259.
13. 'What has not been noticed is that the reason Mill gives for supposing that mental pleasures are more valuable than bodily ones can very naturally be interpreted as reinstating the identification of value with quantity of pleasure that he ostensibly rejects.' (Quinton, op. cit., p. 43) Actually, as Quinton himself notes elsewhere, this point had been noticed by John Grote, in his *Examination of the Utilitarian Philosophy* (1870). 'Grote neatly argues that Mill's criterion in terms of the preference of qualified judges is in fact quantitative, since in simply preferring 'higher' to 'lower' pleasures the judges are simply asserting the former to be more pleasurable.' (Quinton, op. cit., p. 85)
14. See J. Bentham, *The Principles of Morals and Legislation* (1948), chapter 4.
15. Mill, op. cit., p. 262.
16. Bentham (op. cit.) himself gave warning that he should not be taken too literally or scientifically: 'It is not to be expected that this process should be strictly pursued previously to every moral judgement, or to every legislative or judicial operation. It may, however, be always kept in view; and as near as the process actually pursued on these occasions approaches to it, so near will such process approach the character of an exact one.' (p. 31)

    As James Steintrager cautiously puts it in *Bentham* (1977): 'Strictly speaking, it would be impossible [to employ the calculus] even on his own terms since he consistently admitted that one of the elements to be considered in measuring the value of pleasure, namely, intensity, could not be assigned any value or, at best, a nominal one. It is doubtful whether Bentham ever expected the calculus to be strictly and consistently applied, although he certainly believed that it was a fruitful model for the legislator and ... that the more closely it was approximated the more likely it would be that the greatest happiness of the greatest number would result.' (pp. 30, 31)

    In a letter to his brother Samuel, Bentham writes: 'I need not tell you that it is impossible to form any tolerable estimate of the quantity of happiness that the saving, supposing the exact sum of it could be known, would produce in this way; we are not however to conclude that this quantity, because difficult to adjust, is unreal or inconsiderable'. (Correspondence, Vol. 1.1, 4th Nov. 1773, ed. T.L.S. Sprigge, 1968)

    W.T. Stace (*The Concept of Morals*, 1937) is suitably trenchant: 'I am quite prepared to admit that the notion of a calculus of satisfactions and dissatisfactions is impossible. But I cannot conceive why any philosopher should want to have one ... It is said that if you cannot make a calculation of the relative amounts of pleasure and pain ... you cannot know which actions are good, which bad. This, however, is a very shallow argument. In the first place, even if you cannot measure pleasures and pains, this does not prevent you from knowing that some pleasures or pains are greater than others. A man does not need a thermometer to know that he is being frozen to death or boiled alive.' (pp. 131–2)

Quinton (1973) comments: 'Arithmetical terminology abounds in [Bentham's] discussion. But it is not at all clear that it is meant to be taken with absolute literalness'. (p. 33) Again 'despite his lip-service to the validity of the circumstantial argument for the superiority of mental to bodily pleasures, Mill does not believe in the hedonic calculus with which it is associated. He insists that pleasures and pains are far too heterogeneous for any mechanical routine of computation to yield acceptable estimations of their quantity of the sort Bentham had in mind. But to deny that pleasure and pain can be appraised by a numerical calculus is not to deny that they can be compared in a more total and impressionistic way and any such comparison will be rational just to the extent that it takes relevant factors other than intensity into account.' (p. 43) Abraham Tucker, in the *Light of Nature Pursued* (1768) was amongst the first to see that calculation of the amount of value resulting from an action had to be impressionistic rather than mechanical.

17. J.J.C. Smart, ('An Outline of a System of Utilitarian Ethics', 1973) suggests that 'what utilitarianism badly needs, in order to make its theoretical foundations secure, is some method according to which numerical probablilities, even approximate ones, could in theory, though not necessarily always in practice, be assigned to any imagined future event ... Until we have an adequate theory of objective probability utilitarianism is not on a secure theoretical base'. (pp. 40, 41) This seems to me wholly (and, given the author, unexpectedly) incorrect. First, I see no argument, in Smart or anywhere else, to support the specific idea of numerical probabilities being assigned; second, I do not see the necessity (though it would be convenient) for any mode of accurately or impressionistically determining probabilities: aesthetic theory is not exploded by the impossibility of assessing relative quantities of beauty. Above all, I find the reference to making 'the theoretical foundations secure' misconceived. The theoretical foundations of utilitarianism are no more and no less secure for turning the theory into a science. It would not be the theoretical foundations, but the practical consequences of the utilitarian position that would be affected by the systematic assigning of numerical probabilities to future events.

18. Mill, op. cit., p. 275.

19. Quinton (1973) op. cit.; Stace (1937) op. cit.

20. Bentham, op. cit., pp. 30–32. Quinton (1973) op. cit., remarks: 'It has often been pointed out that, if the certainty of a future pleasure or pain is allowed for, its propinquity is irrelevant.' This is true, but since the certainty rating may be low in a particular case, there is a natural tendency to compensate for this by reference to relative propinquity.

21. Perhaps one should say that, in a sense, Mill was embarrassed by the charge! But at any rate he vehemently denied its truth.

22. Bentham, op. cit.

8. Does the Utilitarian Recognize Other Values Besides Happiness?

The issues that have been discussed so far have mainly related to the interpretation, coherence and hence adequacy of utilitarianism as an ethical theory, rather than directly to its claims to being the most plausible or acceptable account of the nature of moral obligation. It is arguable, however, that some resistance to the theory is based less on argument about its internal coherence, than on argument about the extent to which it squares with our preconceptions.[1] This kind of argument may border on rationalization at times, and seem to involve psychological rather than logical objections. It is therefore necessary to point out that, just as Galileo's discoveries were in no way invalidated by the fact that they upset people, so the validity of the utilitarian position is in no way necessarily affected by the fact that it might entail re-thinking some of our current assumptions. Nonetheless, my first step will be an attempt to defuse the situation somewhat, by pointing out that certain popular assumptions about utilitarianism that might suggest it is counter-intuitive, such as that it is a godless doctrine, Philistine, monolithic and inclined to sacrifice the innocent, are false. I shall return in the final chapter to the question of whether utilitarianism, properly understood, is nonetheless an impoverished ethical theory and, if so, whether and in what ways this matters.

It is surprisingly often presumed that utilitarians, because they claim that happiness is the only thing that is good in itself, do not adequately recognize other kinds of value, such as those of aesthetics, social convention and truth. They reduce the value of art, social conventions and truth, the charge runs, to the properties these domains have in respect of contributing to people's enjoyment. Thus for example, Roland Gissing, the popular Canadian painter, known therefore as 'The people's painter', may be reckoned superior to Rembrandt, or the best selling novelist Judith Krantz superior to James Joyce. But this line of reasoning is simply false.

We need to remind ourselves that utilitarianism is an ethical theory, and not an all-encompassing theory of value. It is concerned to offer an explanation of what makes actions right, morally, not with what makes them prudential, aesthetically pleasing, religiously acceptable and so forth. It is only the moral worth of activities that, utilitarians maintain, has to be assessed by reference to the criterion of happiness. This is so, notwithstanding the fact that utilitarians such as Bentham emphasize the psychological claim that pain and pleasure are our sovereign masters in everything.[2] For to believe this, regardless of whether it is true or false, no more prevents one from seeing that aesthetic value must be tied up with the distinctive properties that constitute what we understand as art, than it prevents one from seeing that a good chef or a good cricketer is only partially, if at all, defined in terms of his crowd-pleasing ability. A utilitarian might conceivably (though this is in fact most improbable) want to argue that people ought to aspire to be popular cricketers, trying to build a case to the effect that this would be a productive means to the sum of human happiness. But this can scarcely be understood to suggest that being a good cricketer is to be defined in terms of pleasing the crowd, rather than in terms that derive from the way in which we understand the concept of cricket.

Similarly, utilitarians certainly value truth for, at the very least, they think it important that their doctrine should be recognized as true. But on this issue a certain amount of clarification is needed. First, we have to distinguish between the question of the moral value of telling the truth and the question of the intellectual value of pursuing the truth. The latter derives from, and can readily enough be established by reference to, our understanding of the nature and purpose of rational deliberation. It is a virtue in argument to aim at the truth and to be swayed by considerations of logic, consistency and coherence. But it is not a peculiarly moral virtue: it is a criterion of good scholarship.

Second, when we turn to the issue of telling the truth, we need to consider carefully what this notion comprises. The notion that one ought always to tell the truth might after all be taken to mean anything, from the claim that one should gratuitously reveal everything one knows to everybody concerned, to the claim that one should respond truthfully when asked a direct question. Similarly, one might distinguish between telling a lie and refusing to speak. Again, some conceptions of telling the truth might be so extreme as to classify joking, playfulness, generalizing and so forth as instances of not telling the truth. Given these considerations, one may well imagine that neither utilitarians nor many other people would give unqualified allegiance to the proposition that one ought always in all circumstances to tell the truth, notwithstanding the fact that *prima facie* truth telling is a widely recognized moral value.

If we presume that a narrower conception of truth telling is involved, say, for example, that when one is engaged in serious discussion about matters of importance and professes to be telling the truth, one should do so, it is reasonable to suppose that a utilitarian might as readily regard this as a moral duty as anyone else. That is to say a utilitarian might argue that, as with some rule about promise keeping, a rule to the effect that one should not in such circumstances lie or misdirect would be necessary to attaining the ideal of a happily functioning society. Hence it would be one's duty never to lie or misdirect in such circumstances, whatever the consequences in terms of unhappiness in particular circumstances. Only on those occasions when this rule runs into conflict with another (say the rule relating to promise keeping) as a result of human imperfection and the confusions and shortcomings of real life, would it be morally acceptable (and sometimes morally justified) to break the rule.[3] For the moment, however, the point to stress is that utilitarians may and do value truth as readily as anyone else, and may in principle value truth telling too. The only distinctive thing about them in this context is their belief that, in the latter case, such moral value as telling the truth has is ultimately a matter of its contribution to happiness. In the former case, their reasons for valuing truth are no different from anybody else's.

As Mill observed, in itself utilitarianism implies nothing about religion.[4] It is certainly illegitimate to dismiss it as a 'godless doctrine',[5] but it would be equally wrong to assume it presupposes, requires or is necessarily enhanced by the notion of a God. The fact is that religion and morality are logically distinguishable, as almost all philosophers would now concede, regardless of what contingent links there may be, so that the explication of the one in any terms implies nothing necessarily for the other.[6] It might be suggested that in practice utilitarian ethics are likely to be rather different from Christian ethics (though Mill seems to try to suggest otherwise). But that is not the same thing as denying the existence of a Christian God, let alone others. If it were the case, as it might be, that utilitarianism led to the conclusion that it was sometimes morally legitimate to commit adultery, it is evident that that would be in conflict with at least one view of part of what Christian ethics demands. One could, of course, counter this by pointing out that interpreting Christian ethics is in itself a complex business, that it is not clear that all Christians will take their ethical commandments directly from the New

Testament, that it is not clear why they should, and so forth. But the argument that a philosopher would most naturally turn to would be that, while there may be a God, while He may be as the Christians conceive Him, and while He may want them to refrain from adultery, the fact remains that if that is a moral wish on His part, we still have to explain what makes it moral. Either God sees that it is moral and thus wills it, in which case why it is moral still needs to be explained, or else He is not making a moral demand, or else we assume that moral means 'whatever God wants' which, besides being counter-intuitive, seems to give us (especially atheists) no reason other than fear for doing what is moral.

The fundamental point here is that values in any sphere arise out of the nature of the enterprise in question, as was indicated in the reference to art and cricket above. A good baseball player is defined in terms of the successful execution of certain behaviours that are involved in the definition of the game of baseball. A good Christian is defined by reference to what Christianity involves; a good painting by reference to what art is about; good manners by reference to a particular notion of civilized behaviour. This business of extrapolating evaluative criteria from the nature of the enterprise formally exactly parallels the process that a moral philosopher employs. For what is the utilitarian, in common with other philosophers, doing other than seeking to establish that such and such is morally right, because such and such is the nature of morality?

The utilitarian seeks to establish that the nature of morality, what we understand morality to be, is best understood and most credible (not, by the way, most obviously understood) in terms of the promotion of happiness. The art critic talks about how to understand paintings, and his value judgements are inextricably bound up with his conception of art. It is possible that one who is drawn towards an explanation of morality in utilitarian terms might be similarly drawn to a utilitarian theory of value in the realm of aesthetics, but there is no necessary reason why he should be. He would not be likely, for example, to arrive at a theory of educational success based purely on the criterion of happiness.[7] His utilitarianism might lead him to object to certain particular practices on the grounds that they involve needless suffering, and he might even argue that education ought to be conducted in such a way that it promotes happiness. But there is no reason why he should, and he is not likely to, attempt to conceive of education in terms of people's happiness. And if he recognizes that education is actually concerned with such things as promoting understanding and developing the mind, it is by reference to those criteria that he will judge a good education. Similarly, good medical practice is clearly not to be identified with administering *placebos*. Perhaps making the patient feel happy is a part of good practice, but it is at best a part and, in many instances, whether the patient or anyone else derives happiness, in the long or short term, from medical treatment is simply irrelevant to the question of its quality. Thus, while a person might hold a utilitarian theory of aesthetics, which is to say, roughly, the view that aesthetic quality resides in the tendency to provide enjoyment, whether this was a plausible theory would have to be determined by examination of the nature of art and aesthetics and, as such, would be quite distinct from the question of the plausibility of a utilitarian theory of ethics.

There is however a different question to consider, and that is whether what may be agreed to be true art and, as such, rich in aesthetic quality defined without reference to happiness, has moral worth. This question should also be distinguished from yet a third, which is whether one type of value, such as aesthetic value, is more or less important than another type, such as economic value, or indeed moral value. I shall consider both these questions *pari passu*.

In general, the question of whether one kind of value is more valuable than another seems to me to be one that we should acknowledge we cannot satisfactorily answer, and had therefore better not ask. It must be the case that we cannot answer it, because questions of relative worth presuppose common criteria of evaluation (that is why you cannot compare chalk with cheese, except in respect of their use for some common purpose such as providing sustenance). But we do not have a general theory of value involving a set of common criteria, in the light of which we may consider the general relative worth of beauty and profit. One could devise one, and indeed some people have done so. (Not infrequently, and somewhat ironically in view of these remarks, people have from time to time proposed to set up utilitarianism as a general theory of value. But that is another story, and as such it requires a separate argument.) I do not here claim that it would be impossible to convincingly establish such a general theory of value, although I think it would. I merely observe that, until such a general theory is accepted, it is futile to compare apples and oranges.

It is certainly not my contention that all value is reducible to considerations of happiness, and that we can therefore in principle establish that, say, economic value is superior to aesthetic value, or that a Rembrandt, though superior as art, is inferior in general terms to the comic strip Peanuts. Those who maintain that all value judgements are simply a matter of opinion are plainly incorrect; it is an objective fact, for example, that Donald Bradman was a better cricketer than I, as is easily enough shown through an understanding of what cricket is; similarly, provided we have an understanding of what art involves, we are able to make certain objective judgements, however difficult they may sometimes be to discern. But judgements about the relative value of economic and aesthetic value must be a matter of opinion, until such time as we are persuaded to adopt some particular overarching theory of value.

The only *prima facie* exception to the above is ethical value. It might be argued that ethical values are necessarily superior to other kinds of value, because ethics is about what ought to be done. It would seem odd to say 'this action is morally right, but that is less important than the fact that that action is expedient', in a way that it does not seem odd to say 'this is aesthetically superior, but that is better entertainment; I value the latter more'. However, despite the *prima facie* oddity, I am not convinced that it makes much sense to regard even moral value as a superior kind of value to others. Many years ago, a favourite question at the University of Oxford was 'why ought I to be moral?', usually receiving an answer along the lines 'the nature of morality is such that it doesn't make sense to recognize an obligation as moral, and yet not see a reason for complying with it. To recognize moral obligation is to see a reason for action'. As far as it goes, that is correct. But the matter becomes different once a particular moral theory has been expounded. 'Why should I promote the general happiness?' for example, whatever else it is, is not an incoherent question, and does not rule out the possibility of answering 'I do not see any compelling reason to do so'. Certainly, the statement 'I believe this action to be right, because it is productive of happiness, but I live for art, placing it even above morality, and therefore will not perform the action', seems to me strange rather than absurd.

But whatever the case may be here, the more immediate point is that the utilitarian moral theory does not commit one either to a general utilitarian theory of value or a utilitarian aesthetic theory of value, and the question may therefore reasonably be asked as to whether various pursuits, such as the arts, often taken to be intrinsically valuable, have any worth in the moral scale of things. On most ethical views the answer would seem to be straightforwardly 'no'. There is nothing in Christian ethics, Kantian ethics, or Aristotelian ethics, for instance, that would lead one to suppose that a society would be morally better or worse for the presence of art. This is not to deny that art might serve certain moral purposes. Aristotle, for example, clearly thought that the cathartic effect he attributed to tragedy had desirable moral consequences.[8] And any ethical theorist might see opportunities for art to promote morality. But our concern here is with the rather different idea that the mere existence of good art is a moral good. G.E. Moore[9] believed this, though he did not offer anything more than an appeal to intuition to support the belief. But utilitarianism does at least allow the possibility of arguing that art and certain other definable pursuits, such as rational inquiry, do have a specifically moral value. And I believe that the argument has strong plausibility.

The manner of the argument here will come as no surprise to the reader, and I do not intend to try to make my case so much as to sketch it out. All that one would need to convince oneself of would be the contingent claims that art is in some clear sense a civilizing influence, and that people thus civilized are in a stronger position to achieve the ideal. This does not imply any claim to the effect that if only Inuits would take in a bit of Beethoven they would be the happier for it. The utilitarian view, as has been explicitly argued, allows for many different species of, and ways of achieving, happiness, and hence for various morally acceptable modes of societal existence. Furthermore, while one may believe in a general concept of art that is not culture-bound, and in objective judgements about art, this need not involve a denial of the fact, to which any historian of art would have to accede, that there are many distinct types, species or forms of art. My suggestion that art, by being a civilizing influence, may have moral value does not therefore involve me in a wild ethnocentric claim, for I am not committing myself to any particular culture's species of art, nor to any particular culture's sources of pleasure.

The suggestion is based on contingent and generalized assumptions about the pleasure to be derived from a developed aesthetic sense and about features of societies that have some such sensibility. For example, aesthetic pleasure, experience suggests, is high in fecundity, purity, certainty and propinquity, to refer again to Bentham's terminology, and a strong case could be made for saying that, historically, societies that do not value the aesthetic also tend towards being relatively unpleasant, even as judged by members of the society. The claim would remain unmoved by rejoinders about culture-mad Nazis, with the implication that there is one example of a society of misery that nonetheless valued art. In the first place, one could reasonably argue that the Nazi hierarchy did not have aesthetic sensibility. Enjoying Brahms, collecting paintings, attending Bayreuth and so forth, which we know that Hitler's circle did do, are not to be identified with appreciating a work of art in aesthetic terms, which we might have little independent reason to assume they did. In the second place, it would make no material difference to the present argument if they did have genuine aesthetic appreciation, for the claim is not that culture leads necessarily to happiness (let alone to morality). The claim is that there is reason to suppose that a society would, and evidence to support the idea that societies do, by and large, benefit from a developed sense of art, in terms of happiness, which is a good.

However, my concern here has not been to establish the superiority of high culture over low, nor even to insist that the former is necessary to the happiness of a society. My point has been that the suggestion that utilitarians necessarily see no value in art *qua* art is false, and the suggestion that they would see no moral importance in promoting art is logically conceivable, but highly implausible. Taking account of both points, this means that by and large there is reason to suppose that we are the beneficiaries of high culture in terms of happiness but, even if we were not, there is no reason why a utilitarian should not value art. In order to have a reason for according moral value to art, we would not need to establish (what is certainly false) that it invariably leads to happiness, nor should we be required to 'prove', in some inappropriately scientific sense of that word, that it does anything. We need only to argue that it seems reasonable to suppose, given what we know about human beings, the nature of art and aesthetic response, and various societies, that one contribution to the ideal would be to develop a widespread aesthetic sensitivity.

If it were to be asked why the utilitarian would not in that case prefer to promote the popular culture enshrined in television and what G.H. Bantock once called 'the ephemeral products of the railway bookstall',[10] the answer is twofold. First, the utilitarian does not necessarily have anything against popular culture (which, for simplicity, I am here distinguishing from art or high culture by stipulation). If it makes people happy, at no cost to the community in terms of happiness, taking into account all the aspects of calculation we have referred to, then it contributes to the good, and the utilitarian is in favour of it. But, second, the point of my initial suggestion here was that, on reflection, it may seem that, however much certain individuals do enjoy popular culture in this society at present, the likelihood is that the community as a whole would come much nearer the ideal, if individuals could be brought to experience the same intensity of pleasure in high culture. This would be because of the likelihood of a high culture that is appreciated producing more happiness on balance, when we take into account duration, certainty, extent, propinquity, fecundity and purity of pleasure.

Some, who have experience of both high and popular culture, to reintroduce an argument which it is hoped will no longer be misinterpreted,[11] might go further and suggest that even the intensity of pleasure gained from the former is greater. It may be acknowledged that, if it were established that art did absolutely nothing for us in respect of happiness, the utilitarian would have no moral concern at all about whether it flourished or died; and, if it were established that it was a strong force for unhappiness, the utilitarian would have moral objection to the concern for art. But the latter contention is implausible, and the former, though scarcely less so, would in any case not prevent us from valuing art, albeit not for moral reasons. In point of fact the utilitarian, unlike other moralists, can without difficulty explain why he believes that art is a force for the moral good, since it clearly is a potential source of happiness.

To return for a moment to the question of truth, we can see that, in exactly the same way, while commitment to truth is not a moral value but a commitment to the canons of rational inquiry as a necessary part of engaging in such inquiry, a case can be made for according moral value to the latter activity on utilitarian grounds. In terms of an intellectual inquiry such as I am now engaged in, it is necessary that I should seek to deceive neither myself nor anybody else, that I should acknowledge the truths I encounter, that I should try to avoid contradiction, ambiguity and incoherence, that I should tease out logical implications and take account of evidence, and so forth. It is plainly culpable to proceed as Cyril Burt is alleged to have done (cooking his data), to bow down to ideological pressure, or to provide socially acceptable science (meaning to confine oneself to questions and answers that do not upset people) rather than scientifically acceptable science. To do such things is to engage in bad rational inquiry. But this is not in itself a moral use of the word 'bad'. The commitment to truth, honesty and the like is the result of what we understand by rational inquiry. Terms such as 'scholarship', 'research' and 'academic' are defined by reference to notions such as truth and logical coherence. One is not doing philosophy if one is not being truthful.

But while the commitment to truth is part of the nature of the activity, rather than an independent moral value, one can accord moral value to the business of inquiring into the truth. Fortunately, there is not a lot that I need to do here, for the argument for so doing has been provided by Mill at his most convincing and his most unequivocally utilitarian. The pursuit of truth is to be morally valued without qualification, not, as some wrongly interpret him, for its own sake, but on grounds of utility.

Mill, as most readers will recall, argues unambiguously for absolute freedom of speech and expression.[12] He does this on the four grounds:

- that the suppression of any opinion might be a suppression of the truth;
- that the suppression of a falsehood may work against the interests of truth;
- that the suppression of a truth prevents it being challenged, however erroneously, and thus debilitates a thorough understanding of it; and
- that debilitated understanding of truths leads in the long run to substantive changes in our perception of the truth.

The whole argument is evidently predicated on the value of truth. But it is necessary to distinguish between valuing something because it is always in itself good and valuing something because it is necessary to the promotion of the good. Furthermore, in the latter case, it is necessary to distinguish further between valuing something because it consistently promotes the good and valuing something because, while it does not consistently promote the good, its capacity to promote the good is dependent on it being untrammelled. This latter distinction has already been drawn attention to in discussing act- and rule-utilitarianism, where it was pointed out that the rule-utilitarian may value a rule such as 'Do not kill', and demand that it be followed without exception, even while acknowledging that on particular occasions to break the rule would be more productive of happiness.

The trouble is that a phrase such as 'absolute value' blurs these distinctions. Mill (and any other comprehending utilitarian) does accord absolute value to truth, in the sense that he believes the pursuit of truth should always be our concern and should never be interfered with. But he does not, and cannot in consistency, regard it as an absolute value in the sense of something that is morally good in itself. For the utilitarian, only happiness has that quality; but the pursuit of truth can be regarded as an absolute value in the other sense, even when we add, what is perfectly obvious, that on specific occasions the pursuit of truth will lead directly to suffering and dismay. The argument, surely one of the most convincing in the utilitarian domain, is that it is logically inconceivable that a society should find the way either to attaining or to maintaining the ideal of full happiness for all, without respect for truth, because even in ideal circumstances to be enmeshed requires the ability to control and predict circumstances, which presupposes a grasp of the truth. In our attempts to attain the ideal in an imperfect world, it is even more apparent that our chances of happiness are tied up with our ability to get things right, in the sense of to understand the truth about things. [13]

In discussing truth, we have moved on from consideration of whether the utilitarian may recognize other, non-moral, values such as aesthetic value, to the question of whether he recognizes other moral values besides happiness. The foregoing discussion makes it clear that the criticism that utilitarianism denies that anything but happiness has moral value, and is therefore to be rejected because there are other values besides happiness, is doubly problematic.

In the first place, the first part of the criticism is false. As we have seen, not only does the utilitarian not deny that there are other moral values besides happiness; he does not even deny that there are other moral values that, in some sense of the words, have 'absolute validity'. Thus, for example, the utilitarian believes in the moral value of impartiality, the pursuit of truth, freedom of expression, promise keeping, friendship and telling the truth. The argument for according them moral value is indeed ultimately based on reference to considerations of happiness. But that does not prevent us from regarding them as morally valuable. In the case of impartiality we even have what some would be pleased to call an independent principle. But that is neither here nor there. The point is that any ethical theory must accept the principle of impartiality, since any ethical theory is concerned with treating people as they ought to be treated, which means treating them the same except where there is good reason to treat them differently, which is the essence of the formal principle of impartiality. The utilitarian is distinctive only in locating 'good reasons' by reference to happiness. The value placed on the pursuit of truth and freedom of speech may, as we have seen, be classified as absolute, in the sense that the utilitarian believes that neither should ever be interfered with. The value of promise keeping might or might not convincingly be seen as absolute, but it will certainly be valued. (I incline to the view that a qualified rule about the obligation to keep promises could be defended as absolute.) The values of friendship and truth telling might likewise be regarded as absolute, with or without qualification. But whatever the final determination of what exactly is being valued, with what qualification, and whether absolutely or not, it is certain that these all represent moral values for the utilitarian.

Second, even if this were not the case, it would not *ipso facto* follow that utilitarianism was to be rejected. Here we revert to the issue discussed above in Chapter 3. An ethical theory is not to be discredited simply by observing that it challenges some of our cherished opinions. If it has no point of contact with any aspect of our moral understanding, we shall obviously reject it, and reasonably so, on the grounds that it does not seem to be a theory about what we understand as moral conduct. But when, as in this case, that is far from being so, we have to accept the challenge and consider anew whether we can either fault the theory as it is presented, in terms of clarity and coherence, or produce an equally strong or stronger argument to defend those assumptions that are now threatened. If utilitarianism leads to the conclusion that our sexual *mores* have no particular moral sanction, and if that offends our moral sensibility, the onus is on us to produce a coherent defence of those *mores* in convincing moral terms.

The above paragraphs are important as an antidote to attempts to refute utilitarianism simply by mistakenly assuming that it leads to no respect or love for various things generally thought to be valuable or important.[14] However, there is one aspect of the matter we have not directly faced. That is the charge that utilitarianism does not allow one to regard such things as friendship, truth telling or promise keeping as morally good in themselves. That is of course true. The premiss all along has been that happiness alone is morally good in itself, and certainly my remarks above are based on the argument that friendship, the pursuit of truth, promise keeping, etc. are desirable because in some way or other they contribute to the ideal.

So what does one say to the correct observation that utilitarianism denies that such things as friendship are morally good in themselves? One goes back to the beginning. One says, yes, that was explicitly stated at the outset. Furthermore, it was pointed out that it seems unintelligible to deny that happiness is morally good in itself, but not to deny that anything else is; and in fact the alleged intrinsic value of everything else, including friendship, has at one time or another been seriously challenged. Following that, we have shown how utilitarianism explains and makes sense of some of our moral assumptions, and reasonably rejects others. We are in the process of showing that, as a whole, the theory makes sense. To throw in this hypothetical list of other things allegedly morally good in themselves is certainly to beg the very question we are examining. In response one has to ask, weakly, what is the argument for assuming the intrinsic moral value of these other things, and strongly, are they truly morally good in and of themselves? I don't know of a convincing answer to either question.

The value of friendship and the pursuit of truth are not in dispute. Nor is our commitment to them. Nor is their status as absolute values. The only thing in dispute is whether something such as friendship is good in and of itself. But the question that insistently arises here is: what is actually meant by the phrase 'good in and of itself'? In the case of happiness, sense accrues to the phrase because it does not appear to make sense to ask for what further reason one values happiness. One does not value it for some extrinsic reason, such as that it will make one rich or famous. One just values it. It is meaningless to ask why. Now, one can understand the psychological state of valuing friendship in and of itself, as one can understand those who believe in the idea of 'my country right or wrong'. But that is not an argument, nor an appropriate kind of consideration. It is not in dispute that different people just like, value or feel committed to various things. What is in dispute is whether it is intelligible to say of something that one can logically question the inherent value of, and that people have been known either not to value or to value only for extrinsic reasons, that it nonetheless has intrinsic value. Despite Moore's convictions, it is plainly intelligible to think that a world might be morally good without friendship. It is perfectly in order to ask someone why he values friendship. And not only is there no obvious argument to establish that friendship does have intrinsic value (the best arguments, such as those of Aristotle,[15] being manifestly extrinsic), but it seems very convincing to maintain (at the level of our current sentiments) that there might be circumstances in which friendship was a thoroughly bad thing.

Be that as it may, to discredit the utilitarian account, which does after all explain the fact of many of our various moral commitments, and which does not deny various other moral and non-moral values, it is incumbent on critics to establish in some way or other that something other than happiness does have moral value in and of itself, and is necessarily good. If it is the case, as I believe, that this is something that has not been, and shows no sign of being, successfully done, then utilitarianism is emerging as the only plausible ethical theory. 'Plausible' is not 'proven', but, as we have remarked before, it may be all that we can expect.

Notes

1. On this issue see also Chapters 2, 3 and 5.
2. J. Bentham, *The Principles of Morals and Legislation* (1948), p. 1.
3. The position might be: it is one's duty always to tell the truth; therefore one ought always to do so; it is right always to do so. If that is the case, according to the argument I am presenting, it can never be justifiable to tell a lie, except when the imperfect conditions of life force one into the dilemma of making a choice between the demands of this rule and another rule. In such a case, one is morally justified in abiding by the rule that does on this occasion lead to the most happiness all told. Moral commendation, however, will be accorded to anyone who sincerely seeks to do what is justified, whether they succeed or not.
4. J.S. Mill, *Utilitarianism*, p. 273.
5. Ibid., p. 273, and e.g. p. 268, 'In the golden rule of Jesus of Nazareth, we read the complete spirit of the ethics of utility.'
6. 'Others besides utilitarians have been of the opinion ... that we need a doctrine of ethics, carefully followed out, to interpret to us the will of God.' (J.S. Mill, *Utilitarianism* op. cit., p. 273) Of course, as Quinton, *Utilitarian Ethics* (1973), has pointed out, there are respects in which Christian ethics is decidedly unutilitarian: its conception of happiness is non-hedonistic, and its view of the status of moral principles as the commands of God is distinctive. But utilitarianism incorporated the altruistic and benevolent content of morality that could be said to stem from Christian ethics.
7. See, for example, R. Barrow, *Plato, Utilitarianism and Education* (1975) or *Common Sense and the Curriculum* (1976). Contrast Amy Gutmann, 'What's the use of going to school? The problem of education in utilitarianism and rights theories', in A. Sen and B. Williams, eds, *Utilitarianism and Beyond* (1982) who seems confusedly to assume that utilitarians turn directly to happiness as a standard 'by which to determine what and how to teach children' (p. 261) and who, equally off beam, queries 'how is society to prepare children for the pursuit of their own self-defined happiness?' (p. 262) As Smart, op. cit., observes 'Even the most hedonistic schoolmaster would prefer to see his boys enjoying poetry and mathematics, rather than neglecting these arts for the pleasures of marbles or the tuckshop'. (p. 18)
8. See Aristotle, *The Poetics*.
9. G.E. Moore, *Principia Ethica* (1903), esp. chapter 6.
10. G.H. Bantock, *Education in an Industrial Society* (1963).
11. See above, Chapter 7, where it was pointed out that experience of both A and B, while not being sufficient, is a necessary condition of judging their respective merits in respect of pleasure.
12. Mill, J.S., *On Liberty* in *Utilitarianism*, op. cit., chapter 2.
13. Harsanyi (1982) defends utilitarianism, but does 'not think it covers all morality'. Specifically he thinks that it does not cover the 'duty to seek the truth and to accept the truth as far as it can be established – regardless of any possible positive or negative social utility this truth may have'. (p. 62) It would help if we were to clearly distinguish between the 'possible utility' a truth may have, and the 'possible utility' the pursuit of truth may have. My position, of course, involves reference to the latter rather than the former, and I find it hard to conceive of the pursuit of truth being separable from positive utility. However, I am more puzzled by why Harsanyi needs to see 'intellectual honesty' as a *moral* obligation, if it is to be placed beyond utility, which is treated by him as the criterion of (other) moral behaviour. As I have suggested, while its utility can scarcely be in doubt, there is no reason why it should not be valued as an intellectual virtue in its own right.

14. According to Mill, Utilitarianism 'maintains not only that virtue is to be desired, but that it is to be desired disinterestedly, for itself.' (*Utilitarianism*, p. 289)
15. On friendship, see Aristotle, *The Nicomachean Ethics*, Books viii and ix.

9. Will the Utilitarian Accept Scapegoats and Will he Perform Acts of Supererogation?

For a long time, a favourite topic of debate in arguments about utilitarianism has been the scapegoat. Utilitarians, it is often claimed, are in principle willing to sacrifice innocent persons for the good of the greater number. This is felt to be self-evidently unacceptable, and hence a blow to utilitarianism. We are invited, for example, to consider the case of a group of individuals shipwrecked on a raft. Circumstances are such that they cannot all survive, but, if one of their number were to be thrown overboard, the others would be able to survive. The utilitarian, it is claimed, would have to approve of this act.

Great ingenuity goes into such a debate, on both sides. Suppose, for instance, we add the consideration that in either case it is only an expectation or a probability that the outcome will be as envisaged. On the face of it, that might give the utilitarian the opportunity of arguing that the act would not clearly be productive in terms of happiness, and hence he would not have to see it as justified. 'Ah,' comes the response, 'but it is always the case, strictly speaking, that outcomes are uncertain. If that is the line of defence, does it not imply that we can never be sure of good reason for acting in a certain way, on utilitarian terms?' Perhaps it makes a difference if the people concerned recognize their problem and agree to draw straws for the role of victim, suggests the utilitarian. 'Perhaps it does, and it may be conceded that utilitarianism does not necessarily imply summary action, and indeed the claims of happiness might seem to require that people come to see the need for certain actions, since they will then experience less resentment. But, on the other hand, why should people agree to abide by a decision just because it is arrived at through discussion, and how does this alter the fact that the theory may condone sending an innocent person to his death?' That is misleading, comes the quick response. The theory does not condone putting an innocent person to death, period. It condones (or may condone) putting someone to death in very unusual and awkward circumstances, which is rather different.

'Be that as it may, the utilitarian is prepared to let an innocent suffer for the sake of others.' Well, is it not the case that others are prepared to let innocent beings suffer for the sake of others, as when they subject monkeys to cruel experimentation and death? 'But they are not humans.' No, but they are innocent and they suffer. Anyway, it is not clear that utilitarians have to accept the hypothesis as presented. They might argue that if one accepted the propriety of throwing someone overboard, that is to propagate the idea that sacrificing a member of a group is morally acceptable, and acceptance of that idea would lead to much uncertainty and anxiety in the world at large. On those grounds we need a rule forbidding this kind of conduct. 'But on those terms you would need rules forbidding anything the possibility of which tended to cause unease. And the point remains that, if happiness is all that matters, sooner or later the determination to provide as much happiness as possible in the world is going to lead to the sanctioning of behaviour that we do not and should not condone.'

Some of the elements in this kind of debate are not directly relevant to the question of the plausibility of utilitarianism, because they are equally problematic for other ethical theories. The question of whether it makes a moral difference if all the people involved agree to a course of action, for example, is one that faces us all. As is the question of whether there is an inconsistency between our professed moral views and our treatment of animals. A utilitarian, I believe, must be concerned about causing suffering to animals; but one does not have to be a utilitarian to share that concern, and it is at least arguable that those who accept certain behaviour towards animals ought likewise to accept it in respect of human beings. If it is morally acceptable to have the dog put down because it is old and feeble and we want to go abroad, why is it not morally acceptable to practise euthanasia on people in certain circumstances? I am not suggesting necessarily that it is, nor that there are not arguments to establish a morally significant difference between the two cases. I am merely observing that the question of whether it is sometimes justifiable to take an innocent life is not peculiar to utilitarianism. Even the business of trying to calculate consequences may be problematic for other, not necessarily consequentialist, theories. For example many people, who would not necessarily see themselves as consequentialists, value freedom, but have to calculate in particular circumstances what the suppression or defence of a particular freedom would lead to.

Nor is it peculiar to utilitarianism that it may sometimes condone acts which clearly contain an element of the morally bad, even on its own terms. If we assume that the utilitarian would condone the sacrifice of the innocent, even he would feel that the suffering of the individual was in itself bad, and he might also regard the act of throwing someone overboard as wrong, considered as a type of act, but justified in these particular circumstances. But other ethical theories too face this kind of tension. Thus, liberalism with its plurality of ultimate principles, such as freedom, equality and, very often, happiness, or Kantian ethics with its list of specific injunctions, such as always keep a promise, never tell a lie and never ignore others in distress, may both face clashes of principle. There will be situations, if we are realistic, in which we cannot both satisfy our commitment to freedom and serve the demands of equality. There will be occasions when telling the truth or keeping a promise will involve us in ignoring someone's distress. In such cases, whatever we do, we do something that ideally we ought not to do, just as, the utilitarian might say, he has to do when faced with the situation on the raft.

The fact is that there are problems in life, which strictly speaking are soluble, though it may be difficult to solve them, and there are dilemmas. Dilemmas are, by definition, situations in which one cannot solve the problem; one cannot do right. And life, I repeat, presents them from time to time. That a theory cannot solve them is not therefore to be held against it. The intuitionist is not discredited by the observation that sometimes he must either sacrifice beauty or people's happiness, both of which, we may suppose, he values. The Ten Commandments are not shown to be false, because it is possible that keeping the Sabbath day holy will conflict with honouring one's father and mother. So, even if the utilitarian were forced to accept that in certain circumstances he would condone an act that contains an element of wrongness, he should not on that account be considered to have been refuted.[1]

However, it may be said that, while it is true that the utilitarian cannot be criticized for accepting the necessity of some wrongness in an action on a particular occasion, the point is being missed. That point is that utilitarianism would not see anything wrong in this action. Certainly, other ethical theories may have to countenance or accept clashes of principle, and the consequent inevitability of some acts of promise breaking, telling a lie or whatever. But they do not claim that such acts are morally justified; they recognize them for what they are: inevitable and unfortunate. The utilitarian, by contrast, maintains that if the sum of happiness is enhanced, the action is right. Therefore he must be maintaining that sacrificing an innocent person may be a morally acceptable action. This claim now needs to be examined.

Let us consider the example again. And let us concede straightaway that act-utilitarianism is open to the objection raised. An act-utilitarian, faced with the situation on the raft, can be rapidly brought to conclude that it is morally right to throw one of the members overboard. For it requires little ingenuity to describe the situation in such a way that the interests of happiness are best served by so doing. And the act-utilitarian has no recourse to arguments concerning the ideal. His thesis is such that the rightness of actions is tied to them being, on each particular occasion, conducive to the most happiness possible. If he were to attempt to argue that one should do that which would on ideal terms produce most happiness his position becomes unintelligible, for the point about particular occasions is that they are not ideal. Of course, even the act-utilitarian will say that, in so far as the scapegoat suffers, or his family suffer indirectly, or his fellows experience feelings of guilt, that is to be deplored and constitutes a diminution of good. But he will have to concede that it is conceivable that such considerations should be outweighed by the happiness of the survivors and their friends and families, and that is sufficient to establish that it may be a right act. It is true also that, with no other principles to refer to, he cannot say 'well I know it was wrong – but I had no choice'. If doing that which, of available options, is most likely to increase the sum of happiness is morally right, then such an action as this may be right.

This conclusion should, however, be construed as another indication of the shortcomings of act-utilitarianism. Not only does it lead to a conclusion that is counter-intuitive (for we do not accept that it can be morally right to kill a person in such circumstances, although we might condone it), it also leads to a conclusion that anybody who grasps the fundamental point about utilitarianism must find wrong-headed. The fundamental point is that, if happiness is the only good, then the ideal must be complete happiness for all, and the right is what is conducive to that ideal. A world in which people are at liberty to make up their own minds on such issues and in which, where the calculation is correct, the act is morally right, is not a world in which the ideal can be attained. A society could not be completely happy, if some individuals might legitimately be dispatched on an arbitrary basis.

We therefore turn to a consideration of the example in terms of rule-utilitarianism. It is evident that the difficulties of calculation, the enormity of the consequences, and concern for the peace of mind of individuals all conspire to make this the kind of situation which requires the clear governance of rules. Granted that there have been societies in which individuals accepted their role as human sacrifices, we are not inclined to suppose that people in general would choose to live in a situation where there is nothing to stand in the way of their being sacrificed for the sake of the happiness of others.

Precisely what the rule should be would go beyond the scope of the present argument. But it is clear that some of the more extreme forms of the scapegoat argument would not get off the ground on rule-utilitarian terms. The maintenance of happiness requires a degree of predictability and conformity, as a consequence of the logical nature of happiness and the actual nature of human beings. It is necessary that we should all drive on the same side of the road, for instance, and in various other respects have similar, or, at least, compatible, expectations and behaviours. It is necessary that we should have some reasonable idea of the consequences of our actions. It is necessary that we should not feel insecure or anxious, and therefore that we should have some idea of what we can count on and certainty that various particular unpleasant fates will not befall us. Thus we must have rules, and thus it is by reference to such considerations that we determine what rules to have.

As in the case of the more specific act of killing (I am assuming that throwing a man overboard is not quite the same thing), a rule against sacrificing innocent people in the interests of the majority might conceivably be qualified. For example, one might feel that there are important differences between the raft example and the example of the need to shoot an innocent person in time of war in order to prevent the killing of several hundred equally innocent people. The latter might possibly be regarded as morally justifiable by the rule-utilitarian, but so it might by many other ethical theories; whether it is in fact is another question, on any view, and one that I do not intend to pursue here. All that is required for the moment is to establish that the sort of example that involves what is conceded to be morally wrong would be covered by a rule, with or without qualifications, on rule-utilitarian terms. And so it would, for it is inconceivable that in ideal circumstances the idea that one innocent person's happiness might reasonably be sacrificed for the sake of an overall gain in happiness should be other than detrimental to the happiness of the community. One needs a rule against such practice (notwithstanding the fact that on particular occasions the practice would produce a net gain in happiness), as surely as one needs some kind of rule against killing.

The same conclusion may be arrived at by recollecting that utilitarianism is understood to incorporate a principle of impartiality. This formal distributive principle gains its substance from happiness: it is in respect of happiness that all are to be treated alike unless relevant reasons for discrimination can be provided. Such reasons can be provided as, for instance, in the case where an individual forfeits his right to equal consideration by his criminal and immoral conduct. A utilitarian can as easily justify imprisoning the thief and the thug as any other system of thought. Certain rules of conduct are determined by the theory, and the issue of paying a penalty is determined by the nature of rules: rules that people are allowed to break with impunity are not rules. But in this case we are dealing with innocent persons, persons who by definition have not forfeited their right to impartial consideration. That being the case, it cannot be morally right to sacrifice the interests of one for no relevant reason.

In short, it is not the case that the rule-utilitarian would regard the act of throwing an innocent person overboard as morally right. It offends against the basic tenet that all are to count equally in respect of happiness, and it is a type of action (the arbitrary sacrifice of one innocent for the sake of the happiness of others) that one must have a rule against, if one is attempting to envisage a society that allows of complete happiness for all. One might add that even on the more traditional but mistaken assumption that one sets about devising rules in the context of the actual world, as opposed to the conceivable and in principle attainable ideal world, the case would probably not be different. Even as things are, that is to say, it is reasonable to surmise that in the long run, taking all factors relevant to estimating happiness into account, we gain in terms of happiness from a rule forbidding such an action.

As has already been indicated, it is possible to redraw the example in such a way that it is not clear that it should be covered by a rule forbidding the action. If we imagine that one of the survivors on a raft is not quite so innocent, or if we imagine that the survival of some is necessary to the survival of an entire community, or if we imagine that one individual is going to die anyway within six months, one might be tempted to reconsider the case. But then, when we produce such particular and extreme possibilities, anybody working on any theory might be tempted to rethink the situation. Certainly one does not have to be a utilitarian to take seriously the possibility that, for instance, in such extreme circumstances one might throw a known murderer overboard or an unconscious and terminally ill survivor. Conversely, it is by no means certain that a rule-utilitarian would. Whether he would belongs to argument within utilitarianism rather than about its plausibility as a theory.

It is important to remember that the particular argument we are concerned with here is one that seeks to show that utilitarianism leads to intuitively unacceptable consequences. But, as I hope is by now clear, that is not the case in respect of rule-utilitarianism interpreted in terms of the ideal. The only position that can maintain the view that it leads to unacceptable consequences is an ethical theory that asserts simply and categorically that under any circumstances at all to throw anybody off the raft is wrong. But simply to hold that view is to beg the question at issue rather than to argue about it; it is not a view that actually many people would hold; and, in fact, it is possible that a rule-utilitarian might come to the same conclusion.

Indeed, ironically perhaps, utilitarianism might be one of the few theories that could provide a plausible argument for such a conclusion. For most of us, the example of the survivors on a raft, if drawn in careful detail, can represent a real moral dilemma. That is to say, the situation can be described in such a way that, while on the one hand we are repulsed by the very idea of sacrificing one life for the sake of others, on the other hand we sense a case for doing so. As I have been at pains to stress, for most of us, on any ethical view, there are such cases of insoluble conflict to be faced. On other views it is impossible to see how one could provide even a rational argument for acting in one way rather than another. But the utilitarian could at least try to mount a rational argument to the effect that, however understandable and however justified in terms of immediate happiness throwing an individual overboard would be, we cannot countenance such an act, taking into account the long-term and indirect consequences of taking that position. Alternatively, he could argue in favour of the action. Whatever his conclusion, which, as I say, is not our immediate concern, he does at least have a mechanism or procedure for coping with the situation. And, in the terms outlined in Chapter 2, his conclusion would represent a course of action that was morally intentioned and that might in principle be morally justified, in a dilemma where there is no possibility of carrying out our duty or doing what we know to be unequivocally right. I do not say that such an argument would necessarily be persuasive for either course of action but it would at least be a coherent and respectable kind of argument.

However, the previous paragraph takes us beyond our present concern. Utilitarianism, in common with certain other theories, such as Ross's intuitionism, but by no means all, does enable us to attempt to work out what is morally justifiable in a systematic and rational way. But, as was pointed out at the outset, the credibility of a theory is not to be reckoned by reference to such a feature, for all that it presents a bonus that will recommend itself to some. The credibility of the theory, in this instance, is to be assessed in terms of whether it leads to self-evidently unacceptable claims. But it does not. Utilitarianism can very convincingly formulate certain rules that would cover and forbid certain kinds of action that the scapegoat argument is designed to show it would morally approve.

It is conceded that situations may be envisaged in which rule-utilitarianism does not seem to give clear guidance. With time and patience some of these problems might be resolved by conscientous thinking within the utilitarian framework: a morally justified form of conduct would be established, notwithstanding the fact that there would be an acknowledged admixture of moral badness in the action. (What I refer to as 'morally justified', it will be recalled, is defined in terms of admixture.) If, on occasion, we cannot resolve the problem, even on rule-utilitarian terms, we have a moral dilemma. But moral dilemmas are a feature of human existence. We cannot wish them away and, by defini-tion, no system of ethics can cope with them. They therefore represent no particular reproach to utilitarianism. Furthermore, faced with a genuine dilemma, the utilitarian can at least proceed in a morally commendable way, by sincerely aiming at as much happiness for all concerned as he can, albeit we know, and he knows, that he will make an imperfect job of it.[2]

No more will be said about the scapegoat. I turn from consideration of the complaint that utilitarians would do things that they clearly should not, to consideration of the claim that they should do a great deal more in the way of promoting the good than they generally seem to suppose. If striving towards a reasonably clear ideal is what we ought to be doing, then ought we not, rather more specifically, to be out in the world taking positive steps to promote the ideal?[3]

If the promotion of happiness (in the sense and in the manner that has been elucidated) is our moral duty; if, that is to say, we are doing right when we are acting in ways that, within the restraints of the possible, are most conducive to the ideal, does it not follow that we should be travelling the globe doing things that can reasonably be said to yield large happiness dividends, rather than sitting at home selecting actions from a limited range of options all of which affect only a few people? Is it not evident that, while taking my family out for a picnic is preferable to indulging myself alone at a movie, neither comes near the advantage to the world of volunteering for the Peace Corps, in utilitarian terms? Is it not my moral duty to stop living as I do, even allowing that I bring happiness to myself, my family and friends, and get out into the world to make a more dramatic and positive contribution to the diminution of world suffering? In short, is it not the case that I should engage in what are termed acts of supererogation? (that is, strictly speaking, 'good works beyond what God requires', and thus, by extension, taking active steps to find good to do).[4]

This, I frankly admit, I find a difficult question on any ethical view. Certainly, it seems odd on the face of it to say an ideal world would be one in which all were equally and fully happy, and that therefore one ought to do that which will maximize happiness, but then not go further and say that therefore one ought to seek out ways to devote one's life to promoting that happiness. However, by the same token, it seems odd to say that an ideal world would be one that fully realized Christian values, therefore one ought to be Christian, but then not go further and say that therefore one ought to give away one's worldly goods and become a priest. More generally, it seems odd to say that this is the moral good which, by definition, we want to maximize, and yet hold back from any attempt to contribute in a decisive way to the promotion of that good.[5]

There is, of course, some difference between saying that one ought to do X (e.g., promote happiness) and saying that one ought to proselytize for the doing of X (e.g., promote the promotion of happiness). Yet that distinction is not necessarily at issue. Perhaps one does not have a moral duty to preach for happiness, but still does have one to spread more happiness than we typically try to do. However, despite misgivings, I intend to argue that we are not morally obliged to choose a way of life that is predicated on the positive advancement of as much human happiness as we could individually hope to advance.

As we have seen, rule-utilitarianism not only leads to the formulation of certain rules which, once determined, have to be obeyed absolutely (regardless of qualification to the rule itself), but also to the conclusion that where there is no utilitarian argument for a rule, the individual should proceed as an act-utilitarian. One important question for the utilitarian is therefore the basic one of what actions should be rule-governed. But another important question is whether there are not some types of action that, in principle, on utilitarian terms, should not only not be rule-governed, but should actually be treated as neutral. In other words, one might argue that in the interests of happiness people should be free over a range of activities to ignore the question of how much happiness accrues to whom. To put it yet another way, one might argue for a rule to the effect that when one's choice is between a number of behaviours, none of which obviously adversely affect anyone, one should do what one pleases.

Thus, whether I should read a book, go swimming or go to the pub, should not be determined by subtle attempts to estimate long-term and indirect consequences. Similarly, whether my family goes for a picnic or stays at home at the weekend should be a matter denuded of any moral significance. Such a view should, I think, be adopted, and can be cogently explained on utilitarian terms. People being as they, broadly speaking, are, it is in the interests of happiness to do this. People might of course be different. That was conceded in Chapter 5, when it was pointed out that many, but not any, types of society might be envisaged, each of which represents the utilitarian ideal. But since people, as things are, do tend to enjoy freedom in such matters, and do tend to resent the idea of a life lived entirely with an eye on obligation and a heavy degree of self-sacrifice, we should aim for a form of the ideal which takes account of this. Nor is there any problem in this, since one can well imagine a society in which everybody is completely happy on these terms. We cannot imagine a society in which individuals are free to steal what they want or kill whom they please being completely happy. But we can imagine a society in which individuals are free to go fishing, visit friends or paint the house, when they see fit, as being completely happy. And at the level of the real world, we can also reasonably surmise that our society is the happier for such an attitude to a wide variety of everyday activities.

It seems then that, on utilitarian terms, one can argue for a whole range of actions and choices not being invested with moral significance. But what, more particularly, can be said about the idea that one has a moral duty to leave a life largely consisting of such neutral activities behind, in order to do good? There is surely no case for adopting a moral rule to govern this issue. That is to say, there is no case for adopting a rule of the form 'Always seek out that place in the world where you can promote most happiness.' For utilitarian considerations lead to the rejection of such a rule. A combination of contingent (but in some cases seemingly fairly inevitable) facts about human nature, logical and contingent facts about the smooth running of societies, and logical facts about interrelationships between various types of activity, makes it absurd to maintain that we should all act all the time in this way. If we did, we would all be running in different directions to help each other, the normal running of society would break down, a large number of people would be dissatisfied and resentful, and it is probably fair to add that most people just would not enjoy themselves. To formulate and tabulate a precise set of reasons as to why this could not work would be extremely difficult, even, I dare say, impossible. But it is nonetheless surely, in the literal sense, inconceivable that a society or a world should be fully happy on such terms. There is a real logical incoherence about the idea of adopting such a rule in the interests of happiness.

I conclude, then, that utilitarianism itself leads to a rejection of the idea that we should abide by a rule such as 'Always seek out that place in the world where you can promote most happiness.' But, if it cannot reasonably be said to be a rule, then the question of whether one should go to Nicaragua, for example, or to Ethiopia, to fight for a cause, to help feed the starving, or whatever, becomes a question to answer for oneself.

The suggestion that this kind of decision might be classified as neutral would not, I think, be convincing. The individual should (morally) face the question of whether he should not change his life dramatically and engage in some supererogatory action. But in facing the question, the individual becomes an act-utilitarian, and one trying to determine, not what is morally right, but what his moral obligation is. He therefore takes into account neither the question of what would happen if others acted as he does, nor the question of what kind of conduct would be necessary in an ideal world. Rather, he attempts to weigh up his own happiness and that of his family and the wider community in which he lives, taking such things as intensity and duration into account as best he may, and to compare that with the likely sum of happiness if he makes the move.

It seems entirely reasonable to suppose that in the great majority of cases the individual will correctly decide that staying at home will produce more happiness for those affected than making the move would do.[6] Lest that conclusion seem too casuistic and self-serving, let me add that I believe that in many instances such a process of reasoning, fairly conducted, would lead us to concede that we ought to do something more than we do to make the world a happier place. Speaking for myself, for example, I am sure that I ought to do more than I do in my local community, and the fact that I don't is straightforward selfishness and lack of moral will. But I am equally certain that there is no good reason for me to go to Nicaragua.

The preceding few paragraphs speak to the question of whether the individual should, on utilitarian grounds, seek out good to do in the world. The conclusion is that he very possibly should do more than he does for the good of the world, but he is under no obligation to seek out the most productive way of life he could in terms of promoting the good, and in most cases he would be justified in, broadly speaking, continuing with his normal way of life. Such a conclusion allows us to defend utilitarianism against the charge that it leads to a demand for the impossible or that, in consistency, utilitarians should all devote their lives to humanitarian causes. On the other hand, of course, it opens the theory up to the charge that it does not make sufficient moral demands on us. As to that, I can only say that I am not persuaded of the view that we ought to be engaging in supererogatory acts as a matter of course.

But let us now remind ourselves that not only does utilitarianism not require us always to put ourselves forward to alleviate distress throughout the world; it also does not require that each individual should always be actively engaged in generating as much happiness as he could conceivably do in the situation in which he finds himself. To recapitulate, the only straightforward requirement that follows from utilitarianism is that the individual should follow certain specific rules. And beyond that there is only a general requirement that he proceed as an act-utilitarian in situations that pose options that are not regarded as morally neutral. There are no other requirements. Thus, in practice, the utilitarian proceeds much as others would do: he abides by certain rules of conduct, and when faced with uncertain moral territory tries to do what would be most conducive to the general good.

Finally, if it could be successfully argued that the world would be a happier place if people were to devote their lives to supererogatory acts, it would follow, on utilitarian terms, that we should do so. If I am wrong in my suggestion that the hypothesis is implausible, I would say, notwithstanding my admission that I am not personally of the view that we should be engaging in acts of supererogation, that this does not discredit utilitarianism so much as ourselves. For I would say that if the argument takes us that way, we must accept that we are wrong in our sentiment that we have no such obligation, rather than conclude that our sentiment, unbacked by reasoning, should be taken as sufficient to discredit the theory.

Notes

1. 'Mackintosh [see James Mill, *A Fragment on Mackintosh*, London, 1835] holds that there are some, intrinsically base, things, which a truly moral man would never do, however they contributed to public utility. [James] Mill replies, in effect, that this is frivolous if the public utility is really at stake.' (A. Quinton, *Utilitarian Ethics*, 1973, p. 37) Quinton comments, 'A large issue is raised here but not very deeply explored.' That is true enough, but the significance of Mill's response is perhaps not duly appreciated. Who really wants to say that it is self-evident that

there are some acts one should never perform, even if, as a consequence of not doing them, society will totally disintegrate? and what are these acts?

2. J.J.C. Smart, 'An Outline of a System of Utilitarian Ethics' (1973), gives serious attention and due weight to H.J. McCloskey's presentation of a case for saying that utilitarianism could have some 'very horrible consequences' ('A note on Utilitarian Punishment', *Mind*, 72, 1963). 'Suppose,' writes Smart, 'that the sheriff of a small town can prevent serious riots (in which hundreds of people will be killed) only by "framing" and executing (as a scapegoat) an innocent man'. (p. 70) He points out that there are various considerations that make the scenario contingently implausible. But 'McCloskey can always strengthen his story to the point that we would just have to admit that if utilitarianism is correct, then the sheriff must frame the innocent man ... However unhappy about it he may be, the utilitarian must admit that he draws the consequence that he might find himself in circumstances where he ought to be unjust'. (pp. 70, 71) Smart, while stressing how very unhappy he is about it, points out, as I do above, that one must be equally unhappy about 'the anti-utilitarian conclusion. For if a case really did arise in which injustice was the lesser of two evils (in terms of human happiness and misery), then the anti-utilitarian conclusion is a very unpalatable one too, namely that in some circumstances one must chose the greater misery, perhaps the very much greater misery, such as that of hundreds of people suffering painful deaths'. (pp. 71, 72)

I should add that both McCloskey and Smart believe that the same problem applies for the rule-utilitarian. 'An unjust system of punishment might be more useful than a just one.' (p. 70) A system of punishment, however, is not an instance of, or the embodiment of, rule-utilitarianism. I am uncertain whether it is plausible to maintain that a society might find long-term advantage in a rule demanding that there sometimes be scapegoats (and how the 'sometimes' would be given extension). Certainly, I cannot imagine that there would be room for such a rule in the ideal circumstances that we should envisage when determining what is morally right.

3. As Anthony Quinton (*Utilitarian Ethics*, 1989) puts it: 'Ordinary Utilitarianism ... implies that in every situation in which action is possible one should choose that possibility which most augments the general welfare. That would rule out as morally wrong not only harmless self-indulgences like sitting in the sun, reading for pleasure and non-strenuous walks in the countryside (since in each case one could be working or begging for Oxfam), it would also override most of the altruistic things we do for people to whom we are bound by ties of affection.' (p. xi) Quinton, writing 'from a position sympathetic, but not wholly committed, to utilitarianism', tends towards a reformulation of the theory in terms of the negative purpose of eliminating suffering. There is a lot to be said for such a view, but I hope that what I say in the text also provides a reasonable way of avoiding the objection raised against 'ordinary utilitarianism' here. Note also Quinton's similar conclusion that 'The morally heroic or supererogatory conduct of the saint is rational only for those whose direct concern for the welfare of others is of a scope and intensity which are not to be found in the structure of interests derived from the innate constitution and moral education of most of us.' (p. 71)

Compare Bernard Williams's formulation of 'the notion of negative responsibility', which he believes to be essentially involved in consequentialism: 'if I am ever responsible for anything, then I must be just as much responsible for things that I allow or fail to prevent, as I am for things that I myself, in the more everyday restricted sense, bring about.' ('A Critique of Utilitarianism', 1973, p. 95)

4. Rawls (1971), for example, suggests that traditional utilitarianism imposes unnecessarily strict moral standards on us. And Harsanyi (1982), endorsing the point, remarks, when I feel like reading a book 'I must always ask whether my time could

not be more usefully devoted to looking after the poor'. He proceeds to suggest that 'any reasonable utilitarian theory must recognise that people assign a nonnegligible positive utility to free personal choice, to freedom from unduly burdensome standards trying to regulate even the smallest details of their behaviour'. (p. 60) Though this claim is no doubt contingently true of our society, it is not a necessary truth. The point rather, as I argue in the text, is that there is no moral case for such regulations: there is no case for saying that we require such rules in order to ensure overall happiness.

5. J. Raz ('Right-based moralities' in Frey, R.G., ed., *Utility and Rights*, 1985) argues that rights-based moralities 'cannot account for the nature of supererogation and its role in moral life'. 'Acts are supererogatory if their performance is praiseworthy and yet it is not morally wrong to omit them. There is no obligation to act in a supererogatory way. Indeed supererogation is identified with action beyond the call of duty'. (p. 44)

Quinton, in his preface to the second edition of *Utilitarian Ethics* (1989), explains that his 'principal point of disagreement' with utilitarianism is that, as he sees it, 'morality is not concerned with the maximisation of positive well-being, utility, welfare, happiness, pleasure, desire-satisfaction or whatever, but has a negative purpose: the elimination of suffering ... On that view, the promotion of positive well-being is admirable, but it is not morality. Furthermore, not causing suffering is morally compulsory in a way that the charitable relief of suffering for which one is not personally responsible is not'. (pp. x, xii) The view I expound in the text has something in common with Quinton's. There are, however, some difficulties with the idea of negative utilitarianism. See, e.g., R.N. Smart, 'Negative Utilitarianism', *Mind*, 67 (1958). K.E.M. Baier, *The Moral Point of View* (1958) suggests that act-utilitarianism leads to the conclusion that we should at all times be engaged in good works (and rejects it accordingly). He is possibly correct, though J.J.C. Smart has pointed out that not only the intrinsic pleasure of relaxation and play, but also their possible long-term consequences in terms of the more effective doing of good works, have to be taken into account. ('An Outline of a System of Utilitarian Ethics', p. 55) But Baier's point does not, in any case, relate to the rule-utilitarianism with which I am concerned.

6. 'The occasions on which any person (except one in a thousand) has it in his power to do this [multiply happiness] on an extended scale, in other words to be a public benefactor, are but exceptional; and on these occasions alone is he called on to consider public utility; in every other case, private utility, the interest or happiness of some few persons, is all he has to attend to.' (John Stuart Mill, *Utilitarianism*, p. 270)

10. Does Utilitarianism Offer an Impoverished Conception of Morality?

I have argued that it is highly misleading to summarize utilitarianism by means of traditional formulae such as 'the greatest happiness of the greatest number'.[1] It is not the doctrine that one should simply do whatever will maximize happiness, even if it were clear what that meant. It is not, essentially, concerned with what the individual should do in specific real life situations, although of course it speaks indirectly to that issue. Being an ethical theory it is to be construed as an explanation of what in principle makes actions morally right. It therefore, like any other ethical theory, has to be interpreted in terms of a conceivable ideal.[2] Working in this way, we see the need to adopt rule-utilitarianism[3] and to reject the idea of distinguishing between qualities of happiness,[4] on utilitarian grounds. We also see that most of the traditional objections then fall by the wayside, being seen to be false, irrelevant, or no more a problem for utilitarianism than any other theory. Thus, as we have seen in previous chapters, it is not true that utilitarians think it morally acceptable to sacrifice innocent scapegoats;[5] it is not true that they do not value non-moral qualities such as beauty, or other moral principles such as that of keeping promises;[6] and it is not true that the theory is necessarily conservative.[7]

Nonetheless, though the nature of the preceding argument should have done something to weaken the prejudice, utilitarianism is always up against the intuitive suspicion, the established sentiment, that it is lacking in what might be described as a familiar savour of moral texture. People are wedded to the idea that moral rules, whatever they may be, ought to be respected because they are moral rules, not because they make the world a pleasanter place. Rules, furthermore, ought to be rules, not calculated risks. And happiness, desirable as it is, seems altogether too self-indulgent a matter to form the apex of morality. Morality ought to come hard.

One might be deflected into speculation about the origins of such convictions. Is this the real legacy of Christianity? Is our puritan heritage here to haunt us? And one might suggest that they are not particularly well founded. Morality is concerned with doing what is right, which is to say what is conducive to the good. Is there any obvious reason to suppose that the good should be demanding rather than welcome, or that doing what is right should feel like an obligation just because it is one? Utilitarian rules are rules, for all that devising them requires some calculation, and they are obeyed because they are moral rules, not because it necessarily pleases us to obey them. Why do people fear that the theory is not moral enough?

But it seems to me that the sensible and important thing to do at this point is to go back to the beginning and ask ourselves what an ethical theory is supposed to be doing; for we should not confuse a theory about the nature of morality, with a prescriptive theory about what we ought to do. As we have said,[8] if utilitarianism is accepted, then we can set about the task of establishing specific principles and rules of conduct within the terms of the theory, and hence arrive at some specific prescriptions. But the prior task is to establish the plausibility of the theory as an account of moral right and wrong. Too many critics seem to have compared Mill with the Bible, so to speak, and found him less inspiring and, yes, less moral. But he and the authors of the Bible were engaged in very different tasks. The latter were delivering prescriptions without an argument. He was producing an argument for establishing principles of procedure for the ultimate generation of specific prescriptions.

At the end of the day, any view of morality (how it works, what it enjoins, why it does so) has to come up against the bar of our moral sentiments.[9] Nazi values just do not seem morally acceptable to most of us; the view that moral judgements are merely a matter of opinion just does not seem plausible; the view that something is morally right simply because God wants it done just does not convince. When a theory challenges such widespread and ingrained convictions it is bound to lose credibility. But while that is so as a matter of psychological fact, we must acknowledge that our sentiments cannot be allowed to be the sole determinants of the acceptability or otherwise of a theory. Logically it is possible that our sentiments are flawed. And it is the business of an ethical theory, in seeking to explain what makes actions morally right, to sift through our sentiments, discriminating between the sound and the unsound. It seems that utilitarianism, understood in the manner ex-plained, does not in all probability offend grossly against current sentiment.[10] But in so far as it does, we must simply learn to accept that an account that is clear and coherent, and largely in accord with our instincts, and which shows some small part of our ingrained view of the matter to be inconsistent, is to be reckoned more worthy of our approval, as rational beings, than unsubstantiated intuitions.

Similarly, it may be acknowledged that, an ethical theory being what it is, it is to be expected that its dry and abstract account of how one determines what is morally right should prove less emotionally satisfying, less enticing, less substantially moral, than a prescriptive code or a theory that is set out with a great many specific injunctions derived from it. It is forgotten that were utilitarianism once generally accepted and taken for granted, as at certain periods of history various religious views have been, then the utilitarian philosopher could proceed to the secondary task of building a prescriptive framework of rules and a list of examples of morally right and morally justified acts, which might well be as appealing and psychologically comforting as, say, the Ten Commandments. It is not a utilitarian code of life that is cold and uninspiring. It is the detached exercise of explaining and arguing for the theory that necessarily lacks a certain substantive moral flavour.

In short, we should be wary of allowing the presumption that utilitarianism offers an impoverished conception of morality to be accorded too much respect. It arises partly out of a failure to appreciate the nature of ethical theory and partly out of an unwillingness to recognize that our current convictions may be misplaced. Obviously, an audience that is wedded to the idea that various things are good in themselves, and that certain actions are right in themselves, is going to have some psychological resistance to any ethical theory that suggests that that is, in a sense, not the case. But let us at least recognize it for what it is, psychological resistance, unless, of course, an independent argument can be produced either to discredit utilitarianism or to support our current beliefs.

But, having said that, let me return to the theme that the presumption is in any case ill founded. Though the outline of utilitarianism as an explanation of what truly constitutes moral conduct may seem arid, the moral system(s) that it leads to will share many features of a traditional morality, as I hope to have brought out already, and might in principle have them all. Thus a utilitarian might be prepared to go to the stake for the principle of free speech as readily as the next man. He explains the moral value of free speech in a different way from some, maintaining that it is valuable because of its relationship to happiness rather than in itself, but he does not value it any the less for and of itself. He too believes that freedom of speech should always be preserved, whatever the consequences in particular situations; he might even say that in a particular case freedom of speech should be defended because it is freedom of speech. It is only at the higher level of explaining the grounds for treating this as an absolute principle that he differs from some. He does not differ in regarding it as an absolute principle.

The utilitarian will deplore murder as vehemently as his neighbour. The nature of his reaction will be no different. He will be morally outraged; he will say that such things ought not to be. He will classify the act as wrong, and he means by that that, being the act it is, it ought not to occur. In this he does not differ from other ethical theorists or the man in the street. He differs only in explaining at another level why it is to be regarded as wrong. It is in the account he gives of why it is reasonable to have such a sentiment, that he is distinctive, not in having some different sentiment. Kant, St Paul, John Stuart Mill and John Doe all believe that we ought to keep promises. It is morally right to do so. None can avoid the possibility of a dilemma, when in real life the obligation to keep a promise clashes with some other obligation, though sometimes the utilitarian has what may be seen as an advantage over others, in that he has a rational way of turning what seemed like a dilemma into a soluble problem. But, generally, the commitment to the value of promise keeping, and the intensity of that commitment, does not differ at all between such gentlemen. Mr Mill is as outraged by the barefaced liar as St Paul would be. It is only when it comes to explaining the grounds for this outrage that they differ.

Loving one's neighbour as oneself, honouring one's father and mother, helping people in distress, telling the truth, keeping promises, refraining from murder and theft, these and many other such established values are all as likely to be held by the utilitarian as anyone else. Those values that, on the face of it, the utilitarian might not see reason to share are precisely those that, while sincerely held by some, are plainly contentious. For instance, it is not certain that a utilitarian would see reason to share Kant's conviction that suicide is morally wrong, or the Catholic view of the sanctity of marriage. But then it is very far from certain, on any view, that these are plausible moral values. A theory that explains and confirms the majority of our actual moral sentiments, that allows the normal range of moral attitudes, and that demands most of the kind of conduct that we intuitively recognize as moral, cannot reasonably be said to offer an impoverished conception of morality.

The issue for debate should not, then, be whether utilitarianism squares with our current beliefs. In the first place it does, generally speaking. In the second place, it might be suggestive, but it would not be conclusive, if it did not. The issue should be whether this is a plausible explanation of what makes actions morally right, whether we should be persuaded of the soundness of this ethical theory.

It will be noted that I do not raise the question of whether the theory is proven. In common with most philosophers, I believe that, while there may be a question of truth here, it is inappropriate to look for 'proof' in the narrow sense of 'unequivocal demonstration' that the term usually carries these days. It makes sense to suppose that the utilitarian theory (or any other) might be true or false. But the nature of ethical theory is such that it does not seem appropriate to look for an unequivocal demonstration of the truth or falsity. We do not know, or we are not agreed on, in what such a demonstration might consist. But we can ask of a theory whether it is clear, whether its implications are recognized and acceptable to us, whether it is consistent, both in itself and with a sufficient number of our wider set of beliefs and understanding, and whether it is in other respects coherent. The argument in the previous chapters has been designed to show that many criticisms of utilitarianism are based on misunderstanding (or, alternatively, apply only to poorly conceived versions of the theory). An account of it can be provided that meets the criteria referred to, and that account, in meeting the criteria, makes utilitarianism a far more plausible theory than any other we have been presented with.

The theory is founded on the scarcely disputable, and in any case not sincerely disputed, truth that happiness is morally good. Happiness is something that we think people ought to have. Other theorists, while acknowledging this, seek to add other moral goods. But they are unable to establish by reasoning that these other values obtain, which they need to do, since these other values, unlike happiness, are not universally shared and can logically be questioned. Furthermore, a strong case can be made for saying that, in the final analysis, when people do not simply assert the self-evidence of what is not evident to all, they are driven to defending these other values by reference to what looks suspiciously like happiness, even if the word itself is not used.[11]

From that foundation, the ethical theory of utilitarianism emerges. It has been objected that the theory has no principle of justice. I should rather say that the principle was so obvious to the founding fathers of the theory that they failed to articulate it explicitly. In any event, utilitarianism is to be understood as embodying a principle of impartiality or fair distribution.[12] The happiness of every individual is to count equally. At this point it becomes essential to recognize that trying to work out what further principles and values are enjoined by the theory necessitates a consideration of the matter in possible but ideal conditions.[13] It is impossible and misleading to attempt to work out what actions will or will not necessarily contribute to happiness in the context of an imperfect world. The utilitarian recognizes that the nature of happiness is such that individuals may gain it in different ways.[14] Nonetheless, there is reason to suppose that, assuming we have to live with the contingent necessities of this earth and certain general characteristics, some logically and some contingently necessary, of human beings, there will be some rules and some particular actions in particular situations that will necessarily contribute to happiness in principle. That is, there are rules that, if they were followed consistently in a community, would thereby promote happiness. These rules are those that one should therefore follow; the actions they enjoin are actions that should be performed, even if on occasion in an imperfect world they cause distress. From this framework a substantive notion of justice necessarily emerges.

The theory does not imply that our natural moral sentiments are necessarily without foundation, or that they should not take the emotive form that they do. It suggests only that they are best explained as deriving, not historically or psychologically, but logically, from the notion of a world in which all are completely happy. This is a way of making sense of at least the majority of them and providing comprehensible grounds for questioning the remainder. The theory also leads to a view of the respects in which moral judgements are objective or subjective, relative or absolute, which again seems to have plausibility and to be reasonably in accord with our intuitions, without being enslaved to them. We treat various principles, such as that of freedom of speech, as absolute, meaning that we ought always in all societies and under all circumstances to abide by them because, we argue, this must be in the interests of happiness in ideal terms. But it is recognized that cultural variations in respect of various specific actions are not only a fact of life, but a morally legitimate fact of life. Because, while there are some conditions that obtain in any time and place and which may affect happiness, there are others that do not. It is not plausible to suggest that any society could be happy without subscribing to a notion to the effect that promises should be kept; but it is entirely plausible to suggest that a society might be happy with a monogamous institution of marriage, or with polygamy, or without any concept of marriage.

Much has been made of the distinction between the ideal and the actual, imperfect world in the previous pages, and the question 'what ought a utilitarian do in an imperfect world?' deserves some kind of response, notwithstanding the point that to work out a utilitarian code of conduct is to go beyond the task of explicating and arguing for utilitarian theory, which has been the focus of this book. The utilitarian should, in the first instance, abide by certain rules, consistently and in all circumstances. I do not claim to have fully substantiated the case for any particular rule, nor to have even considered a large number of possible rules. But I am fairly confident of the reasonableness of the following partial list: one ought never to cause gratuitous suffering; one ought never to kill, except possibly in self-defence or time of war; one ought always to keep promises; one should never tell a lie when engaged in serious discussion of matters of moment; one should never account one person's happiness as in itself more worthy of consideration than another's; one should always act with a view to promoting the happiness of all persons immediately affected by an action.

These rules vary in their explicitness and in their capacity to yield precise guidance to action, and all require some further conceptual work. There is room for argument, for instance, both about what constitutes 'gratuitous suffering' and what will in fact cause particular people to suffer. The question of where 'immediately affected by an action' begins and ends is difficult to answer. The whole issue of what, if anything, is justified in time of war, including the question of whether there is a distinction to be made between just and unjust wars, would require several books to discuss. Nonetheless, these rules are all reasonably clear at the verbal level: we are not mystified about what we are being asked to do, merely aware that sometimes they will be difficult to interpret in terms of particular actions. That difficulty faces any theory's list of demands and is not to be held against it. It is the consequence of life, including our conceptual armoury, being complex, rather than the consequence of the theory being inadequately formulated.

The point to insist on is that these are plain and positive prescriptions for everyday life (even when phrased negatively). There is a moral obligation on the utilitarian to act in accordance with these rules, even if all around him are thereby caused great dismay. To pick up on the distinction introduced in Chapter 2, these are his duties, and that means, in my terminology, what he ought always to do. Only when he cannot do his unalloyed duty, because the imperfection of human society has produced a situation in which two or more duties clash, is he justified in not doing so. In such a case what he ought to do is what will generate the most happiness.

Beneath these universally binding rules will be a far greater number of rules that are equally binding but only within the context of particular societies. Thus some rules of conduct will be necessary to govern the community in the interests of happiness, but what form they take will legitimately vary, because circumstances and people's natures vary. A society, therefore, will generate rules governing everything from driving to personal relationships, predicated on the need for uniformity. It does not matter what side of the road we drive on, but we have to agree on one or the other. It does not matter whether we classify ignoring people or exposing their private parts as socially acceptable or unacceptable, provided the people concerned can in principle live happily with either arrangement, but it is necessary that we should agree which it is to be. 'Rudeness' being by definition objectionable and upsetting, we must arrive at some common understanding of what acts are rude. Any society, in the interests of happiness, needs to formulate rules governing rude behaviour. And the utilitarian ought never to be rude.

This differs from, say, the rule that one should always act with a view to promoting the happiness of all persons affected by an action, in that the latter, though it may lead to different actions in different circumstances, has universal application as it stands. What constitutes happiness conceptually does not vary, though what makes people happy may. But in the case of rudeness what varies is the form it may take. One cannot, even within a society, entirely convert the general principle of promoting happiness into a set of specific actions (unless it so happens that all individuals in the society are exactly alike in respect of what makes them happy). But one can and needs to establish a common understanding of what acts are rude within a society. Thus the latter rule will be couched in culturally specific terms. For example, in our society it is probably safe to say that ignoring people when they address one, spitting at people, and abusing them are all rude. As such we may state categorically that the utilitarian in our society ought never to engage in such behaviour. Never, even when we have reason to suppose it would make a lot of people happier if we did. It is not, of course, being suggested that ignoring people who address one is always and necessarily morally wrong in itself, still less that it is inherently immoral to drive on the wrong side of the road. But it is morally wrong to break the respective rules.

Much of our daily conduct will be covered by such universal or culturally specific rules, especially since we have determined that we are not morally obliged to engage in acts of supererogation.[15] However, it is obvious that in practice we will encounter many problematic situations which are not governed by a rule or which, entirely because human beings are not perfect, involve a clash between rules. In such cases the utilitarian's moral duty is to estimate as best he can what is most conducive to the general happiness. This is where formulae such as 'the greatest happiness of the greatest number' do come into play (not before), and it is freely admitted that they are imprecise and imperfect. That is because they are introduced as approximate guides to help us in avowedly problematic situations. It is not possible to state clearly and categorically what a person should do in a situation where one's duty to keep a promise would conflict with one's duty not to cause gratuitous suffering, although it is worth suggesting that such clashes of principle are usually brought upon us by ourselves; it would be sensible not to make promises that might lead us into this kind of trouble. But if we are faced with such a clash, we have a dilemma on our hands, and there is no correct answer to the question of what one ought to do. If, on the other hand, it is not a dilemma, but a problem, such as whether to tell an unpalatable truth to someone, that we are faced with, then the utilitarian must do that which he believes will most contribute to the sum of human happiness. His calculation will be inadequate and he will never know whether it was correct. But he must act in accordance with it. To do so is to act morally, and for doing so he is to be morally commended, regardless of the actual consequences of his action. If in fact the consequences are as he predicted (or if we believe them to be so) then we would classify his action as morally justified.

While in the realm of what utilitarianism implies for everyday life, it is worth commenting on two popular principles which it does not endorse. Although again I have not argued the point, it does not seem likely that on utilitarian terms one could establish that one ought always to tell the truth (assuming this rule is not carefully qualified in some way, as above) or that one should never take a human life.[16] A world in which people were completely happy, even though it countenanced euthanasia and abortion, presuming both to be clearly delineated and limited in scope, seems entirely conceivable. There is therefore no obvious case for a universal rule forbidding such practice. Further, it seems entirely possible that a particular community would gain in terms of happiness from a rule allowing such practices under certain circumstances. In considering the question we have to take into account not only what people do feel now, but also what they might feel if circumstances changed for, as we have been at pains to stress in discussing the concept of happiness, what makes people happy changes to some extent as their expectations and beliefs change. Thus, in convincing people that abortion is morally acceptable, we contribute to making it so for, regarding it as morally acceptable, they are less upset by it. But the argument here would simply be that on utilitarian grounds a society might well deny that these practices are morally reprehensible. Similarly the notion that one ought always to tell the truth, pro-actively, under any circumstances seems, on the face of it, implausible on utilitarian terms. For it is evident that such a principle would generate a great deal of misery on occasion, and yet the absence of such a principle in no obvious way militates against happiness.

To some, this admission will appear to be further evidence that utilitarianism is not truly moral, or not moral enough. 'What! Telling the truth, that fundamental requirement, dismissed as a moral principle? Approval for the killing of innocent embryos and the aged and infirm, who cannot help themselves?' One can only say that in recognizing that these issues are open ones, which is all that denying that there is a rule that settles the issue amounts to, the utilitarian would seem to be in step with the majority of informed opinion. Nobody that I know of has produced an incontestably persuasive argument to support the view that all instances of euthanasia and abortion are morally objectionable, despite the fact that many individuals insistently believe that they are. The utilitarian is therefore not alone in concluding that he does not see a case for such a principle. Beyond that, his presumption that the issue should finally be resolved, if it can be, by reference to considerations of human happiness is not out of tune with the kinds of consideration that most people involved in the debate in fact resort to. Only those who are committed to the intuition that such acts are always self-evidently wrong, being instances of the taking of human life, can coherently argue that the utilitarian position necessarily misses the essence of morality, and such people, by definition, have no supporting argument to offer.

On an appropriately happier note, let me conclude by listing some of the things that utilitarians are likely to regard as being morally good. It will be recalled that, while only happiness is believed to be morally good in itself, many other things are regarded as morally good, often without qualification, by the utilitarian. It is simply that he sees their goodness as being derivative of their relationship to happiness. Beauty, friendship, kindness, humour, education, loyalty, trustworthiness, integrity, sympathy and love are all likely to be regarded as morally desirable. Nor is it accidental that the list consists of what we are usually inclined to regard as normative concepts. Of course utilitarians value beauty rather than ugliness, friendship rather than enmity, and humour rather than dullness. Who could not? For while one may argue about what things are beautiful or what jokes are funny, it is clear that, by definition, these normative terms represent something desirable and hence conducive to happiness. It is not of course the case that particular people necessarily need friends to be happy, or that everybody needs to be surrounded by what is conventionally regarded as beautiful. Nor is it the case that the utilitarian thinks it morally incumbent on us to try to be funny and to cultivate friendship. But he does see a world in which such things thrive as being necessarily preferable to a world full of their opposites, and likely to be preferable to a world of uniform neutrality in such respects. Consequently, he values them for their no doubt massive contribution to the sum of human happiness.

Such then is utilitarianism as I understand it. Not a matter of the selfish pursuit of pleasure, not a Philistine creed of calculated enjoyment, not a non-moral doctrine that denies our moral sentiments, but a reasonable and plausible account of what lies behind our moral instincts, the majority of which may, in the light of the theory, be seen to be well founded. The strength of the theory is that, in contrast to many, perhaps all others, it has no very obvious defect.[17] Perhaps that is why it refuses to go away.[18]

Notes

1. See above, Chapter 3. D.G. Brown ('What is Mill's Principle of Utility?', *Canadian Journal of Philosophy*, 1973, Vol. 3, pp. 1-12) claims that there are 'fifteen possible formulations (of the Principle of Utility) which Mill seems committed to regarding as equivalent'. Brown himself finds none of them to be entirely satisfactory.
2. See above, Chapters 2 and 3. A. Quinton, *Utilitarian Ethics* (1973) writes: 'the utilitarian end is not the achievement of total and unqualified happiness but its maximisation to the greatest possible extent ... an ideal of conduct does not have to be strictly attainable to be effective: doctors are right not to yield to any discouragement arising from the knowledge that all men are mortal.' (p. 45) The second observation is well taken. It is, in a way, at odds with the first, which attempts to replace a strictly unattainable ideal with something that is, by definition, attainable ('to the greatest possible extent'). In any case, as I argue above, the formula is to be resisted: the utilitarian end *is*, ideally, the achievement of total and unqualified happiness, and that is what we, like the doctors, *mutatis mutandis*, should keep our eye on.
3. See above, Chapter 6.
4. See above, Chapter 7.

5. See above, Chapter 9.
6. See above, Chapter 8.
7. See above, Chapter 5.
8. See above, Chapter 3.
9. On the issue of the relationship between ethical theory and ingrained moral sentiment, see also above, Chapters 2 and 3.
10. As Harsanyi (1982) says 'rule utilitarianism comes fairly close to traditional morality in recognising the importance of social institutions which establish a network of moral rights and moral obligations among different people in society, and in maintaining that these rights and obligations must not be infringed upon on grounds of immediate social utility'. (pp. 59, 60) He adds 'with the possible exception of some very rare and very special cases', but, as argued in the main text, there is no need to admit of any moral exceptions and, were one to do so, the coherence of the utilitarian theory would be in jeopardy. It makes sense to limit the theory to the ethical domain, as I have done, or to argue that some values conventionally seen as moral are not in fact so, as I have also done. I am not sure that it does make sense to proclaim that utilitarianism is an ethical theory that does not cover 'all morality', as Harsanyi does. (p. 62)
11. For fuller discussion of the points summarized in this paragraph, see above, Chapter 4.
12. See above, Chapter 3.
13. See above, Chapters 2 and 3.
14. See above, Chapter 4.
15. See above, Chapter 9.
16. In referring to a rule against killing, except in self-defence (above, Chapter 6) I was merely illustrating the difference between a qualified rule and a qualified injunction to obey a rule. I was not presuming to argue that killing could never be permissible except in self-defence. The moral acceptability of, e.g., abortion and euthanasia, at any rate, seem to me to require considerably more discussion.
17. In 1960, Mary Warnock wrote, in *Ethics Since 1900*: 'If hostility could nullify the influence of a philosophical view, then utilitarianism ought by now to be stone dead.' That it is very far from being so is evident from the appearance since that date of such publications as J.J.C. Smart, 'An Outline of a Utilitarian System of Ethics' (1961, reprinted 1973), David Lyons, *The Forms and Limits of Utilitarianism* (1965), Ian Narveson, *Morality and Utility* (1967), D.H. Hodgson, *Consequences of Utilitarianism* (1967), R.B. Brandt, *A Theory of the Good and the Right* (1979), R.M. Hare, *Moral Thinking* (1981), Amartya Sen and Bernard Williams (eds), *Utilitarianism and Beyond* (1982), R.G. Frey (ed.), *Utility and Rights* (1985), and James Griffin, *Well-Being* (1986). As Anthony Quinton, *Utilitarian Ethics* (2nd ed., 1989) observes: 'For utilitarianism, then, there has been a remarkable restoration of status'. (p. ix)
18. 'The day cannot be too far off when we hear no more of it,' wrote Bernard Williams hopefully in 1973 ('A Critique of Utilitarianism', p. 150). I doubt whether the passing of more time will make that judgement look any the less misplaced.

Bibliography

Acton, H.B. (1963), 'Negative Utilitarianism', *Proceedings of the Aristotelian Society*, Supp. Vol. XXXVII, pp. 83–94.

Anscombe, G.E.M. (1958), 'Modern Moral Philosophy', *Philosophy*, Vol. 33, pp. 1–9.

Aqvist, Lennart (1969), 'Improved Formulations of Act Utilitarianism', *Nous*, Vol. 3, pp. 299–323.

Aristotle (1953), *The Nicomachean Ethics*, trans. J.A.K Thomson. Harmondsworth: Penguin.

Aristotle (1962), *The Politics*. trans. T.A. Sinclair. Harmondsworth: Penguin.

Aristotle (1965), *The Poetics*. trans. T.S. Dorsch. Harmondsworth: Penguin.

Austin, Jean (1968), 'Pleasure and Happiness', *Philosophy*, Vol. 63, pp. 51–62.

Ayer, A.J. (1936), *Language, Truth and Logic*, London: Victor Gollancz.

Baier, Kurt (1958), *The Moral Point of View: A Rational Basis of Ethics*, Ithaca: Cornell University Press.

Baier, Kurt (1962), 'Pains', *Australian Journal of Philosophy*, Vol. 40, pp. 1–23.

Bailey, Stephen K. (1976), 'Educational Purpose and the Pursuit of Happiness', *Phi Delta Kappan*, (September), pp 42–7.

Baker, J.M. (1971), 'Utilitarianism and "Secondary Principles"', *The Philosophical Quarterly*, Vol. 21, pp. 69–71.

Bantock, G.H. (1963), *Education in an Industrial Society*, London: Faber.

Barrow, Robin (1975), *Plato, Utilitarianism and Education*, London: Routledge & Kegan Paul.

Barrow, Robin (1976), *Common Sense and the Curriculum*, London: George Allen & Unwin.

Barrow, Robin (1980), *Happiness*, Oxford: Martin Robertson.

Barrow, Robin (1983), 'Does the Question '"What is education?" Make Sense?', *Educational Theory*, Vol. 33.

Barrow, Robin and Milburn, Geoffrey (1986), *A Critical Dictionary of Educational Concepts*, Brighton: Wheatsheaf.

Barry, Brian (1962), 'Preferences and the Common Good', *Ethics,* Vol. 72, pp. 141–2.

Barry, Brian (1965), *Political Argument,* London: Routledge & Kegan Paul.

Barry, Brian (1973), *The Liberal Theory of Justice,* Oxford: Oxford University Press.

Bayles, Michael (ed.) (1968), *Contemporary Utilitarianism,* Garden City: New York.

Bayles, Michael (1969), 'A Rule Utilitarian Moral Code', *Journal of Value Inquiry,* 3, pp. 259–69.

Bedau, Hugo (1963), 'Justice and Classical Utilitarianism', in Friedrich, C. (ed.) *Nomos VI: Justice,* New York.

Benditt, Theodore (1974), 'Happiness', *Philosophical Studies,* Vol. 25 (January), pp. 1–20.

Bennet, John (1965–1966), 'Whatever the Consequences', *Analysis,* Vol. 26, pp. 83–102.

Bentham, Jeremy (1838–1843), 'A Plea for the Constitution' in Bowing, John (ed.), *The Works of Jeremy Bentham Vol. IV,* Edinburgh: William Tait.

Bentham, Jeremy (1948), *The Principles of Morals and Legislation,* New York: Hafner.

Bentham, Jeremy (1968), *Correspondence,* ed. by T.L.S. Sprigge, London: Athlone Press.

Bertman, M.A. (1972), 'Pleasure and two Happinesses in Aristotle', *Apeiron,* 6 (Summer), pp. 30–36.

Bradley, F.H. (1927), *Ethical Studies,* 2nd ed. revised, Oxford: The Clarendon Press.

Brandt, R.B. (1959), *Ethical Theory,* Englewood Cliffs, N. J.: Prentice-Hall.

Brandt, R.B. (1963), 'In Search of a Credible Form of Rule-Utilitarianism' in Nakhnikian, G. and Castenada, H. N. (eds), *Morality and the Language of Conduct,* Detroit.

Brandt, R.B. (1964), 'Utility and the Obligation to Obey the Law', in Hook, Sidney (ed.) *Law and Philosophy,* New York.

Brandt, R.B. (1967), 'Some Merits of One Form of Rule Utilitarianism', *University of Colorado Studies Series in Philosophy,* No. 3, Denver.

Brandt, R.B. (1969), 'A Utilitarian Theory of Excuses', *The Philosophical Review,* Vol. 78, pp. 337–61.

Brandt, R.B. (1979), *A Theory of the Good and the Right,* Oxford: Oxford University Press.

Braybrooke, David (1967), 'The Choice Between Utilitarianisms', *American Philosophical Quarterly*, Vol. 4, pp. 28–38.

Britton, Karl (1958), 'J.S. Mill: A Debating Speech on Wordsworth, 1829', *Cambridge Review*, Vol. LIXXIX.

Brody, B.A. (1967), 'The Equivalence of Act and Rule Utilitarianism', *Philosophical Studies*, Vol. 13, pp. 81–7.

Broiles, R.D. (1964), 'Is Rule Utilitarianism Too Restricted?', *Southern Journal of Philosophy*, 2, pp. 180–97.

Bronaugh, R.N. (1974), 'The Utility of Quality', *Canadian Journal of Philosophy*, (December), pp. 317–25.

Brown, D.G. (1973), 'What is Mill's Principle of Utility?', *Canadian Journal of Philosophy*, Vol. 3, pp. 1–12.

Cohen, Brenda (1962), 'Some Ambiguities in the Term "Hedonism"', *The Philosophical Quarterly*, Vol. 12, pp. 239–47.

Cooper, Neil (1969), 'Mill's "Proof" of the Principal of Utility', *Mind*, Vol. 78, pp. 278–9.

Cowan, J.L. (1968), *Pleasure and Pain*, London: Macmillan

Dearden, R. (1972), 'Happiness' in Dearden, R.F. et al. (eds) *Education and the Development of Reason*, London: Routledge & Kegan Paul.

Diggs, B.J. (1964), 'Rules and Utilitarianism', *American Philosophical Quarterly*, Vol. 1, pp. 32–44.

Donagan, Alan (1968), 'Is There A Credible Form of Utilitarianism?' in Bayles, M. (ed.), *Contemporary Utilitarianism*, Garden City.

Donagan, Alan (1977), The *Theory* of *Morality*, Chicago: University of Chicago Press.

Dworkin, Ronald (1977), *Taking Rights Seriously*, Cambridge, Mass: Harvard University Press.

Elster, J. (1978), *Logic and Society*, London: Wiley.

Elster, J. (1982), 'Sour Grapes – Utilitarianism and the Genesis of Wants' in Sen, A. K. and Williams, Bernard (eds) *Utilitarianism and Beyond*, Cambridge: Cambridge University Press.

Ewing, A.C. *Reason and Intuition*, out of print

Ezorsky, Gertrude (1965), 'Utilitarianism and Rules, *Australasian Journal of Philosophy*, Vol. 43, pp. 225–9.

Feinberg, Joel (1967), 'The Forms and Limits of Utilitarianism', *The Philosophical Review*, Vol. 76, pp. 36–81.

Flatham, Richard (1965–1966), 'Forms and Limits of Utilitarianism', *Ethics*, Vol. 76, pp. 309–17.

Flew, Antony, (ed.) (1979), *A Dictionary of Philosophy*, London: Pan Books.

Foot, Philippa (1978), *Virtues and Vices,* Oxford: Blackwell.

Frey, R.G. (1985), 'Introduction' in Frey, R.G. (ed.), *Utility and Rights,* Oxford: Blackwell.

Fromm, Erich (1942), *Fear of Freedom,* London: Routledge & Kegan Paul.

Gauthier, D.P. (1963), *Practical Reasoning,* Oxford: Clarendon Press.

Gauthier, D.P. (1964–1965), 'Rule Utilitarianism and Randomization', *Analysis,* Vol. 25, pp. 68–9.

Gauthier, D.P. (1967–1968), 'Progress and Happiness: A Utilitarian Reconsideration', *Ethics,* Vol. 78, pp. 77–82.

Gibbard, A.F. (1965), 'Rule Utilitarianism: Merely an Illusory Alternative?', *Australian Journal of Philosophy,* Vol. 43, pp. 211–20.

Goldstein, Irwin (1973), 'Happiness: The Role of Non-hedonic Criteria in its Evaluation', *International Philosophical Quarterly,* 13, (December), pp. 523–34.

Goldworth, Amnon (1969), 'The Meaning of Bentham's Greatest Happiness Principle', *Journal of the History of Philosophy,* Vol. 7, pp. 315–21.

Gosling, J.C.B. (1969), *Pleasure and Desire,* Oxford: Clarendon Press.

Graham, K. (1977), *J.L. Austin: A Critique of Ordinary Language Philosophy,* Brighton: Harvester Press.

Gray, John (1983), *Mill on Liberty: A Defence,* London: Routledge & Kegan Paul.

Griffin, James (1986), *Well-being: Its meaning, importance and measurement,* New York: Oxford University Press.

Grote, John (1870), *Examination of the Utilitarian Philosophy,* Cambridge

Gutmann, Amy (1982), 'What's the Use of Going to School?' in Sen, A. K. and Williams, Bernard (eds), *Utilitarianism and Beyond,* Cambridge: Cambridge University Press.

Hall, J.C. (1966–1967), 'Quantity of Pleasure', *Proceedings of the Aristotelian Society,* Vol. 67, pp. 35–52.

Halliday, R.J. (1976), *John Stuart Mill,* London: George Allen & Unwin.

Hamlyn, D.W. (1961–1962), 'The Obligation to Keep a Promise', *Proceedings of the Aristotelian Society,* Vol. 62, pp. 179–94.

Hammond, P.J. (1981), 'Liberalism, Independent Rights and the Pareto Principle' in Cohen, L.J. et al. (eds), *Logic, Methodology and the Philosophy of Science,* Amsterdam: North Holland.

Hampshire, Stuart (1982), 'Morality and Convention' in Sen, A.K. and

Williams, Bernard (eds), *Utilitarianism and Beyond*, Cambridge: Cambridge University Press.

Hare, R.M. (1952), *The Language of Morals,* Oxford: Oxford University Press.

Hare, R.M. (1963), *Freedom and Reason*, Oxford: Oxford University Press.

Hare, R.M. (1981), *Moral Thinking: Its Levels, Method and Point,* Oxford: Clarendon Press.

Hare, R.M. (1982), 'Ethical Theory and Utilitarianism' in Sen, A.K. and Williams, Bernard (eds), *Utilitarianism and Beyond,* Cambridge: Cambridge University Press.

Harrod, R.F. (1936), 'Utilitarianism Revised', *Mind*, Vol. 45, pp. 137–56.

Harsanyi, John C. (1976), *Essays in Ethics, Social Behaviour, and Scientific Explanation*, Dordrecht: Reidel.

Harsanyi, John C. (1982), 'Morality and the Theory of Rational Behaviour' in Sen, A.K. and Williams, Bernard (eds), *Utilitarianism and Beyond,* Cambridge: Cambridge University Press.

Hart, H.L.A. (1979), 'Between Utility and Rights', *Columbia Law Review*, Vol. 79, pp. 828–46.

Hart, H.L.A. (1980), *Essays on Bentham: Jurisprudence and Political Theory,* Oxford: Clarendon Press.

Haworth, Lawrence (1968), 'Utility and Rights' in Rescher, Nicholas (ed.), *Studies in Moral Philosophy,* Oxford: Blackwell.

Henson, Richard (1971), 'Utilitarianism and the Wrongness of Killing', *The Philosophical Review*, Vol. 80, pp. 320–37.

Hilgard, Ernest (1977), *Divided Consciousness,* New York: John Wiley.

Hodgson, D.H. (1967), *Consequences of Utilitarianism,* Oxford: Clarendon Press.

Hospers, John (1970), *Human Conduct*, London: Hart-Davis.

Hudson, W.D. (1967), *Ethical Intuitionism,* New York: St Martin's Press.

Hudson, W. D. (1970), *Modern Moral Philosophy*, London: Macmillan.

Hutcheson, F. (1973), *Concerning Moral Good and Evil* (part 2 of the *Inquiry into the Original of Our Ideas of Beauty and Virtue,* The Hague: Martinus Nijhoff.

Institute for Social Research Newsletter (1974), No. 2, University of Michigan.

Jack, H.J. (1971), 'Utilitarianism and Ross' Theory of "Prima Facie" Duties', *Dialogue*, Vol. 10, pp. 437–57.

Kant, Immanuel (1959), *Foundations of the Metaphysics of Morals,* trans. Lewis Beck White, Indianapolis: Bobbs-Merrill.

Kaplan, E.A. (1960), 'Hypnosis and Pain', *Archives of General Psychiatry,* 2

Kaplan, M.A. (1960–1961), 'Restricted Utilitarianism', *Ethics,* Vol. 71, pp. 301–2.

Kenny, A. J. P. (1965–1966), 'Happiness', *Proceedings of the Aristotelian Society,* Vol. 66, pp. 93–102.

Kerner, George (1971), 'The Immorality of Utilitarianism and the Escapism of Rule Utilitarianism', *The Philosophical Quarterly,* Vol. 21, pp. 36–50.

Kleinig, John (1970), 'The Fourth Chapter of Mill's *Utilitarianism*', *Australasian Journal of Philosophy,* Vol. 48, pp. 197–205.

Lyons, David (1965), *The Forms and Limits of Utilitarianism,* Oxford: Oxford University Press.

Mabbot, J. (1937), 'Is Plato's Republic Utilitarian?' *Mind,* Vol. 46.

MacIntyre, Alasdair (1964), 'Against Utilitarianism' in Hollins, T.H.B. (ed.), *Aims in Education: the philosophical approach,* Manchester: University of Manchester Press.

MacIntyre, Alasdair (1965), 'Pleasure as a Reason for Action', *Monist,* Vol. 49, pp. 215–33.

MacIntyre, Alasdair (1981), *After Virtue,* London: Duckworth & Co.

Mackie, J.L. (1977), *Ethics: Inventing Right and Wrong,* Harmondsworth: Pelican.

Mackie, J.L. (1978), 'Can There Be a Rights-based Moral Theory?', *Midwest Studies in Philosophy,* 3.

Mandelbaum, Maurice (1965), 'Rule-Utilitarianism', *Australasian Journal of Philosophy,* Vol. 43, pp. 220–25.

Mandelbaum, Maurice (1968), 'On Interpreting Mill's *Utilitarianism, Journal of the History of Philosophy,* Vol. 6, pp. 35–46.

Mandelbaum, Maurice (1968), 'Two Moot Issues in Mill's *Utilitarianism* in Schneewind, J.B. (ed.), *Mill: A Collection of Critical Essays,* Notre Dame: University of Notre Dame Press.

Mandelbaum, Maurice (1971), *Values and Conduct,* Oxford: Oxford University Press.

Margolis, Joseph (1971), *Values and Conduct,* Oxford: Clarendon Press.

McGill, V.J. (1967), *The Idea of Happiness,* New York: F. A. Praeger.

McCloskey, H.J. (1963), 'A Note on Utilitarian Punishment', *Mind,* Vol. 72.

McPeck, J. (1978), 'Can Robin Barrow Be Happy and Not Know It?', *Proceedings of the American Philosophy of Education Society.*

Mill, James (1835), *A Fragment on Mackintosh,* London.

Mill, John Stuart (1962), *Utilitarianism* and *On Liberty*, edited by Mary Warnock, London: Collins, The Fontana Library.

Montague, Roger (1966–1967), 'Happiness', *Proceedings of the Aristotelian Society,* Vol. 67, pp. 87–102.

Moore, G.E. (1903), *Principia Ethica,* Cambridge: Cambridge University Press.

Moore, G.E. (1912), *Ethics,* Oxford: Oxford University Press.

Moore, G.E. (1960), *Philosophical Studies,* London: Routledge & Kegan Paul.

Murdoch, Iris (1970), *The Sovereignty of the Good,* London: Cambridge University Press.

Narveson, J.F. (1965), 'Utilitarianism and Formalism', *Australasian Journal of Philosophy,* Vol. 43, pp. 58–72.

Narveson, J.F. (1967), *Morality and Utility,* Baltimore: Johns Hopkins Press.

Narveson, J.F., (1970), 'Utilitarianism and Moral Norms', *Journal of Value Inquiry,* Vol. 4, pp. 273–82.

Perry, D.L. (1967), *The Concept of Pleasure*, The Hague: Mouton.

Plato (1960), *Gorgias*, (trans. W. Hamilton), Harmondsworth: Penguin.

Plato (1974), *The Republic,* (trans. Desmond Lee), Harmondsworth: Penguin.

Prichard, H.A. (1968), *Moral Obligation and Duty and Interest*, Oxford: Oxford University Press.

Quinton, A. (1973), *Utilitarian Ethics*, London: Macmillan.

Quinton, A. (1989), *Utilitarian Ethics*, 2nd ed., London: Duckworth.

Rawls, John (1971), *A Theory of Justice*, Cambridge, Mass.: Harvard University Press.

Raz, J. (1985), 'Right-based Moralities' in Frey, R.G. (ed.), *Utility and Rights,* Oxford: Blackwell.

Robinson, John, and Shaver, P.R. (1978), *Measures of Social Psychological Attitudes,* Michigan: University of Michigan.

Ross, W.D. (1930), *The Right and the Good*, Oxford: Oxford University Press.

Ross, W.D. (1939), *Foundations of Ethics*, Oxford: Oxford University Press

Russell, Bertrand (1975), *The Conquest of Happiness*, London: Allen & Unwin.

Ryan, Alan (1966), 'Mill and the Naturalistic Fallacy', *Mind*, Vol. 75, pp. 422–25.

Ryan, Alan (1990), 'Positive Scepticism', *Oxford Today*, Vol. 2, No. 2, p. 30.

Scanlon, T.M. (1982), 'Contractualism and Utilitarianism', in Sen, A.K. and Williams, Bernard (eds), *Utilitarianism and Beyond*, Cambridge: Cambridge University Press.

Schick, Frederic (1971), 'Beyond Utilitarianism', *The Journal of Philosophy*, Vol. 68, pp. 657–66.

Sen, A.K. (1979), 'Utilitarianism and Welfare', *Journal of Philosophy*, Vol. 76, No. 9, pp. 463–89.

Sen, A.K. (1981), 'Plural Utility', *Proceedings of the Aristotelian Society*, Vol. 81.

Sen, A.K. (1982), 'Rights and Agency', *Philosophy and Public Affairs*, Vol. 11.

Sen, A.K. and Williams, Bernard (1982), 'Introduction: Utilitarianism and Beyond', in *Utilitarianism and Beyond*, Cambridge: Cambridge University Press.

Sidgwick, Henry (1962), *Methods of Ethics*, 7th edition reissue, London: Macmillan.

Simpson, Robert (1975), 'Happiness', *American Philosophical Quarterly*, April, pp. 169–76.

Singer, Peter (1977), *Animal Liberation*, New York: Avon Books.

Singer, Peter (1979), *Practical Ethics*, New York: Cambridge University Press.

Smart, J.J.C. (1960–1961), 'Extreme Utilitarianism: A Reply to M.A. Kaplan', *Ethics*, Vol. 71, pp. 133–4.

Smart, J.J.C. (1967), 'Utilitarianism' in Edwards, Paul (ed.), *The Encyclopedia of Philosophy*, London: Collier Macmillan.

Smart, J.J.C. (1973), 'An Outline of a System of Utilitarian Ethics' in Smart, J.J.C. and Williams, Bernard, *Utilitarianism For and Against*, Cambridge: Cambridge University Press.

Smart, R.N. (1958), 'Negative Utilitarianism', *Mind*, Vol. 67.

Sobel, J.H. (1968), 'Rule-Utilitarianism', *Australasian Journal of Philosophy*, Vol. 46, pp. 146–65.

Sprigge, T.L.S. (1968), 'Professor Narveson's Utilitarianism', *Inquiry*, Vol. 11, pp. 332–46.

Stace, W.T. (1937), *The Concept of Morals*, New York: Macmillan.

Stearns, J.B. (1965), 'Ideal Rule-Utilitarianism and the Content of Duty', *Kant-Studien*, Vol. 66, pp. 50–70.

Steintrager, James (1977), *Bentham,* London: George Allen & Unwin.

Stern, Kenneth (1966), 'Testing Ethical Theories', *The Journal of Philosophy,* Vol. 63, pp. 234–8.

Sumner, L.W. (1971), 'Cooperation, Fairness and Utility', *Journal of Value Inquiry,* Vol. 5, pp. 105–19.

Sumner, L.W. (1985), 'Rights Denaturalised' in Frey, R.G. (ed.), *Utility and Rights,* Oxford: Blackwell.

Taylor, C.C.W. (1963), 'Pleasure', *Analysis,* Vol. 23 Supplement, pp. 2–19.

Taylor, Charles (1982), 'The Diversity of Goods' in Sen, A.K. and Williams, Bernard (eds), *Utilitarianism and Beyond,* Cambridge: Cambridge University Press.

Telfer, E. (1980), *Happiness,* London: Macmillan.

Thomas, D.A. Lloyd (1968), 'Happiness', *Philosophical Quarterly,* 18, No. 71, April.

Tucker, Abraham (1768), *Light of Nature Pursued.*

Urmson, J.O. (1953), 'The Interpretation of the Moral Philosophy of J.S. Mill', *Philosophical Quarterly,* Vol. 3, pp. 33–9.

Von Wright, G.H. (1963), *The Varieties of Goodness,* London: Routledge & Kegan Paul.

Wall, G.B. (1971), 'More on the Equivalence of Act and Rule Utilitarianism', *Philosophical Studies,* Vol. 22, pp. 91–5.

Warnock, G.J. (1967), *Contemporary Moral Philosophy,* London: Macmillan .

Warnock, G.J. (1971), *The Object of Morality,* London: Methuen & Co.

Warnock, Mary (1960), *Ethics Since 1900,* London: Oxford University Press.

Watkins, J.W.N. (1963), 'Negative Utilitarianism', *Proceedings of the Aristotelian Society,* Vol. 37, pp. 95–114.

Williams, Bernard (1972), *Morality: An Introduction to Ethics,* New York: Harper & Row.

Williams, Bernard (1973), 'A Critique of Utilitarianism', in Smart, J.J. C. and Williams, Bernard, *Utilitarianism For and Against,* Cambridge: Cambridge University Press.

Williams, Bernard (1976), 'Persons, Character and Morality', in Rorty, A. (ed.), *The Identities of Persons,* Berkeley: University of California Press.

Williams, Bernard (1976), 'Utilitarianism and Moral Self-Indulgence', in Lewis, H.D. (ed.), *Contemporary British Philosophy,* Series 4, London: Allen and Unwin.

Williams, Bernard (1981), *Moral Luck*, Cambridge University Press.
Wilson, John (1968–1969), 'Happiness', *Analysis*, Vol. 29, pp. 13–21.

Name Index

Subject Index

Act-Utilitarianism *see* Utilitarianism, Act/rule
Acts *see* Justified acts; Morally intentioned acts; Right acts
Aesthetic theory 12, 47, 95, 138
Aesthetic value 4, 9, 41, 44, 47, 55, 95, 139, 140, 142, 143–47
Analytic philosophy 1, 2, 27, 28, 32, 41–3, 66–8
  see also Conceptual analysis
Animals 50, 75, 99, 155
Autonomy 5, 19, 20, 49, 51, 53, 55

Beauty 20, 40, 41, 42, 44, 45, 51, 55, 69, 74, 92, 126, 132, 143, 177

Conceptual analysis 1, 4, 8, 27, 28, 31, 32, 41–3, 66–8, 74–5, 77–81, 95
  see also Analytic philosophy; Linguistic analysis
Conservatism and Utilitarianism *see* Utilitarianism, Conservatism
Contentment 41, 68, 70, 72, 74, 75, 81–2, 91, 128, 129
Cultural differences 4, 13, 14, 15, 45, 50, 51, 69, 92–104, 108, 117, 145, 163, 173, 175
  see also Relativity (of moral judgements)

Deontological/Teleological theories 15, 16, 19, 29, 30, 40
Dilemmas 26, 29, 45, 59, 108, 109, 134, 152, 156, 160, 161, 171, 176
Distribution (of happiness) *see* Happiness
Divine discontent 41, 88

Duty 15, 21–3, 48, 49, 56, 65, 94, 102, 103, 117, 118, 119, 120, 141, 160, 161, 163, 174

Ecstasy 68, 74, 82, 91, 129
Education 6, 8, 9, 10, 36, 59, 72, 79, 103, 128, 142, 143, 152, 178
Emotivism 4, 26
Equality 5, 43, 44, 50, 61, 107, 119
Ethical Theory (nature of) 7, 12–38, 45–7, 52–6, 96, 138, 155–6, 168–78
  see also Sentiment, moral; Ideal, the (in relation to ethical theory)
Ethical Theory (proof of) 7, 12, 30–38, 85, 86, 134, 151, 160, 161, 172

Fairness 29, 44, 49, 50, 53, 92, 173
Felicific calculus 8, 99, 130, 131, 132–5, 137, 138
Formulaic versions (of principle of utility) 21, 40, 45–7, 49, 50, 53, 59, 65, 168, 98, 176
Freedom 5, 31, 43–5, 50, 56, 83, 84, 112, 132, 148–9, 155, 156, 170, 171
Friendship 8, 9, 18, 20, 27, 40, 44, 45, 51, 74, 118, 119, 149, 150, 151, 177

Good, the 9, 11, 13, 16–24, 29, 41, 42–6, 49–51, 56, 84–5, 119

Happiness 5, 6, 8, 14–21, 30, 39–54, 65–90, 91, 112, 124, 125, 177
  Being and feeling happy 75–6
  Degree of intensity 72–3